Landmarks in Classical Literature

TO JEM

Landmarks in Classical Literature

Philip Gaskell

Fitzroy Dearborn Publishers
Chicago·London

© Philip Gaskell, 1999

Published in the United Kingdom by
Edinburgh University Press
22 George Square, Edinburgh

Published in the United States of America by
Fitzroy Dearborn Publishers
919 North Michigan Avenue,
Chicago, Illinois 60611

Typeset in Futura and Sabon
by Bibliocraft Ltd, Dundee, and
printed and bound in Great Britain
by MPG Books Ltd, Bodmin

A Cataloging-in-Publication record for this book
is available from the Library of Congress

ISBN 1-57958-192-7 Fitzroy Dearborn

Contents

Abbreviations

...   ellipsis in the original
[...]   editorial ellipsis

Preface

Landmarks in Classical Literature is the last in a set of three books about the major authors of European literature and their works, from ancient times until the early twentieth century. Despite their similarities, each of these three volumes of 'landmarks' approaches its subjects in a slightly different way.

Landmarks in English Literature (1998) is a survey of the major British and Irish authors from Chaucer to the 1920s, together with explanations of how the three main genres of literature – fiction, poetry, drama – actually work. Then *Landmarks in European Literature* (1999) discusses thirty-two key works of European literature from Dante to Brecht, translated from six languages other than English, putting them into the contexts of their times and places. Now *Landmarks in Classical Literature* surveys the most influential authors of ancient Greece and Rome, and says something about their environment, and about translations of their work.

All three books are aimed at 'general readers' and students of all ages, people who want to discover the delights offered by literature, old as well as new. All three base their discussions on the texts of English literature, and of foreign and ancient literature in translation, that are available nowadays in well-edited paperback editions. And the prime purpose of all three is, not to be a substitute for reading these wonderful books, but to help and encourage readers to explore and enjoy the great literary heritage of the west for themselves.

Acknowledgements

I am most grateful for help and advice kindly given by John Davey, Pat Easterling, Margaret Gaskell, Neil Hopkinson, Jackie Jones, Jenny Shearan, Alison Sproston, and Robin Waterfield.

For permission to reprint copyright material, the publishers would like to thank: Penguin Books for Homer, *Iliad* 6.503–16, 20.407–18, translated by Alexander Pope © 1996, Penguin Books Ltd; *Iliad* 6.503–16, 20.407–18, translated by Martin Hammond © 1987, Penguin Books Ltd; *Iliad* 6.503–16, 20.407–18, translated by Robert Fagles © 1990, Penguin Putnam; Homer, *Odyssey* 23.39–57, translated by E. V. Rieu and D. C. H. Rieu © 1991, Penguin Books Ltd; Pindar, *The Odes*, translated by C. M. Bowra © 1969, Penguin Books Ltd; Sophocles, *Oedipus the King*, translated by Robert Fagles © 1982, Penguin Books Ltd; Sophocles, *Oedipus Coloneus*, translated by Robert Fagles © 1982, Penguin Books Ltd; Herodotus, *Histories* 7.208–9, 7.211–13, translated by Aubrey de Sélincourt, revised and annotated by John Marincola © 1996, Penguin Books Ltd; Thucydides, *History* 2.37, 40, translated by Rex Warner, revised by M. I. Finlay © 1972, Penguin Books Ltd; Xenophon, *Anabasis* 4.5, translated by Rex Warner, revised by M. I. Finlay © 1972, Penguin Books Ltd; Plato *The Last Days of Socrates*, translated by Hugh Tredennick and Harold Tarrant © 1993, Penguin Books Ltd; Cicero, *Selected Political Speeches*, translated by Michael Grant © 1969, Penguin Books Ltd; Theocritus, *Idylls* 3.1–9, 52–4, translated by Robert Wells © 1988, Penguin Books Ltd; Virgil, *Eclogues* 1.1–5, translated by Guy Lee © 1980, Penguin Books Ltd; Virgil, *Georgics* 4.3–5, 88–89, 559–66, translated by L. P. Wilkinson © 1982, Penguin Books Ltd; Virgil, *The Aeneid* 6.847–53, translated by David West © 1990, Penguin Books Ltd; *Virgil's Aeneid*, translated by John Dryden © 1697, Penguin Books Ltd; Horace, *Satires* I.6.45–64, 132–46, 3.131–6, 140–53, translated by Niall Rudd © 1973, Penguin Books Ltd; Horace, *Odes* I.29, translated by W. G. Shepherd © 1983,

Penguin Books Ltd; Horace, *Odes* I.9, translated by James Michie ©
1964, HarperCollins; Ovid, *Amores* I.1.1–4, 25–30, translated by A. D.
Melville © 1990, Penguin Books Ltd; Ovid, *Amores* III.12.1–14,
translated by Peter Green © 1982, Penguin Books Ltd; Ovid, *Amores*
III.12.41–2, translated by E. J. Kenney; Ovid, *Tristia* IV.10.1–2,
115–32, translated by Peter Green © 1994, David Higham Associates;
Tacitus, *Annals* 11.31–2, translated by Michael Grant © 1956, revised
1989, Carcanet Press; Suetonius, *The Twelve Caesars*, Augustus 65,
Nero 53–4, translated by Michael Grant © 1957, revised 1979,
Penguin Books Ltd; all reprinted by permission of Penguin Books Ltd.

Oxford University Press for Homer, *Iliad* 6.503–16, 20.407–18,
translated by Robert Fitzgerald © 1974, Oxford University Press;
Homer, *Odyssey* 23.39–57, translated by Walter Shewring © 1980,
Oxford University Press; Hesiod, *Theogony and Works and Days*,
translated by M. L. West © 1988, Oxford University Press; Herodotus,
Histories 8.105–6, translated by Robin Waterfield © 1998, Oxford
University Press; Plato, *Symposium*, translated by Robin Waterfield ©
1994, Oxford University Press; Virgil, *Aeneid*, translated by C. Day
Lewis © 1952, Peters, Fraser and Dunlop; Catullus, *The Complete
Poems*, translated by Guy Lee © 1990, Oxford University Press;
Horace, *Epodes* 2 1–16, 67–70, translated by David West © 1997,
Oxford University Press; Ovid, *Amores* I.1.1–4, 25–30, translated by
A. D. Melville © 1990, Oxford University Press; Ovid, *Metamorphoses*
IV.96–104, XV.871–9, translated by A. D. Melville © 1986, Oxford
University Press; Tacitus, *Histories* 1.12, 49, translated by W. H. Fyfe,
1912, revised by D. S. Levene © 1997, Oxford University Press;
Plutarch, *Greek Lives*, Alexander 1, translated by Robin Waterfield
© 1998, Oxford University Press; all reprinted by permission of
Oxford University Press.

Loeb Classical Library for *Greek Lyric*, vol. 1 and 2, translated by
David A. Campbell © 1982, reprinted by permission of Loeb Classical
Library; the Society of Authors for Horace, *Odes* IV.7, translated by A.
E. Housman, *Poems* © 1997, reprinted by permission of The Society of
Authors as the literary representative of the Estate of A. E. Housman;
Faber & Faber for Ovid, *Metamorphoses* I.1–4, paraphrased by Ted
Hughes in *Tales from Ovid* © 1997, reprinted by permission of Faber
& Faber.

Every effort has beeen made to trace copyright holders but if any have
inadvertantly been overlooked, the publishers will be pleased to make
the necessary acknowledgements at the first opportunity.

The bad effects which, generally, result from the present system of [classical] education are the following; a blind and bigotted attachment to authorities, names, and antiquity: disputes merely verbal: and, consequently, the continuance of error and prejudice.
(William Stevenson [father of Elizabeth Gaskell], *Remarks on the Very Inferior Utility of Classical Learning*, 1796)

The special benefit which these [classical] studies are supposed, and in some cases justly supposed, to confer, is to quicken our appreciation of what is excellent and to refine our discrimination between what is excellent and what is not.
(A. E. Housman, 'Introductory Lecture' as Professor of Latin at University College, London, 1892)

Introduction

Reading the classics today

The civilisation and literature of ancient Greece and Rome, along with the Judaeo-Christian religion, have been the bedrock of the thought and culture of the western world since the high Middle Ages, and they still underlie the way Europeans and Americans think and write. Until quite recently the classics have also under-pinned western education, first-hand experience of at least a few Roman authors in the original Latin being the basic requirement of anything more advanced than elementary schooling.

But, although western culture is based on the classics, not many schoolchildren now learn Latin, and very few indeed learn Greek; while the ancient languages are long gone as a requirement for university entrance. And because the Greek and Latin languages are taught to so few pupils at school, the history and culture of the ancient civilisations tend also to be disregarded, both in school and afterwards. It is true that the classics are still taught on a small scale in British secondary schools,[1] and that there are some twenty-five university departments of classics in Britain (few of them large on the scale of the major humanities and science departments); but it is also true that the classics are no longer taught to anything like the extent that they once were. An important part of our heritage – the basis of much of our thought and art – is in danger of being forgotten.

The purpose of this book is to make available the work of some of the most important Greek and Roman writers, chosen both for their intrinsic quality and for the influence they have had on the

---

[1] In 1998 there were 10,945 UK candidates for GCSE Latin, 3,529 for Classical Civilisation, and 980 for Greek; compared with (to the nearest thousand) 1,006,000 for Combined Science, 638,000 for English, 491,000 for English Literature, 385,000 for Design and Technology, 336,000 for French, and 134,000 for German (*The Times*, 27 August 1998).

development of our own cultural history; and to present it against a background of the history – political, social, and cultural – of the ancient world.

A novel or a poem or a play, while it is being experienced, is an event in time like a piece of music, not a thing. (Of course the text of a work of literature can be written down, as can a musical score, and it may appear to be a thing in that state; but it remains a thing only so long as it is unread or unheard, when it becomes an event once more.) Now these events will have certain effects, depending on the skill and understanding of the readers or listeners, who will experience intellectual, imaginative, emotional, and even physical responses to them. It is obviously important that readers and listeners should hold themselves open to these responses during such events, and should welcome the interest, wonder, pleasure, amusement, anger, or whatever that may result from reading or hearing works of art. This is what I hope readers of this book will do when I suggest that a work is good, and worth their attention.

What cannot be explained is why a particular work of art is beautiful. Beautiful works can induce a transcendental state of happiness in experienced and receptive listeners or readers that goes beyond the describable pleasures of the intellect, imagination, and emotion. There are no words that can usefully say why Bach's B-minor Mass is beautiful – though there are plenty that can say why it is interesting or satisfying or well made or well performed – and the problem of explaining the beauty of works of literature is essentially the same.

The classical canon

The acknowledgement of the most important writers of any period – of canonical writers, as they are called – both forms and safeguards its cultural tradition. Some of the canonical authors of the ancient world were identified as being canonical even in their own time, a position which the writers and critics of later periods have confirmed by acknowledging them to be their greatest and most influential predecessors. The epic poets Homer and Virgil are the most classical – in that their works have always been considered valuable and exemplary as well as traditional – of the primary writers discussed here, but the eight others follow closely behind them: the lyric poets Pindar and Horace, Ovid the poet of love and myth, the dramatist Sophocles, the philosophers Plato and Cicero, and the historians Herodotus and Tacitus. These ten are given the most space here, but a further twenty-five Greek and Latin writers are also discussed in connection with them: the didactic poet Hesiod; the Hellenistic poets Callimachus, Apollonius Rhodius, and Theocritus; the lyricists Sappho, Anacreon, and Catullus, and the satirist Juvenal; the dramatists Aeschylus, Euripides, Aristophanes, Plautus, Terence, and Seneca (as playwright); the historians Thucydides, Xenophon, Caesar, Sallust, Livy, Plutarch, and Suetonius; the novelists Petronius, Apuleius, and Longus; and the philosophers Aristotle and Seneca (as philosopher).

Technicalities

The rest of this Introduction considers a number of technical matters. They are dealt with here rather than in appendices because they are the sort of things which can puzzle or put off new readers of the classics, and which are best explained at once for those who would like to know more about them. These matters are: (1) reading classical authors in translation rather than in the original; (2) the form and pronunciation of Greek and Latin names; (3) metre in classical verse; (4) dates; (5) Roman numerals; and (6) maps.

(1) The classics in translation

Because few people can read Greek and Latin, our authors are necessarily approached through translation; and their distance from us means that their work has to be introduced by explanations that are longer than would be required for the discussion of more recent literatures.

We have to accept that translation is an imperfect medium for the transmission of even the simplest literature written in prose, and that it is especially inadequate for expressing the poetry of one language in terms of another. Hardly any but simple words for concrete things translate directly between languages without some distortion of meaning, and even simple words tend to have subsidiary senses that differ from language to language. Furthermore, as C.D.N. Costa remarked in connection with translating Seneca's Latin prose:

> The more brilliant and distinctive an author the harder it is to translate him adequately, and Seneca is no exception. There is in any case the general problem of translating from an inflected into a virtually uninflected language. For example, inflection allows variations in word order for special effects of emphasis or surprise that are difficult to achieve in the far more

fixed word order of a language like English.[2] When to this general difficulty are added Seneca's numerous and highly sophisticated mannerisms – word play, pungent aphorism, elaborate sentence structure combined with elliptical phraseology – we are faced with sometimes daunting problems. (Seneca, *Dialogues and Letters*, ed. and trs. by C.D.N. Costa, 1997, Penguin Classics p. xxv)

For poetry the situation is even worse: the rhythms, sounds, puns, nuances, and emotional charges of poetry simply cannot be translated from one language to another, and cannot easily be mimicked in the inevitably different modes of another language.[3] G.H. Lewes summed the problem up in connection with translating the poetry of Goethe:

> A translation [of a poem] may be good *as* a translation, but it cannot be an adequate reproduction of the original. It may be a good poem; it may be a good imitation of another poem; it may be better than the original; but it cannot be an adequate reproduction; it cannot be the same thing in another language, producing the same effect on the mind.[4]

The difficulties and imperfections of literary translations are bad enough between modern languages, but between ancient and modern languages they are compounded because the cultural environments are further removed from each other by time as well as place.

Translations are what we have to deal with, however, and we are fortunate in having plenty of good ones easily available. There is also a real advantage in being able to approach the riches of classical literature through the medium of these translations. This is that everyone – including those who have been taught some Greek and Latin – can read so much more of it, and read it so much more easily, than they could if they had to pick their way through the varieties of the ancient languages in which the classics were originally written.

Those with some knowledge of Greek and Latin may choose to use the admirable series of Loeb Classics (with the original texts on the left-hand pages and prose translations – in some cases rather dated – on the right, in dozens of handy volumes, bound in green for

---

[2] On inflections and word order, see pp. 20–1, 124–6 below.

[3] The practical difficulties of translating poetry from one language to another are discussed at greater length in my *Landmarks in European Literature*, Edinburgh University Press 1999, pp. 2–6.

[4] G.H. Lewes, *The Life and Works of Goethe*, Everyman's Library, 1908 and reprints, p. 483. The philosophy of translation is considered at length in George Steiner's erudite *After Babel*, rev. ed., Oxford University Press 1991.

Greek and red for Latin). But for most people it will be more practical to read the fine paperback translations, mostly annotated and without the original texts, that are available in Penguin Classics and Oxford World's Classics; and in fact all but one of our ten principal authors are included in both series (the exception being Pindar, translations of whose poems appear in Penguin Classics but not so far in Oxford World's Classics); and most of the additional twenty-five writers appear in one or other of these series, or in both. Both series are keeping up to date with recent translations and revisions, the Penguin series covering a larger number of works than the Oxford World's Classics. Sections on these translations are added to the discussions of the main and additional authors.

(2) The form and pronunciation of Greek and Latin names

Many of the Greek and Latin names appearing here are generally familiar in anglicised spellings and pronunciations which have little to do with their original forms. Our ten main writers, for instance are commonly known as Homer (HOHMə), Pindar (PINdah), Sophocles (SOFəkleez), Herodotus (heRODətəs), Plato (PLAYtoh), Cicero (SISəroh), Virgil (VURjil), Horace (HORis), Ovid (OVid), and Tacitus (TASitəs).[5]

There are two main reasons for the confused state in which Greek and Latin names have reached us: alterations made to the forms of the names, and changes of pronunciation. With regard to form, some Greek names have been Latinised, the -os termination for instance being changed to -us (Kronos, Cronus), or in a more extreme case Polydeukes becoming Pollux. Where the name has not been anglicised, the Latin form is sometimes used (Hercules rather than Herakles or Heracles). But some of the most familiar Greek names have been anglicised – Homer (Homeros in Greek), Pindar (Pindaros), and Plato (Platon) in the list given above – and then it is the anglicised forms that are usually preferred. Similarly, many of the most familiar names of Roman writers are normally used in their anglicised rather than in their original Latin forms, including Virgil (Vergilius), Horace (Horatius), and Ovid (Ovidius) in our list.[6] On

---

[5] See the beginning of the Index on pp. 213–14 for the phonetic equivalents for these simplified phonetic spellings. Phonetic spellings using the same system are given for all the Greek and Latin names that are used in the book following their entries in the Index. The symbol 'ə' stands for the neutral vowel in English.

[6] See pp. 127–8 for more about Roman names.

the other hand the names of some ancient places have to be distinguished from those of their modern successors, so that we say Ithaca
rather than Itháki; Massalia (or Massilia) rather than Marseilles;
Eburacum rather than York; and so on (though we have anglicised
Gallia as Gaul).

The pronunciation of Latin by English speakers has undergone
changes that have left their mark on the way we pronounce common Latin words and phrases – especially legal and medical terms –
and the Greek and Latin names discussed in the last paragraph.
Until the late nineteenth century Latin was pronounced in Britain
with English vowel sounds: 'PAYtə' for *pater*, 'reJEYEnə' for
regina, 'BOHnə' for *bona*, 'veyediLEYEset' for *videlicet*, and so
on. Then a 'reformed' Latin pronunciation was introduced in
schools with Continental vowel sounds, hard 'c' and 'g', and 'w'
for 'v'; which gave 'PAHtə', 'reGEEnə' (hard 'g'), 'BONə', 'wee-
dayLEEket', and so on.

Used strictly, the reformed Latin pronunciation (which was an
attempt to reconstruct the pronunciation of the Romans) does not
use the neutral vowel 'ə' to the extent that I have done here, but
suggests 'PAHtair' rather than 'PAHtə' for *pater*, and 'reGEEnah'
rather than 'reGEEnə' for *regina*, and so on. This can sound
pedantic, and I have opted for a more relaxed form of the reformed
pronunciation in this book, with a liberal use of the neutral vowel,
because this is what most people actually say.

The introduction of the reformed pronunciation has resulted in
many inconsistencies in the way that we pronounce Latin words
and phrases today. For instance, *prima facie* retains its old English
pronunciation 'PREYEmə FAYsi', not the reformed 'PREEmah
FAKee-ay; and for *faeces* we say 'FEEseez', not 'FEYEkayz'. On
the other hand for *fecit* (as part of the signature on an engraving) we
are more likely to say 'FAYkit' than 'FEEsit'. In some cases both
pronunciations are current: *nisi* is pronounced both 'NEYEseye'
and 'NEEsee'; *opus* is both 'OHpəs' and 'OPoos'; and Newton's
book is sometimes the 'prinSIPi-ə', sometimes the 'prinKIPi-ah'.
And, as a further complication, there is Church Latin, which uses
Continental vowels (with a few alterations), and 'tsh' for 'c': thus
for *pace* we have 'PAYsi' ('English'), 'PAHkay' (reformed), and
'PAHtshay' (Church).[7]

---

[7] Another oddity is the common pronunciation 'rashonAHL' for the Latin word
rationale, presumably in the belief that it comes from French; the English
pronunciation was 'rashoNAYli', the reformed would be 'ratioNAHlay'.

The outcome is that the pre-reform pronunciation of Latin names, and of the Latin forms of Greek names, also survives in the common forms of many Greek and Roman names today; which is the reason why the names listed at the beginning of this section are pronounced as they are, and why we say 'meyeSEEnee' not 'miKEEneye', and 'SEEzə' not 'KEYEzah', for *Mycenae* and *Caesar*; and so on.[8]

A point, finally, about the spelling of names in this book: there is a convention that spells the possessive case of ancient Greek and Latin names ending in -s as -s'; but it is, it seems to me, a bad and outdated convention. We do not say *Sophocles' plays* or *Athens' temples* any more than we say *Polonius' speech* or *John Jones' house*. We say *Sophocles's plays, Athens's temples, Polonius's speech, John Jones's house*, and so on, as we do for the possessive case of almost all singular proper names and other nouns ending in -s. For this reason I have spelled the possessive case of Greek and Latin names ending in -s as -s's.

(3) Metre in classical verse

The metre of Greek and Latin verse is based on patterns of 'long' and 'short' syllables in a line, not (as in English verse) on patterns of stressed and unstressed syllables, or (as in French verse) on the number of syllables in a line.[9] This arrangement was appropriate for ancient Greek, which was not a stressed language; but it was also adopted for classical Latin verse, in imitation of the Greek model, even though classical Latin was normally spoken with stress. A resulting complication is that 'there are good reasons for believing that the Romans read their [Latin] poetry with the stress accent of their normal speech, the quantitative metre (originally Greek) being heard as a counterpoint or undercurrent.'[10] However that may be, what follows here is a much simplified account of the basics of classical quantitative metre, which applies to both Greek and Latin verse, and which explains the origin of certain features of the Homeric verse that we shall be considering in Chapter 3.

In classical 'quantitative' verse (as it is called), patterns of syllables containing long and short vowels were arranged in groups called

---

[8] For the application of these principles to some of the 900 names in Homer's *Iliad*, see p. 28 below. For an explanation of the forms of Roman names, see pp. 127–8.
[9] For an explanation of how the metre of English verse works, see my *Landmarks in English Literature*, Edinburgh University Press 1998, pp. 70–5; and for French verse, see *Landmarks in European Literature*, Edinburgh University Press 1999, pp. 20–1.
[10] L.P. Wilkinson in his edition of Virgil's *Georgics* (1982), Penguin Classics p. 55.

'feet', in which one long syllable (roughly equivalent, for instance, to the long 'ee' in the English word 'seat', as opposed to the short 'e' in 'set') was taken to be equivalent to two short syllables. A single foot might contain, for instance, one long and two short syllables, dah-di-di, which was called a 'dactyl' (the English stress-dactyl 'dánger-ous' is similar to a classical dactyl in that its stressed syllable is long – but the stress-dactyl 'ínterest', with its stressed syllable short, is not). Or a foot might contain two short syllables and one long, di-di-dah, an 'anapaest' ('intercéde', but not 'intermít'); or two longs, dah-dah, a 'spondee' ('áll óut'). Each line of verse was then made up of a particular number and arrangement of feet. The line normally used for epic poems, and also for didactic, satirical, and bucolic poetry, was the six-foot dactylic 'hexameter' (the word is Greek for 'six feet'), which had a slight pause (or 'caesura'), usually in the middle of the third foot. In a simple form it might go:

> dactyl/dactyl/dactyl(paused in the middle)/dactyl/dactyl/spondee

Writing the names of the feet out like this is clumsy, so in 'scanning', or analysing, lines of classical verse, symbols are used: — for a long syllable, ∪ for a short syllable, × for a syllable that may be either long or short, | as a divider between feet, and ⁞ for a caesura. Thus a dactyl is shown as — ∪ ∪ an anapaest as ∪ ∪ —, a spondee as — —, and so on. Using this system, our simple hexameter would be shown as:

$$— ∪ ∪ \mid — ∪ ∪ \mid — \; \vdots \; ∪ ∪ \mid — ∪ ∪ \mid — ∪ ∪ \mid — —$$

Because one long syllable was taken to be the equivalent of two short syllables, dactyls, anapaests, and spondees were often interchangeable; a variety of other hexameter patterns was therefore possible.[11] To give a particular example, the first line of Virgil's *Aeneid* is scanned:

$$— \; ∪ \; ∪ \mid — ∪ ∪ \mid — \; \vdots \; — \mid — — \mid — \mid ∪ \; ∪ \mid — —$$
Arma   virumque cano,   Troiae qui primus ab   oris

(Arms I sing, and the man who first from the coasts of Troy)

Besides the dactylic hexameters of epic and other formal classical verse, other metrical systems were used for less formal types of poetry, using other types of feet (such as 'iambs', short-long, and 'trochees', long-short) and other line-lengths, with or without caesuras:

---

[11] Although anapaests were not used in hexameters.

odes, elegiacs, lyrics, speeches in drama, scurrilous verse, and so on. Their complex technicalities are chiefly of interest to classical specialists.[12]

From the Renaissance onwards, poets continued to attempt to write verse in quantitative metres, whether or not their languages were stressed; it probably worked best in French, which is not a stressed language. The poet who was most successful in giving the effect of classical hexameters in English was A.H. Clough, who substituted stressed for long syllables in, for instance, *The Bothie of Tober-na-vuolich* (1848, 1863):

> Spare me, O great Recollection! for words to the task were unequal,
> Spare me, O mistress of Song! nor bid me remember minutely
> All that was said and done o-er the well-mixed tempting toddy.
>
> (I.82–4)

More recently Cecil Day Lewis similarly recalled classical metres in his translations of Virgil. His version of *Eclogue I* (1963) begins:

> Tityrus, here you loll, your slim reed-pipe serenading
> The woodland spirit beneath a spread of sheltering beech [...][13]

and the first line of his version of the *Aeneid* (1952) is:

> I tell about war and the hero who first from Troy's frontier [...]

There is a full and expert discussion of the problems of translating Latin hexameters into English verse in Niall Rudd's Translator's Preface (1991) to the Oxford World's Classics *Juvenal: The Satires*, pp. xxix–xxxv.

(4) Dates

We use the abbreviation 'BC' for years before the beginning of the Christian Era, and 'AD' for the years after it; but we then have to remember that dates BC are counted backwards, so to speak. The first century BC ran from the year 100 down to the year 1 BC (there was no year 0), the first century AD from 1 up to 100 AD. It is then usual (if not strictly correct) to speak of centuries and millennia

---

[12] The technicalities of classical metres are explained in considerable detail in the current editions of *The Oxford Classical Dictionary* and *The Oxford Companion to Classical Literature*, s.v. Metre.

[13] *Tityre, tu patulae recubans sub tegmine fagi*
siluestrem tenui musam meditaris auena [...]
For another translation of this passage, see p. 157 below.

with unchanged first digits, saying that the second century BC ran from 199 to 100 BC (rather than 200 to 101) and the second century AD from 100 to 199 AD (rather than 101 to 200), and so on. Thus we say that the fifth century BC ran from 499 to 400; that the third millennium AD will run from 2000 to 2999 AD; that the third millennium BC ran from 2999 to 2000 BC; and so on. Note also that the Roman Emperor Tiberius, who was born on 16 November 42 BC and died on 16 March 37 AD, was aged 42 + 36 = 78 at the time of his death (there being no year 0); that 1450 BC was in the middle of the fifteenth century BC, just as 1450 AD was in the middle of the fifteenth century AD; but that, while 410 AD was near the *beginning* of the fifth century AD, 410 BC was near the *end* of the fifth century BC.

(5) Roman numerals

The Romans recorded numbers by using seven symbols (letters of the alphabet and other sigla). These came to be represented by:

I = 1, V = 5, X = 10, L = 50, C = 100, D = 500, M = 1000

There was no symbol for zero.

In ancient times the method preferred for expressing other numbers in formal documents and inscriptions was by adding the symbols together, so that the first ten digits were:

I, II, III, IIII, V, VI, VII, VIII, VIIII, X

with XXXXVIIII for 49, MCCCCLXXXXVIIII for 1499, and so on.

But alongside the additive method, a subtractive method was developed for less formal use. The convention was that, of two number symbols, the smaller one was subtracted if it stood to the left of the larger one, but added if it stood to the right (IX = 9, XI = 11); and that if a smaller number stood between two larger ones, it was substracted from the one on its right (LIX = 59). This reduced the number of symbols required for some numbers, so that the first ten digits could be written:

I, II, III, IV, V, VI, VII, VIII, IX, X

with IL for 49, MCDXCIX for 1499, and so on. This combined system, using both addition and subtraction, eventually superseded the purely additive method, and has been in use from the Middle Ages to the present time.

(6) Maps

Adequate maps will not fit comfortably into a book of this size, and readers are advised to consult a general atlas, or better still a specialist atlas of classical history such as the paperback atlases mentioned on p. 211, for the locations of Greek and Roman cities and other matters of ancient geography.

I The Homeric age

1 The spread of civilisation

The past in the present

Today buses carry the tourists up to the ancient site of Delphi, a few miles north of the Gulf of Corinth. There they are shown the ruins of the sanctuaries of Apollo and Athena, and the usual scattering of foundations and the drums of stone columns, much like other sites they have been taken to see elsewhere in Greece. Suffering a little from the heat, they admire the spectacular setting – a great natural amphitheatre beneath the 2,460-m summit of Mount Parnassus – listen to the winged words of the lecturer, visit the archaeological museum, and are then returned, tired but culturally enriched, to their air-conditioned ship or hotel.

Their predecessors in ancient times were the pilgrims and suppliants who climbed the Sacred Way on foot to worship at Delphi, the mid-point of the classical world, and to consult the miraculous oracle of Apollo. For more than eleven hundred years, from some time in the eighth century BC until the site was closed by the Christian Emperor Theodosius at the end of the fourth century AD, Delphi was revered as a religious centre of supreme authority and importance, supporting the worship of the Olympian gods, especially the cults of Apollo and Dionysus, and giving advice and encouragement to those who asked for it. In its great days there were sanctuaries, temples, treasuries for the worshippers' offerings, free-standing columns and statues, and a stream from the Castalian Spring for purification; all attended by the priests of Apollo, and the Pythia, the priestess who revealed the sometimes ambiguous prophecies imparted to her by the god.

If we now look back some nineteen hundred years, to about 100 AD, we discover that one of the priests of Delphi was a middle-aged philosopher and historian called Plutarch, a Greek who was proud to have the status of a Roman citizen. Coming from a distinguished

14

and prosperous family settled in the small city of Chaeronea, 30km east of Delphi, Plutarch was well known and well travelled in the Roman Empire, which was now at the height of its greatness. He admired the power of Rome and its complement, the culture of Greece; and he wrote about both of them with elegance and charm. His writings were so much appreciated, both in antiquity and afterwards, that a considerable number of them have survived, including a series of *Parallel Lives*, biographical sketches of pairs of Greek and Roman worthies whose careers, he felt, shed light on each other and would provide moral lessons for the educated Romans of his day. The first two biographies in his chronological sequence were those of Theseus, the mythical hero who made Athens great, and Romulus, the supposed founder of Rome.

Theseus, as Plutarch scarcely needed to remind his readers, was the Athenian prince, heir to King Aegeus, who volunteered to join the seven youths and seven maidens who were sent from Athens every nine years as tribute to King Minos of Cnossus in Crete. According to the old story – though Plutarch, who was something of a revisionist, gave little credit to it – these young people were loosed to the Minotaur, a bull–man monster which usually killed them in its labyrinth; but courageous Theseus killed the Minotaur, escaped from the labyrinth with the help of Ariadne's thread, and freed Athens from its subservience to the Minoans.

This takes us back another stage, to the Cretan civilisation which, from about 2000 BC, was centred on a number of 'palace' complexes such as Cnossus – our tourists may have been there too – and had access from its central position in the Mediterranean both to the barbarian north and west, and to the already ancient civilisations to the south and east. These Minoans, who spoke and wrote an unknown language, were in contact with the Egyptian empire, which in turn had relations with the literate civilisations of the Ancient Near East: the Sumerians, and later the Hittites and the Assyrians, with their traditions of literature, mathematics, and medicine. Now we are taken back, not just nineteen hundred years to Plutarch and Imperial Rome, or two-and-a-half thousand years to Classical Greece, but more than six thousand years to the very beginnings of what eventually became our own civilisation, when the irrigation of the deserts of southern Iraq provided a surplus of food sufficient to support the earliest Sumerian cities, and their palaces, temples, crafts, and traders.

From neolithic tribalism to the first cities

Europe, in these earliest times, was a sparsely populated world of neolithic tribes, many of which spoke the Indo-European tongues that were to develop into the major Balto-Slavic, Celtic, Germanic, Greek, Indo-Iranian, and Italic groups of languages. These people, while they were capable of the organisation required to build Stonehenge and Carnac, lived in relatively small settlements, herding animals and growing crops. They were illiterate, and their contact with the developing civilisations of the Near East was limited to little more than the occasional passage of trade goods – stone, amber, metals, and manufactures such as ceramics, articles carved in wood and ivory, and jewellery. The parts of Europe that were the earliest to progress beyond this tribal culture were those nearest to the examples and technologies of Egypt and the Near East: the island of Crete, followed by mainland Greece. The first stage was the acquisition of metal technology (first copper, and then Bronze-Age techniques spreading northwards from the fourth to the third millennium BC), which provided better tools and weapons. It was the application of this technology that appears to have provided the food surpluses which could support classes of people who were not primarily engaged in farming. The non-farmers – who came to include rulers, priests, craftsmen, traders, and soldiers – gathered round centres of power, which eventually became the city-states of Archaic and Classical Greece. The chronological chart opposite shows how these developments were related to each other in time.

The Minoans

Crete was settled by Neolithic peoples from c. 7000 BC, who acquired the beginnings of a metal technology (chiefly copper) from about 3500, and a full Bronze-Age technology from 2500. A civilisation based on Cnossus (which had been settled from the earliest time of human occupation) and several other 'palace' sites was flourishing by 2000 BC, and is called 'Minoan' (after the legendary King Minos); the main external influences having come from Egypt and Asia Minor. Cnossus itself remained the prime centre, with a 'palace' floor area of nearly two acres, a city covering 185 acres, and a population of perhaps 12,000 at its height in the fourteenth and thirteenth centuries. The buildings were well made, with painted murals, and the Minoans produced fine statuettes,

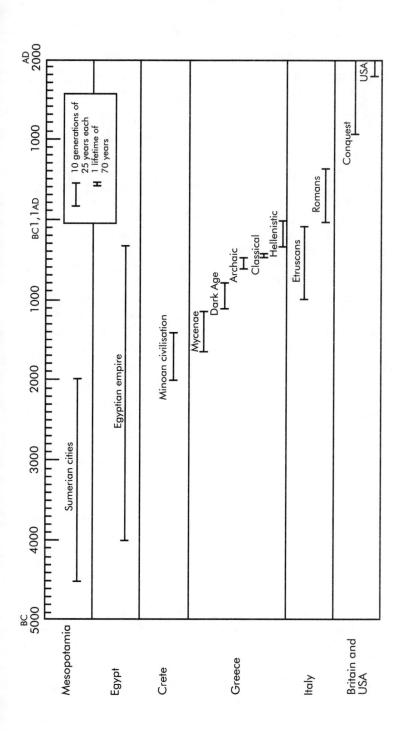

pottery, and jewellery, which are also found in some Aegean islands that appear to have been under Minoan influence; for the Minoans carried on a flourishing ship-borne trade with Greece, Egypt, and the Near East.

Whether the Minoan 'palaces' were primarily the homes of rulers or religious centres is unclear, but in either case they included substantial store rooms, the contents of which were recorded on clay tablets in a script known as 'Linear A'. The Minoan language of these records (which may have been a non-Indo-European tongue brought by early Cretans from the east) is unknown and Linear A, which appears to have been used solely for bureaucratic purposes, has not been deciphered. The archaeological record shows a number of disasters – mostly earthquakes – which afflicted the Minoan centres, but they were rebuilt, and survived until the fourteenth century, when there is evidence of occupation by Mycenaean Greeks and a sharp decline of the Minoan civilisation. Cnossus itself was an important trading centre until the beginning of the Iron Age (c.1000 BC); but from then on Crete became something of a backwater, remaining outside the mainstream of Greek civilisation.

2 The Greeks

Greece – that part of the Balkan peninsula comprising the Peloponnese south of the isthmus of Corinth, a central region north of the isthmus from Attica to Thessaly, and the outlying parts north of Thessaly including Thrace and southern Macedonia, plus the islands of the Aegean Sea – was first invaded by a Bronze-Age, Indo-European people, coming perhaps from southern Russia, around 2200 BC. They spoke an early version of the Greek language, and did what they could with the poor soil and mountainous terrain of their new country, herding sheep and cattle, growing barley in small pockets of arable land, and cultivating olive trees and vines on the dry hillsides. By the middle of the second millennium BC some of them had become productive enough to be able to concentrate their settlements into the first Greek cities.

The Mycenaeans

The principal Bronze-Age citadels in mainland Greece, smaller but more strongly fortified than the Minoan centres by which they were influenced, were at Mycenae (after which the culture is named), Tiryns, and Pylos in the Peloponnese; and at Athens, Thebes, and Orchomenus, north of the isthmus in Attica and Boeotia. Mycenaean civilisation, which lasted from about 1650 to 1150 BC and was at its height from 1400 to 1200, is chiefly known from its sturdy ruins, its pottery, and its rich grave goods that show advanced techniques of metal-working. Although the Mycenaeans took over the Minoan Linear A syllabary and adapted it for writing their early form of Greek (when it is known as Linear B), their written records were limited again to such things as inventories of stores, and they left no written literature. Nevertheless, it is likely that the surviving eighth-century poems of Homer and Hesiod were preceded by a long tradition of oral poetry, which probably went right back to Mycenaean times.

Mycenaean civilisation came to a fairly abrupt end in the twelfth century BC, perhaps at the hands of a further wave of invading Greeks from the north, the Dorians, the final destruction of Mycenae and Tiryns taking place in the late twelfth century.

Dark-Age Greece

The invaders of the twelfth century BC were illiterate, and Greece was plunged into a Dark Age lacking written records. It began with the fall of Mycenae in c.1125 BC, and may be said to have lasted for about 250 years, until the emergence of Athens as a major cultural force c.875 BC; for, although Greek history and literature were not written down until about the middle of the eighth century or even later, the history of Athens in the ninth century was still sufficiently well remembered when written records began.

The Greek language

We have said that Greek is an Indo-European language, and that it represents one of the major Indo-European language groups. This means that it is not closely related by *descent* to any of the other major Indo-European language groups. However, Greek is similar in *type* to, for instance, Latin (which comes from the Italic group of languages), in that both Greek and Latin are 'inflecting' languages, in which grammatical relationships are expressed by changing the structure of the words, for instance by changing their endings.

To take examples from Classical Latin – which are, perhaps, easier to follow than Greek ones would be – the verb form *amo* means 'I love', *amas* 'you [singular] love', *amat*, 'he [or she] loves'; the noun *homo* means 'man' in the subject case, *hominem* 'man' in the object case; and *femina, feminam* mean 'woman' in the subject and object cases respectively. Putting these Latin words together in a sentence, *homo amat feminam* means 'the man loves the woman' (Latin does not have a word for 'the'); and, because the nouns are inflected for case but the verb is inflected only for person and number, not for gender, the meaning remains the same whatever order the three words are put in: *homo feminam amat* (the usual word-order in Latin), *feminam amat homo, feminam homo amat, amat homo feminam,* and *amat feminam homo* all mean 'the man loves the woman'. To say 'the woman loves the man', the cases of the nouns have to be changed round: *femina hominem amat* (or the same three words in any other order). The fact that word-order is relatively unimportant in inflected languages means that their words can be easier to fit into the metrical schemes of poetry than the words of uninflected languages such as English, where part of the meaning is carried by word-order.

Going back to Classical Greek, nouns and adjectives had five main cases, and were arranged into classes (called declensions) according to the endings of the root words. There were three genders, masculine, feminine, and neuter (as there are in modern German); and two numbers, singular and plural (and in early Greek a 'dual' number as well). Verb formations were extremely complicated, indicating action (ongoing, finished, and others); time (past, present, and future); mood (indicative, subjunctive, and others); voice (active, passive, and middle); and person (first, second, and third, in both singular and plural). All this makes ancient Greek quite a difficult language to learn, but a precise and flexible one once it is understood.

The different waves of Greek invaders brought their own dialects of the language with them – Aeolic, Ionic, Attic, Doric, and so on – but the dialects were mutually comprehensible and shared much the same word stock. Much of the literature that we shall be considering was written in the Attic (Athenian) dialect, but we shall also come across major writers in, for instance, the Ionic dialect. Homeric Greek, the 'epic dialect', is a special case, which we shall look at in the next chapter.

The Greek alphabet

The words of a language can be written down in various ways. In logographic systems each word has a separate written sign, of which several thousand are therefore required; basic Chinese can be written with 2,000 signs, but many more are needed for special subjects. Syllabic systems (such as Linear A and B) have a different sign for each syllable, and require anything from fifty up to several hundred signs; syllabic systems are simpler than logographic ones, but are still fairly clumsy. Alphabets are much more economical, having a sign for each consonant and vowel, and requiring a total of only twenty or thirty signs which can be variously combined to make any of the words of a language.

The earliest alphabets were developed from about 1700 BC for certain semitic languages, but they had signs only for the consonants, which limited their usefulness. When the Greeks adopted one of these semitic alphabets – the Phoenician one consisting of nineteen consonants – in the eighth century BC, they used as signs for vowels some of the Phoenician consonants that they did not need, and at a stroke they created the first fully efficient alphabetical system for writing: the direct ancestor of the Roman capital alphabet, and of the lower-case alphabet in which you are reading these words.

The standard Greek alphabet, which is still in use, is shown in the chart opposite.

We can see that some of the characteristics of the original semitic alphabet have been carried right through into our own time: the forms of the letters A, D, K, O, and T, for instance, and the order of the letters ABC ... (Aleph Beth Gimel ... in Hebrew, Alpha Beta Gamma ... in Greek). Without the Greek alphabet and its descendants, which made literacy relatively easy, western literature would have taken a very different course.

Bronze-Age society and culture

Although Homer's epics ostensibly refer to a late Bronze-Age culture of Mycenaean type, they are an imperfect historical source because Homer applied many of the features of the culture of his own time and place (eighth-century BC Ionia) to the events of the mythical eleventh-century Trojan War and its aftermath. In the absence of contemporary written literature or other social records, the nature of daily life in Mycenae and the other Bronze-Age citadels must remain largely obscure. We know that the Mycenaeans buried their eminent dead, first in shaft graves and later in tall 'beehive' tombs, accompanied by magnificent grave goods; this indicates the emergence of wealthy ruling groups, who appear to have been native to the areas they ruled. The many weapons found among the grave goods suggest a warlike and aggressive society. The citadels, although influenced by Minoan models, were smaller than the palace cities of Crete, and appear to have been ruled by individual 'kings', major landowners who were the direct superiors of most the palace's servants, craftsmen, and field-workers (who might include freedmen but were probably mostly slaves, acquired in war or bought from slave-traders). Society, finally, was essentially patriarchal, ruled by men, with women largely confined to domestic roles; there is indeed no good

Phoenician	Early Greek	Early Latin	Later Greek	Greek Names[1]	Modern Roman
⊲	A	ꓶ	A α	alpha	A a
9	B	B	B β	beta	B b
ꓶ	Γ	<	Γ γ	gamma	C c
Δ	Δ	D	Δ δ	delta	D d
⅃	E	E	E ε	epsilon	E e
Υ	φ	F	Z ζ	zeta	F f
Ꮌ			H η	eta	G g
目	H	H	Θ θ	theta	H h
⸲	I	I	I ι	iota	I i
					J j
Ж	K	K	K κ	kappa	K k
⎩	Λ	↳	Λ λ	lambda	L l
⟩	M	ᴟ	M μ	mu	M m
ካ	N	ᴎ	N ν	nu	N n
o	O	O	O o	omicron	O o
ꓶ	π	Γ	Π π	pi	P p
Ϙ		Q			Q q
⊲	P	R	P ρ	rho	R r
W	Σ C	Ϛ	Σ σ ς	sigma	S s
†	T	T	T τ	tau	T t
	Y		Υ υ	upsilon	U u, Y y
		V			V v
					W w
Ŧ	Ξ	X	Ξ ξ	xi	X x
					Z z
			Φ φ	phi	
			X χ	chi	
			Ψ ψ	psi	
			Ω ω	omega	

evidence for the existence of matriarchal societies or rule by women at this or any other time in the ancient world.

Mycenaean religion

Although traces of the non-Indo-European Minoan religion, which celebrated a mother-goddess, survived in Mycenaean Greece, the names of some of the familiar polytheistic deities of later Greek religion already appear on Linear B clay tablets: Zeus, Hera, and Poseidon, for instance; some of them may indeed have accompanied

[1] For the pronunciation of the Greek names, see the Index.

the early Greek invaders.[2] There is also evidence from Pylos that certain religious customs (such as the order of events at sacrifices to the gods) that are known from later Greek practice were already in use in Mycenaean times. Homer, of course, has much to say about the Olympian pantheon, but as we have seen his frame of reference is more likely to be that of the eighth than of the eleventh century BC; and the beliefs and practices of developed Greek polytheism will be discussed in the next chapter.

---

[2] See the section on Hesiod's *Theogony*, pp. 40–1 below.

3 Homer and epic poetry

The background

Homer's two great poems incorporate both history and myth. They tell the story of certain episodes during and after an aggressive war undertaken by mainland Greeks against the city of Troy in north-west Asia Minor; and they tell it as if it is historical fact concerning the fairly recent past. They also set the story in a framework of divine activity, in which the Olympian gods play an active part in shaping these episodes.

To take the history first, the ten-year Trojan War was believed in classical times to have taken place early in the eleventh century BC. That was about the time of the collapse of Mycenaean civilisation, and of the beginning of the Dark Age. Archaeologists at the probable site of Troy have found a level of the city that was violently destroyed in about 1250 BC, not long before the traditional date. There is no evidence, however, that Troy was destroyed by Greeks; it fell at a time of turmoil in other cities in the area, and may just as well have been attacked from the east. Furthermore, although Homer gives his Troy mainly Greek characteristics, it also has some eastern ones (King Priam's fifty children, for instance); and it may be that the story was influenced by a tradition of early conflict between Greeks and some eastern power at the junction of their territories in the area of the Hellespont, the long strait (later called the Dardanelles) that separates Europe from Asia. There are also historical anachronisms in the stories resulting from the inclusion of eighth-century practices in eleventh-century settings; dead heroes being cremated, for instance, as was normal in the eighth century, not buried as they actually had been in the eleventh. In short, although there may be some historical truth in Homer's tale of the Trojan War, we do not know how much.

As to the poems' overtly mythical elements, they present a fully developed pantheon of Olympians, only a few of whom were mentioned in the Mycenaean records. The gods in Homer are led by Zeus the Father, and they include the other major Greek deities: Hera, Zeus's wife, the sea-god Poseidon, Athena goddess of crafts and battle, Apollo the prophetic god of art and learning, his twin sister Artemis the huntress, Aphrodite the goddess of love, Hermes the herald of the gods, Demeter the corn-goddess, Hephaestus the crippled smith-god, and Ares the god of war. They are presented after the fashion of a human family, with all their faults and jealousies and quarrels; and, although the gods are immortal and are able to meddle in human affairs, the human beings of the story still have some control over what happens to them, either by influencing individual gods to act on their behalf by means of prayer and sacrifice, or by exercising what is allowed them of their own free will.

The Olympians, together with nature spirits represented by the nymphs of trees, springs, rivers, lakes, and mountains, formed the supernatural environment of the Homeric Greeks; and they were taken very seriously. They were worshipped and propitiated by the careful performance of ritual, prayer, and the sacrifice of animals; and indeed the practice of ritual may sometimes have taken the place of a deeper or more personal spirituality. One advantage of this clearly defined religion was that it connected in one great family all manner of Greek-speaking communities which might otherwise have been separated from each other.

The early Greeks' understanding of the afterlife was not encouraging. It was believed that, for most people, death would be, literally, the end. The more prominent souls, however, would find their way to the underworld, Hades, where they would lead a bleak and unsatisfying existence, the shade of Achilles saying in the *Odyssey* that he would rather be the humblest labourer on earth than a king in Hades (11.487–91). There is also mention in the *Odyssey* of Elysium, the Islands of the Blest, but this was reserved for a few heroes who would go there instead of dying, and was perhaps a survival of Minoan beliefs. For most people, there was no prospect of heaven after death, no reward for good behaviour, nothing to hope for but relief from the pain of living. (The doctrine of reincarnation was not current in Homer's time.)

There can be no doubt that the Homeric epics first came into existence as oral poetry. There was a strong tradition of bardic poets who sang their poetry and accompanied themselves on the lyre, a kind of harp. They helped themselves to improvise their own versions of traditional tales by the use of words, phrases, and longer passages which were repeated – sometimes with small but significant differences – to bring the elements of the story together and to fit them into the strict metre of the traditional epic form. Each main character in the story, for instance, would have a set of descriptive epithets of various metrical shapes which could be fitted into different parts of the line as they were needed; and the habitual use of his stock of epithets and phrases would give the poet time to remember or improvise what was to come next. Whole scenes and settings in the stories were also repeated, for several possible reasons: repetition to articulate the narrative and to please the audience by its familiarity; to make a point by subtly changing a verbatim repetition; and perhaps to give the poet space, like the chorus of a song, to proceed with his tale.

But, although characteristics of oral poetry are plain to see in Homer, it is surprising to find oral poems of such great length – some 15,000 lines in the case of the *Iliad*, and 12,000 in that of the *Odyssey*, poems that would take twenty or twenty-four hours to recite, spread over many days. A possibility is that the poet built up the poems in parts over a period of time, and that he was eventually able to put the parts together as complete epics when the invention of alphabetic writing (which occurred at just the right time) enabled him to do so. In any event, the poems certainly existed in written form by the sixth century BC, and probably earlier.

Who, then, was Homer? One poet or many? And when did he live and compose his poems? The idea of multiple authorship for the Homeric epics – or at least for each of them – is now discredited (though of course each poem as it has come down to us was the result of many tellings). The 'epic dialect' is peculiar – it uses a mixture of Greek dialects to construct a special language that was not in general spoken use – and there would seem to be a single intelligence that shaped the *Iliad*, and the same (or possibly another) single intelligence that shaped the *Odyssey*. Various linguistic and other clues point to a time of composition in the late eighth century BC, the *Odyssey* being written down a few years after the *Iliad*; and to a poet who came from the Ionian coast of Asia Minor (now part of Turkey). Although we know nothing else about him, the chances are good that there really was a poet whom we call Homer (as the Greeks of the Classical period were quite sure that there was), and that he was responsible for the *Iliad*, and probably for the *Odyssey* as well.

The *Iliad*

A word, first, about the treatment of the more than 900 proper names that are included in the *Iliad*. English translations of Homer have generally followed one of three main courses for expressing Homeric names. (1) The Greek names are Latinised throughout, with English versions of the Latinisations where they exist and are familiar: thus Pope not only writes Achilles and Hector, but he also gives us the Roman names of the Greek gods and heroes: Ajax (Latin Aiax) for Greek Aias, Jupiter (or Jove, Latin Iuppiter) for Greek Zeus, Minerva for Athena, Pollux for Polydeuces (or Polydeukes), Ulysses (Latin Ulixes) for Greek Odysseus, and so on. (2) The Greek names are transliterated as faithfully as possible. This produces Achaioi for Achaeans, Aineias for Aeneas, Mykenai for Mycenae, and Patroklos for Patroclus. (3) A compromise is sought, avoiding both extreme Latinisation and pedantic transliteration. This course, which is followed here, is unashamedly inconsistent. Greek forms are generally preferred to Roman, but (a) the Latin termination *-us* is used in preference to the Greek *-os*; (b) *k*s are replaced by *c*s; and (c) some Latinised and anglicised forms are used when they are familiar and seem appropriate. The outcome is that the first of the following pairs of names is preferred to the second: Achilles/Akhilleus, Ajax/Aias, Apollo/Apollon or Phoebus, Artemis/Diana, Athena/Athene or Minerva, Castor/Kastor, Hector/Hektor, Hephaestus/Hephaistos or Vulcan, Heracles/Herakles or Hercules, Polydeuces/Polydeukes or Pollux, Priam/Priamos, Thebes/Thebai, and Troy/Troia. 'In the end', as Martin Hammond says in his translation of the *Iliad*, 'the question is an aesthetic one, depending on the balance struck between the proper desire to assert the Greekness of the Greek characters, and proper respect for the long tradition of English literature and literary reference.'[1] It is my intention to strike just such a balance in the use of Greek and Roman names throughout this book.

Returning, then, to Homer's poem: the *Iliad* is the first great work of western literature that is known to us: a huge narrative in verse with a compelling structure, well-developed characters, and a commanding poetic style. It is the story of a few crucial days' fighting in the Trojan War. Nine years before the *Iliad* begins, Helen, the wife of King Menelaus of Sparta, was abducted by Paris, one of the sons of King Priam of Troy; and Menelaus, together with his elder

---

[1] Homer, *The Iliad*, trs. by Martin Hammond (1987), Penguin Classics p. li; see also pp. 5–7 above.

brother King Agamemnon of Mycenae, mounted a joint military expedition against Troy with the aim of recapturing his wife and punishing the Trojans. So far neither side has won, largely because the gods, who are divided in the matter with some supporting the Greeks and some the Trojans, have blocked whichever side seemed to be winning.

Now, as the poem begins, a further problem has arisen: the Greeks' most potent warrior, Achilles the son of the goddess Thetis, has quarrelled with the Greek general Agamemnon. The quarrel is primarily the fault of Agamemnon, who has angered the god Apollo by winning a Trojan girl as a battle honour. She is Chryseïs, the daughter of one of Apollo's Trojan priests. In his indignation Apollo (who generally supports the Trojan side) has inflicted a plague on the Greek camp, so obliging Agamemnon to return the girl to her father. To make up for his loss of face Agamemnon arbitrarily seizes Briseïs, another Trojan girl whom Achilles has similarly won. His honour touched, Achilles is outraged and refuses to go out and fight, so exposing the Greeks to the might of the Trojan Hector, Priam's eldest son, whose strength in battle is second only to that of Achilles himself.

Deprived of Achilles's support, the Greeks are driven back to their beachhead by Hector and the Trojans, and their leaders are wounded. Agamemnon considers evacuation, but is persuaded instead to offer to return Briseïs untouched to Achilles, together with a rich treasure, if Achilles will return to the fight. Partly because Agamemnon does not add an apology to his offer, Achilles nurses his anger and still refuses to fight even though his side is losing the battle, so putting himself partly in the wrong. Consequently the Greeks continue to suffer heavy losses, and Achilles is persuaded to give his close friend Patroclus permission to go and fight, and to lend Patroclus his armour. Hector kills Patroclus; Achilles is devastated and, although Patroclus's disarmed body is recovered with great difficulty by the Greeks, he decides at last to leave his tent and fight so that he can take revenge on Hector; and to help him his divine mother Thetis fetches a new and splendid set of armour specially made by the smith-god Hephaestus. Achilles, gleaming and terrible, takes the field and not only kills Hector but subjects his corpse to the gross indignity of tying it by the heels to his chariot and dragging it in the dust.

Honour satisfied and Patroclus cremated, funeral games are held; and after them King Priam comes to the Greek camp to beg for

Hector's body. Achilles's anger is finally spent, and he feels a common humanity with Priam. Hector's body is taken back to Troy, and the *Iliad* ends with his funeral.

Such, in bare outline, is the tragic story of Homer's first, majestic epic; and it is told with narrative drive, carefully structured elements, realistic development of the main characters, gripping scenes of argument and battle, and brilliant language, rich in simile. The structure of the *Iliad* is built on contrasts between opposites: first, general oppositions such as war and peace, Greeks and Trojans, gods and human beings, realistic description and myth; and secondly the personal oppositions of Achilles/Agamemnon, Achilles/Hector, Athena/Apollo, Menelaus/Odysseus, Hector/Paris, Andromache/Helen, Agamemnon/Priam – the list could go on. These contrasts deepen and enrich the simple chronological narrative.

As to character, not only do the passions of Achilles and Agamemnon draw us into the depths of their quarrel, but a large cast of other characters is brought to vivid life: among the Greeks Menelaus, not always as brave as he would like to be, and the persuasive Odysseus who fights on despite his tactical prudence, Ajax and Diomedes who are stand-up fighters second only to Achilles and Hector, and Thersites the insolent ordinary soldier. The Trojans, less hard-headed than the Greeks, include the truly noble Hector and his wife Andromache whom he must leave for honour's sake, Paris who deserts honour for the sake of a Helen dominated by Aphrodite, and the elderly Priam and Hecuba, the sad monarchs whose sons are sacrificed to a war they had not sought.

And then there are the gods, some of them meddling and quarrelsome to the point of frivolity, their careless immunity contrasted with the piteous fragility of the human condition: stern Zeus, Apollo and Athena who are seriously determined to help the Trojan and the Greek causes respectively, and Achilles's mother Thetis who feels a mother's despair at knowing of the death that is decreed for her son.

The rhetoric of the arguments and discussions between the actors in the drama is ornately magnificent, and is even carried into battle, where the major combatants commonly address each other at length before they set to with their spears and swords. The battle scenes are otherwise grimly realistic, all sweat and cries of pain, giving gory anatomical details of exactly what happens when a warrior's spear-thrust or sword-chop connects with a particular part of his opponent's body. (An example is given in the section on translations, pp. 32–4 below.) But even the goriest battle scenes are pervaded with sentiments of pathos, humanity, and compassion, universal and timeless in their application.

And finally there is the language of the poem, simple but exuberant, adorned with moving similes. We have already mentioned the repetitions of the epithets for the various characters, whereby in Book I Achilles is described (in Robert Fagles's translation) as 'Peleus' son', 'brilliant', 'the swift runner', 'the matchless runner', 'the headstrong runner', 'the proud runner', 'godlike', 'blazing', 'the best of the Achaeans'; while Agamemnon is called 'lord of men', 'the fighting son of Atreus', 'the great field marshal', 'King', 'Atrides', 'son of Atreus', 'mighty Atrides'; and so on – epithets which both help the poet on his way and generate for the audience a comfortable familiarity with the heroes. Similar phrases – such as the well-known 'rosy-fingered dawn' and 'wine-dark sea' – and longer repeated passages (the description of the treasure offered by Agamemnon to Achilles, for instance) help in the same ways. Homer's descriptions also depend heavily on metaphor and simile, some of them repetitions, but many unique to their occasions; and they are commonly of great power and beauty – again, a fine example is given in several versions in the section on translations, pp. 34–5 below.

For all these reasons the *Iliad* manages to be an engrossing as well as a stimulating poem, which can carry the modern reader back into the extravagant culture of the Bronze- and early-Iron-age Greeks – an astonishing feat considering its antiquity and its archaic form. Indeed it has been a success right from the start, a national epic treasured by the Greeks, a model admired and built on by the Romans, a work that has been recognised for its seminal importance over the centuries ever since.

Romanticised versions of the story have been current since the Middle Ages, notably the non-classical fiction of Troilus and Cressida,[2] which is related in Chaucer's *Troilus and Criseyde*; and in *Troilus and Cressida*, Shakespeare's outrageous satire based on parts of the *Iliad*.

Translations

Four different English translations of the *Iliad* are currently available in Penguin Classics and Oxford World's Classics. All are agreed to be sufficiently accurate renderings – though 'accuracy'

---

[2] Troilus, a son of Priam, appears as a Trojan hero in the *Iliad*, but his relationship with Cressida (who is a debased version of the Chryseïs captured by Agamemnon) does not.

in translation tends to be an imprecise term – and all have adequate introductions and indexes; but it is worth looking at each one of them both for the way it presents the *Iliad*, and as a background to the whole question of considering translations of classical literature. Taking them in chronological order, the first of them is the classic translation into 'heroic couplets' by Alexander Pope (1715–20, Penguin Classics), which is thought by many still to be the best. It is close to Homer in being set in a highly disciplined form of verse, and it suggests Homer's vigour and panache; but its five-stress couplets sound very different from Homer's unrhymed hexameters, and their relentless rhythmic repetition can have a slightly soporific effect. Pope also translates all the Greek names into their Latin forms (see p. 28 above). Next comes a version in regular five-stress blank-verse lines by an American, Robert Fitzgerald (1974, Oxford World's Classics). This translation is smooth and attractive, but again its very regularity is something of a disadvantage, and it reads perhaps too comfortably. Then there is a fine prose version by Martin Hammond (1987, Penguin Classics). Unhindered by the requirements of verse, he has the freedom to follow Homer's words very closely, and it is hard to see how the *Iliad* could be more faithfully done in prose (though the transliteration of the Greek names is perhaps over-scrupulous); but the truth is, I think, that verse is essential to the poem: the *Iliad* simply does not work so well in prose. Thus brings us finally to Robert Fagles's American translation into six- and five- (and occasionally four- and three-)stress blank-verse lines (1990, Penguin Classics). This irregular verse is a long way from Homer's disciplined hexameters, but the translation has an authentic Homeric feel to it which the others lack, perhaps because of Fagles's clear understanding of and close sympathy with what Homer was doing; it also has a valuable long introduction by Bernard Knox. At all events it is the translation I prefer; but of course the choice is a matter of personal aesthetics, and other readers may not agree with me. To help them choose, here are two passages in each of the four versions, a battle scene in which Achilles kills Prince Polydorus (*Iliad* 20.407–18), and an extended simile illustrating Paris's fleetness of foot (*Iliad* 6.503–16):

> I *The death of Polydorus*
>
> Then fell on *Polydore* his vengeful rage,
> The youngest hope of *Priam*'s stooping age:
> (Whose feet for swiftness in the race surpast)
> Of all his sons, the dearest, and the last.

To the forbidden field he takes his flight
In the first folly of a youthful knight,
To vaunt his swiftness, wheels around the plain,
But vaunts not long, with all his swiftness slain.
Struck where the crossing belts unite behind,
And golden rings the double back-plate join'd:
Forth thro' the navel burst the thrilling steel;
And on his knees with piercing shrieks he fell;
The rushing entrails pour'd upon the ground
His hands collect; and darkness wraps him round.

(Pope, Penguin Classics p. 950)

Achilles turned his spear on Polydorus,
Priam's son. The father had refused
permission to this boy to fight, as being
youngest of all his sons and dearest, one
who could outrun the rest.
                               Just now, in fact,
out of pure thoughtlessness, showing his speed,
he ran the front line till he met his end.
The great battle-field runner, Prince Achilles,
hit him square in the back as he flashed by –
hit where the golden buckles of his belt
and both halves of his cuirass linked together.
Passing through the man, out at the navel
the spearhead came, and on his knees he fell
with a loud cry. The blinding cloud of death
enveloped him as he sprawled out, his entrails
held in his hands before him.

(Fitzgerald, Oxford Worlds's Classics p. 361)

But Achilleus went with his spear after godlike Polydoros, son of Priam. His
father always forbade him to fight, because he was the youngest of the sons
born to him, and the one he loved most: and he was the fastest of all on his
feet. And now in his young folly he was displaying the speed of his legs and
racing through the front-fighters, until he lost the life that was in him. As he
came dashing past, swift-footed godlike Achilleus hit him with his spear in
the middle of the back, where the belt's golden buckles joined and the
corselet opposed a double layer. The point of the spear held on right through
and came out by his navel. He screamed, and dropped on his knees, and a
dark cloud enfolded him: he sank down holding in his entrails with his
hands.

(Hammond, Penguin Classics p. 332)

Achilles rushed with his spear at noble Polydorus
son of Priam. His father would not let him fight,
ever, he was the youngest-born of all his sons –
Priam loved him most, the fastest runner of all

but now the young fool, mad to display his speed,
went dashing along the front to meet his death.
Just as he shot past the matchless runner Achilles
speared him square in the back where his war-belt clasped,
golden buckles clinching both halves of his breastplate –
straight on through went the point and out the navel,
down on his knees he dropped –
screaming shrill as the world went black before him –
clutched his bowels to his body, hunched and sank.

(Fagles, Penguin Classics p. 516)

II *Paris runs out to fight*
But now, no longer deaf to honour's call,
Forth issues *Paris* from the palace wall.
In brazen arms that cast a gleamy ray,
Swift thro' the town the warriour bends his way.
The wanton courser thus, with reins unbound,
Breaks from his stall, and beats the trembling ground;
Pamper'd and proud, he seeks the wonted tides,
And laves, in height of blood, his shining sides;
His head now freed, he tosses to the skies;
His mane dishevel'd o'er his shoulders flies;
He snuffs the females in the distant plain,
And springs, exulting, to his fields again.
With equal triumph, sprightly, bold and gay,
In arms refulgent as the God of day,
The son of *Priam*, glorying in his might,
Rush'd forth with *Hector* to the fields of fight.

(Pope, Penguin Classics pp. 312–13)

Paris in the meantime had not lingered:
after he buckled his bright war-gear on
he ran through Troy, sure-footed with long strides.
Think how a stallion fed on clover and barley,
mettlesome, thundering in a stall, may snap
his picket rope and canter down a field
to bathe as he would daily in the river –
glorying in freedom! Head held high
with mane over his shoulders flying,
his dazzling work of finely jointed knees
takes him around the pasture haunts of horses.
That was the way the son of Priam, Paris,
ran from the height of Pergamus, his gear
ablaze like the great sun,
and laughed aloud. He sprinted on, and quickly
met his brother, who was slow to leave
the place where he had discoursed with his lady.

(Fitzgerald, Oxford World's Classics pp. 111–12)

And Paris did not dally long in his high house, but once he had put on his glorious armour of intricate bronze, he dashed through the city, sure of the speed of his legs. As when some stalled horse who has fed full at the manger breaks his halter and gallops thudding across the plain, eager for his usual bathe in the lovely flow of a river, and glorying as he runs. He holds his head high, and the mane streams back along his shoulders: sure of his own magnificence, his legs carry him lightly to the haunts where the mares are at pasture. So Paris, son of Priam, came down from the height of Pergamos, bright in his armour like the beaming sun, and laughing as he came, his quick legs carrying him on. Then he soon came up with godlike Hektor, his brother, just as he was about to turn from the spot where he talked with his wife. (Hammond, Penguin Classics pp. 103–4)

> Nor did Paris linger long in his vaulted halls.
> Soon as he buckled on his elegant gleaming bronze
> he rushed through Troy, sure in his racing stride.
> As a stallion full-fed at the manger, stalled too long,
> breaking free of his tether gallops down the plain,
> out for his favourite plunge in a river's cool currents,
> thundering in his pride – his head flung back, his mane
> streaming over his shoulders, sure and sleek in his glory,
> knees racing him on to the fields and stallion-haunts he loves –
> so down from Pergamus heights came Paris, son of Priam,
> glittering in his armor like the sun astride the skies,
> exultant, laughing aloud, his fast feet sped him on.
> Quickly he overtook his brother, noble Hector
> still lingering, slow to turn from the spot
> where he had just confided in his wife . . .
>   (Fagles, Penguin Classics pp. 212–13)

The *Odyssey*

To come to the *Odyssey* straight after the *Iliad* can be something of a shock: for it is to come from the great epic of the fighting at Troy, with its gods and kings and heroes, its battles and tragedies, to the story of one man, the ingenious and enduring Odysseus, who has to find his way home from Troy to his wife and son through a multi-tude of troubles and hardships, in an account which is both a tale of high adventure and a romance with a happy ending. From poetic epic to romantic novel: the scope of western literature is prefigured in its first two masterpieces.

Not that the *Odyssey* is without its gods or its killings. The story, which covers a period of about six weeks, begins not with Odysseus himself, but on Mount Olympus, ten years after Troy has fallen to the Greeks, where the gods are discussing Odysseus's plight. All the surviving Greek heroes have returned home except for Odysseus, who has been detained for the last seven years on the isle of Ogygia by the nymph Calypso; while his wife Penelope is being pestered at home in Ithaca by a gang of suitors for her hand, who are eating up his property and threatening his son Telemachus, a baby when Odysseus sailed for Troy and now aged about eighteen. Zeus agrees to send Hermes to tell Calypso to release Odysseus, while Athena (who has always favoured the wily tactician) is to go to Ithaca to put heart into Telemachus and send him off in search of his father. Having failed to persuade the suitors to behave honourably, Telemachus visits Nestor in Pylos, and Menelaus and Helen in Sparta, without finding out anything useful about what has happened to Odysseus.

It is not until this point, when we know how desperately Odysseus is needed at home in Ithaca, that we meet him at the beginning of Book 5, sitting – disconsolate and homesick – on the shore of Ogygia. Hermes delivers his message, and Calypso reluctantly allows Odysseus to build himself a raft and gives him provisions for the voyage. He sets off, but his raft is soon wrecked by the sea-god Poseidon, whom Odysseus has angered by blinding the Cyclops Polyphemus, Poseidon's son. Odysseus, a powerful swimmer, reaches the island of Phaeacia, where Athena arranges that he shall be met by Nausicaa, the king's daughter. Admiring his manly courtesy, she takes him home to the palace of her father Alcinous. Here Odysseus is made welcome, takes part successfully in the Phaeacian games, and is entertained by the bard Demodocus who sings of the frustrated love of the immortals Ares and Aphrodite, and of the Trojan war and Odysseus's crafty infiltration into Troy in the wooden horse. In the evening Odysseus is persuaded to tell the story of his own adventures since leaving Troy.

There follow four books, 9 to 12, which contain Odysseus's vivid account of the attack on the Cicones, the visit to the land of the Lotus-eaters, the dreadful encounter with the Cyclops, the opening of Aeolus's bag of winds which blow them first to the cannibal Laestrygonians and then to Circe's enchanted isle, the visit to the House of the Dead to consult Teiresias where Odysseus meets the shades of his family and friends, the evasion of the Sirens, the narrow escape from Scylla and Charybdis, and finally the sacrilegious slaughter by his crew of the oxen of the sun-god Helios which causes Zeus to destroy the ship and all its company except for Odysseus himself, who is carried on the wreckage to Calypso's isle.

Deeply impressed by his tale, Alcinous gives Odysseus a passage to Ithaca, where he is met by Athena. She disguises him as an old beggar and sends him off to stay with his faithful slave the swineherd Eumaeus. His identity is revealed to Telemachus, who has returned safely from Sparta, avoiding a plot by the suitors to ambush and kill him; and Odysseus, Telemachus, and Eumaeus plan the destruction of the suitors. Odysseus then goes to his palace, where he is recognised by his dog and his old nurse Eurycleia, but not by his wife. Keeping his identity secret, he is mocked as a beggar by the suitors; but in a competition that will decide which of them is to marry Penelope, Odysseus alone is able to shoot an arrow from his own bow through a line of axes; and then, helped by Telemachus and two faithful slaves, he proceeds to slaughter all the suitors in a bloody battle, and then to hang the slaves who had been unfaithful to him. His honour satisfied, Odysseus is reunited at last with his wife and with his father, old Laertes; while Athena prevents the blood-feud that would otherwise have followed the killings. We learn finally that Odysseus, after a journey on the mainland to sacrifice to Poseidon, will return home to Ithaca and die there in old age.

This is by any standards a superb adventure story, and one that can still grip the reader after some 2,800 years. It is also very different from the *Iliad*, which is one of the reasons why it is it sometimes suggested that the Homeric poems were written by two different authors; on the other hand, taking into account that the *Odyssey* was probably written some years after the *Iliad*, and that the language and versification of the two works have greater similarities than would be likely if there were two authors, the chances are that Homer composed them both.

Apart from the adventures, the poem still captivates us with its ingenious structure, the intriguing character of its hero, and the Homeric imagery of its verse. The device of holding back the appearance of the hero until Book 5 works brilliantly: by then we know about the outrages committed by the suitors in his own house, about the threat to the life of his son Telemachus, and about the uncertain rejection of the suitors by his wife Penelope, and we see that it is essential that he should get home and deal with the situation as soon as possible. We also know that, although his detention by Calypso is about to come to an end, he is threatened with revenge by the sea-god Poseidon. How will he get home? Will he be in time? Now the story surges ahead, as Odysseus overcomes one obstacle after another in his race for home, with the interpolation of the magnificent four books in which he relates the adventures he had between leaving

Troy and arriving at Ogygia. The pace is kept up right to the end, when he eventually reaches Ithaca and massacres the suitors in a blood-bath reminiscent of the battle scenes in the *Iliad*.

Just as engaging as the telling of the tale is the unfolding of the character of its hero. In the *Iliad* Odysseus has been presented as a consummate tactician, honey-tongued, the man to send on an awkward embassy, a brave and skilful fighter. Now in the *Odyssey* more of his character is revealed, for he is not only an ambassador, a fighter, and a leader of men, but also a husband, a father, a lover, the firm head of a household, a charming guest. He is moreover a man of resolution, intellectual curiosity, and love of home; a man of endless ingenuity and resource, of indomitable courage and endurance, not unmoved by pity but pitiless when he must be so. But with all this he is a man with human failings who can make mistakes and lose his temper, boast of his trickery, take excessive revenge on his enemies, become despondent and weep with self-pity. Odysseus is, in short, as Joyce said of the hero of *Ulysses*, a 'cultured allround man' with 'a touch of the artist' about him,[3] one with whom we can sympathise and identify even if we cannot aspire to his heroism.

Besides Odysseus himself, the best-defined characters are Telemachus, the youth who has never known his father but must try to take his place in trying cirumstances; Penelope, in conflict between her duties as wife to a man who is probably but not certainly dead and society's expectation that she will remarry; and the old servants Eumaeus and Eurycleia, slaves owned by Odysseus but feeling true affection as well as duty towards their master.

What has been said already about the verse of the *Iliad* applies in general to the *Odyssey* as well, though the imagery is not so consistently high-flown in the later poem, as is appropriate to its very different atmosphere. Again Homer reads fluently, his story winging along with easy assurance, clear exposition, and simple grammatical constructions.

Translations

Unlike the poetic glories of the *Iliad*, the romantic adventure story of the *Odyssey* may be translated very well into prose – better perhaps than in verse. Pope and Fitzgerald and Fagles have all translated it into English verse with the skills they employed in their translations

[3] James Joyce, *Ulysses* (1922), p. 225. Joyce was also punning on an early sense of the word 'artist' (still current in Ireland) as 'one who practises artifice, stratagem, or cunning contrivance' (*OED* s.v. artist, IV. 9).

of the *Iliad*; but the two translations of the *Odyssey* available in
Penguin Classics and Oxford World's Classics are in fact both in
prose. Brought up as I was on the biblical prose of Butcher and
Lang's nineteenth-century version of the *Odyssey* (1879), E.V.
Rieu's modern prose translation of 1946 – the first of all the Penguin
Classics – struck me as an exhilarating breath of fresh air, as it struck
many other readers at the time. It had its minor faults, however, and
it has been revised by E.V. Rieu's son, D.C.H. Rieu, who has
produced a Penguin Classics version (1991) that has purged his
father's text of its occasional inaccuracies. The Oxford World's
Classics version (1980) is by Walter Shewring, who adds an interesting epilogue on translation. It also reads well enough, but I find
that Shewring's heightened, slightly stilted, prose slows up a story
which should race along in its excitement. Again this is my personal
opinion, to be tested against the two versions of a speech at the end
of the poem, in which Odysseus's old nurse Eurycleia tells his wife
Penelope about the slaughter of her suitors (*Odyssey* 23.39–57):

> 'I didn't *see* anything and wasn't *told* anything,' said the dear nurse Eur-
> ycleia, 'but I heard the groans of dying men. We sat petrified in a corner of
> our quarters, with the doors shut tightly on us, till your son Telemachus
> shouted to me to come out. His father had sent him to fetch me. And then I
> found Odysseus standing among the bodies of the dead. They lay round him 5
> in heaps all over the hard floor. It would have gladdened your heart to see
> him, spattered with blood and gore like a lion. By now all the corpses have
> been gathered in a pile at the courtyard gate, while he has had a big fire made
> and is purifying the palace. He sent me to call you to him. So come with me
> now, so that you two may begin a time of happiness together after all your 10
> sufferings. The wish you cherished so long has today come true. Odysseus
> has come back to his own hearth alive; he has found both you and his son at
> home, and in his own palace he has had his revenge on every one of the
> Suitors who wronged him.'
>
> (Rieu, revised, Penguin Classics p. 345)[4]

> Eurycleia answered: 'I did not see; I was not told. I could only hear men's
> dying groans; we women were crouching terror-stricken in a corner of the
> room, locked in behind the close-fitting door, till your son Telemachus called

---

[4] The original 1946 text had the following readings: [line 1] 'I never saw a thing,'
said Eurycleia. 'I knew nothing about it. All I heard was / [line 6] It would have done
you good to see him, spattered with blood and filth like a lion. / [line 9] is fumigating
the palace. / [line 10] may enter into your happiness together after all the sorrows
you have had. The hope you cherished so long is fulfilled for you to-day. /[line 13]
and he has had his revenge in his own palace on every one of the Suitors who were
doing him such wrong.' Some readers may prefer the colloquial simplicity of Rieu
senior to the slightly more mannered style of his son.

me out; his father had sent him to summon me. Then I found Odysseus standing among the corpses of the slain. They lay around him, one above another, over the hard- trodden floor; your heart would have rejoiced to see it. And now the suitors lie all heaped up at the courtyard gates, and Odysseus has had a great fire lit and is purifying the place with sulphur; moreover he told me to summon you. Come down with me, then, so that you two after all your sorrows may tread the pathway of heart's gladness. Your hope deferred is fulfilled at last. He himself is living, is home and is at the hearth; he has found here both you and your son; and as for the suitors who did him wrong, he has taken vengeance on them all in his own house.'

(Shewring, Oxford World's Classics pp. 277–8)

Hesiod

The other poet of Homer's time whose verse has come down to us is his near-contemporary Hesiod,[5] who also used the epic dialect for his two surviving poems, the *Theogony* and *Works and Days*. But, despite the epic dialect and the technical similarity between the verse of the two poets, neither of Hesiod's two poems is an epic, the first being largely a genealogical account of the gods, and the second a collection of a conservative countryman's everyday wisdom. They are quirky and agreeable works, rich in information about the culture of the Homeric period; and they can also serve the modern reader as extended footnotes to the *Iliad* and the *Odyssey*.

Hesiod's father came from the important Aeolian city of Cyme on the coast of Asia Minor but, unable to make ends meet there, he moved to the poor farming village of Ascra in Boeotia where Hesiod and his brother Perses were brought up. Hesiod claims at the beginning of the *Theogony* that his vocation as a poet was revealed to him by the Muses while he was tending his father's flocks on the slopes of Mount Helicon, and that they instructed him to begin by celebrating the family of the immortal gods. This he was to do in passages of great beauty, such as the hymns to the Muses and Hecate, and in the idiosyncracies of his didactic poems. Nothing else is known about him but the few personal details he includes in the two poems, not even the approximate dates of his birth and death.

The *Theogony* continues with an exposition of the Greek creation story, the myth – probably of eastern origin – of what happened before the assumption of power by the Olympian gods, a story that

---

[5] Some scholars think that Hesiod wrote slightly earlier than Homer, others that he wrote slightly later; the matter is unlikely to be resolved.

was of course well known to Homer. It is told how the world came into being from 'chaos' (the Greek word means 'a chasm', not something disordered), out of which came Gaia the earth, Tartarus the underworld, and Eros the omnipotent principle of love. Gaia was enabled by Eros to create Uranus, the heavens; and the children of Gaia and Uranus were the Titans or giants. The last-born Titan was Cronus, who was persuaded by Gaia to castrate his father Uranus. Cronus then had children by his sister Rhea, and he swallowed them all except the last, who was Zeus. Cronus was eventually overthrown by Zeus, who made him disgorge the children he had swallowed; they became the Olympian gods, and chose Zeus as their leader. The *Theogony* goes on to trace the descent and describe the doings of the gods and their associates – it names some 300 of them – and ends by mentioning the godlike men and women who were descended from them, right down to the time of the legendary Oedipus of Thebes, Jason of the Argo, and the heroes of the Trojan War.

Works and Days is a rambling collection of country lore and wisdom, much of it proverbial, ostensibly aimed at Hesiod's idle brother Perses, who has taken more than his share of their inheritance, and at local 'kings' who have been bribed by Perses. The title of the poem refers to the passages on farming practice and on lucky and unlucky days of the month. It begins with a moral-didactic section on the importance and value of work, as opposed to idleness, and goes on to give an account (also perhaps of eastern origin) of the five ages – of gold, silver, bronze, demigods, and iron – which is a fervent expression of the enduring belief that things were better in the past than they are today:

> For now it is a race of iron; and they will never cease from toil and misery by day or night, in constant distress, and the gods will give them harsh troubles. [...] Soon they will cease to respect their ageing parents, and will rail at them with harsh words, the ruffians, in ignorance of the gods' punishment; nor are they likely to repay their ageing parents for their nurture. Fist-law men; one will sack another's town, and there will be no thanks for the man who abides by his oath or for the righteous or worthy man, but instead they will honour the miscreant and the criminal. Law and decency will be in fists. The villain will do his better down by telling crooked tales, and will swear his oath upon it. [...] Decency and Moral disapproval will go to join the family of the immortals, abandoning mankind; those grim woes will remain for mortal men, and there will be no help against evil.
>
> (Hesiod, *Theogony and Works and Days*, trs. by M.L. West, 1988, Oxford World's Classics p. 42)

Hesiod then offers miscellaneous information and advice about how to run a farm; about the need to have good relations with one's neighbours; about the danger of trusting oneself or one's goods to sea voyages; and about choosing reliable servants and a good wife. The farming year is linked to a reliable star calendar, and a more difficult moon calendar; and the treatise ends with a detailed list of the days of the month that are favourable and unfavourable for certain activities. In later centuries Hesiod and Homer were jointly credited, despite their differences of both genius and approach, with creating the form of the early Greek epic, and even with being responsible for allotting names and qualities to the gods, though they must in fact have been building on the work of their predecessors. A wholly improbable tradition of the fourth century BC went so far as to propose that Hesiod and Homer had been contenders in a bardic competition, in which Hesiod was awarded the prize because of the greater morality of his subjects.

Translation

The Oxford World's Classics *Hesiod* (1988) is attractively translated and enthusiastically edited by M.L. West, who says in his note on the text and translation (p. xxiii): 'If I have sometimes made Hesiod sound a little quaint and stilted, that is not unintentional: he is.'

II: Greece in the fifth century BC

4 From Archaic to early-Classical Greece

The Archaic Period is generally taken to have lasted from the end of the Dark Age sometime in the eighth century BC to the final defeat of the Persian invasion at Plataea in 479 BC. At some time before the beginning of the eighth century the 'polis', the Greek city-state, had begun to evolve following the disintegration of Mycenaean civilisation, and to become the focal point for the development of Greek institutions and culture. Whatever its form of government – initially monarchies and autocracies which could themselves evolve into oligarchies and democracies – the 'polis' was (in George Forrest's lucid definition) 'a community of citizens (adult males), citizens without political rights (women and children), and non-citizens (foreigners and slaves), a defined body, occupying a defined area, living under a defined or definable constitution, independent of outside authority to an extent that allowed enough of its members to feel that they were independent'.[1] There were two essentials: the first was a sense of community, the second was a city, usually fortified, at the hub of the surrounding farm-land, which was the seat of government, the meeting place, and the market centre.

The two foremost Greek city-states of the Archaic and early Classical periods, Athens and Sparta, developed in very different directions, as a brief account of their history and constitutional development will show.

Athens

Athens may have been the only major Mycenaean citadel that was not destroyed and depopulated during the Dorian invasions, its

[1] *The Oxford History of Greece and the Hellenistic World*, ed. by John Boardman, Jasper Griffin, and Oswyn Murray, Oxford University Press 1986, p. 13.

45

fortified Acropolis (the word means 'high town') holding out through the troubles of the Dark Age; and it was probably during this period – traditionally the time of the legendary King Theseus – that the farming communities of the peninsula in which Athens is situated were brought under the control of the 'polis' to form the state of Attica. It was not a large country, only some 2,500 square kilometres in extent (the size of an average English county), hilly and dry, fitter for olives than for cereal crops; but it had good harbours and sea fishing, splendid marble quarries, fine potter's clay, rich silver and lead mines, and – above all – active-minded, ambitious, ingenious, and independent people.

In the earliest days Athens was ruled by kings, but at some time in the Dark Age, perhaps in the eleventh century BC, the monarchy was replaced by three (later nine) 'archons' or rulers elected for fixed terms by and from the members of the aristocracy. By the beginning of the sixth century BC the increasing wealth of the rich and the desperate poverty and indebtedness of the poor brought the state close to collapse. The most serious abuse was that a debtor's person was taken as the security for his debt if his possessions did not cover it, whereupon he could be sold as a slave either at home or abroad. The danger was averted by the reforms introduced by Solon, archon for 594–3, which cancelled all debts for which the debtor's land or his person was the security, and prohibited all future borrowing secured on the person of the borrower. The major constitutional reform introduced by the poet-politician Solon was to divide Athenian citizens into four classes in descending order of wealth: large landowners, men who kept horses, men who kept teams of oxen, and landless men; to open eligibility for election to the legislature to the two upper classes; and to re-establish a ruling council of ex-archons (the 'Areopagus'). This brought the rule of the hereditary aristocracy to an end, although there was still some way to go on the road to democratic rule; and the struggle for power following Solon's reforms led to the tyranny[2] of the Peisistratus family and their aristocratic supporters in the mid-sixth century BC.

The chief founder of Athenian democracy was the archon Cleisthenes, who overthrew the Peisistratids at the end of the sixth century BC and grouped the citizens of Attica into ten 'tribes', each containing groups from communities living in different parts of the

[2] A 'tyrant' was simply an absolute ruler who had seized power; the word did not necessarily mean an oppressive or cruel autocrat until later.

country; and each tribe provided fifty representatives chosen by lot for the ruling council of the state, each group of fifty taking it in turn to act for five weeks as an executive committee. The Areopagus of ex-archons was continued but it was, together with the council and its executive, under the supreme authority of the general assembly of all the citizens, which met regularly and decided the most important matters.

Extraordinary as it was, this 'democracy' was not much like the democracies of the modern world. Only a minority of the population (the male citizens) were entitled to be chosen for the ruling council and to vote at the assembly, all the rest being disfranchised; and the citizens did not elect individual representatives to speak and vote for them as we do, but each one of them had (in theory) his own vote in 'parliament'. As there were getting on for 30,000 Athenian citizens in the fifth century BC, there were inevitably caucuses of the rich and powerful who did most of the day-to-day running of the city and country, and had the strongest voice in the major decisions. It was not a perfect system, but it suited the Athenians, and they were proud of it.

They also became, whether or not as a result of their political progress, the intellectual and cultural leaders of Greece, as we shall see as we come to consider their literature, arts, and philosophy. They jostled, moreover, for commercial and political leadership outside Attica, being keen traders, mining their valuable silver, building a powerful navy, and having expansionist designs on other parts of mainland Greece, the Aegean islands, and the Greek Ionian coast of Asia Minor. And here they came up against Sparta, the other, very different, major Greek power.

Sparta

Bypassing Athens, the Dorian invaders of the twelfth and eleventh centuries BC had gone by way of the isthmus of Corinth into the Peloponnese, and groups of them had settled in the southern district of Laconia. Here some of their villages coalesced, probably in the tenth century, into the city of Sparta (or Lacedaemon), jointly ruled by two kings from two royal families, assisted by an oligarchy of 'ephors' (magistrates) and elders over the age of sixty. By about 700 BC most of the southern Peloponnese was under Spartan control, and the original (mostly non-Dorian) inhabitants had become serfs without political rights called 'helots'; they were in effect slaves belonging, not to individual aristocrats, but to the Spartan state, and they were not happy with their lot. There was also a consultative assembly, which had little power, consisting of all the male citizens over the age of thirty, of whom there was a small and declining number: only 8,000–9,000 at the beginning of the fifth century BC, perhaps a third of the number of Athenian male citizens of the same period. However, since the helots did all the work on the land, and a class of free but subservient non-citizens called 'perioikoi' (neighbours) handled business, crafts, and trade, the Spartan citizens were able to devote virtually all their time to military training and warfare. The training began at the age of seven, when every young citizen-to-be was taken away from home and trained with a group of other boys in military discipline and endurance. From twenty-one to thirty he lived as a soldier in barracks, or joined the secret police whose job was to keep down the potentially mutinous helots, who were a source of constant anxiety to the Spartan citizens. At thirty he joined an adult military 'mess' and stayed with it until he was sixty, but was free during this period to marry and beget children. Not surprisingly the result was the finest land army in Greece, expansionist aspirations that conflicted with those of Athens, a declining population, and a withering of the liberal arts.

The Persian Wars, 490–79 BC

Before the Athenians and the Spartans could fight for supremacy in Greece in the Peloponnesian Wars which will be described in Chapter 8 below, they had the Persians to deal with. By the early fifth century BC the Persian Empire encircled the eastern Mediterranean, but the Greek cities on the Aegean coast of Asia Minor assisted by Athens, and Thrace in northern Greece, continued to give the Persians trouble. The Persian King Darius therefore mounted a major invasion of Greece across the Hellespont in 490 BC. In a series of famous campaigns and encounters, the Athenian, Spartan, and allied armies and navies fought far larger and more powerful Persian forces, giving ground when they had to, even evacuating Athens, but winning the land battle of Marathon (490), the naval battle of Salamis (480), and – crucially – the land battle of Plataea (479). After Plataea the Persians had had enough, and King Xerxes (who had succeeded his father Darius in 486) finally withdrew his battered forces from Greece, leaving the triumphant and self-confident Greeks to fight each other.

The most formidable fighting unit of the Greek armies at this time was the 'phalanx' or box of heavy infantrymen called 'hoplites'. The hoplites, who in Athens were free citizens of the third class (men who kept oxen), provided their own armour of helmets, breast-plates, and shin-guards; in battle they stood shoulder to shoulder, their metal and leather shields overlapping, and their pikes sticking out below the shields. Such a phalanx, perhaps fifty men wide and eight deep at this time, was almost unstoppable as it advanced at a steady pace on the enemy, and was vulnerable only to attack, for instance by cavalry, from the flank or rear. The well-trained Spartan hoplites, who were effectively professional soldiers, were the most formidable of all.

But if the Spartans had the best army, the Athenians undoubtedly had the best navy, with from 200 to 300 operational triremes during the mid-fifth century BC. The trireme was a long, narrow fighting ship (27m × 5m) with three banks of oars, fast (9 knots or more) and manoeuvrable, and with an armoured beak for ramming enemy ships. Its well-trained crew numbered about 100: seventy oarsmen, plus sailors, marines, and archers, recruited from the fourth class of free but landless citizens, supplemented as necessary by resident foreigners and slaves: so that in the fifth century the Athenian navy mustered the very large number of 20,000 to 30,000 men.

Women, resident foreigners, and slaves

Besides the four classes of Athenian male citizens devised by Solon totalling perhaps 30,000 in the fifth century BC, there were a rather larger number of women and children (citizens without rights), probably a rather smaller number of 'metics' or resident foreigners, and a much larger number of slaves, perhaps as many as 80,000–100,000 of them.

Women were considered to be inferior to men, not only in strength and intellect, but also as human creatures; for it was generally believed that, in procreation, the woman was little more than the vessel in which the man's seed grew, so that the father, not the mother, was the child's true parent. All this rationalised the inferior status of women, and the contempt in which wives and daughters were frequently held. Citizens' wives were restricted to ordering the household and managing its staff; for a woman might not take part in government, choose her own husband, own property, or conduct a business; and she was encouraged by custom to stay at home and to be, as far as possible, neither seen nor heard in public. Clever and strong-minded women did of course influence their husbands behind the scenes; and upper-class women played an important part, as priestesses or acolytes, in religious rituals, processions, and festivals. Women from the lower orders commonly went out to work, some becoming prostitutes. There was also a class of courtesans ('hetaerae', usually foreigners, slaves, or freed-women), some of whom were accomplished musicians and dancers, who took distinguished lovers in male society.

The free resident foreigners (or 'metics') had some of the duties – such as paying taxes and doing military service – but not the full rights of citizens. They were mostly engaged in commercial and industrial activities, but the class included some major intellectuals, such as the orator Lysias (c.458–380 BC), and Aristotle in the fourth century BC.

The helots who formed the discontented slave society of Sparta have already been mentioned. Slavery in ancient Athens was organised more efficiently. There were several categories of slaves, from the few who were publicly owned and served in the state bureaucracy, through skilled craft workers, military and naval personnel, household slaves, and field-workers, down to the wretched slaves who were hired out by contractors to be worked to death in the mines. Captured in war or supplied by slave-traders, slaves had no rights and were open to every sort of abuse. In Greece, moreover, which was acutely conscious of the social hierachy, there were few opportunities for a slave to gain his or her freedom; yet there were few occasions on which Athenian slaves rebelled against their lot. Slavery existed in Bronze-Age Greece, it was taken for granted by Homer, and – hard as it is for us to understand – it was not seriously opposed by Greek philosophers of the Classical period.

Colonisation

The first great wave of colonists set out from Greek city-states from the mid-eighth to the mid-sixth century BC. They went, not to 'colonise' in the sense of exploiting foreign lands, as the Romans did, and as Spain did later in the Americas and Britain did in India and elsewhere; but to set up daughter-colonies of their home states, as the British did in, for instance, New Zealand. They were continuing the movement of Greek settlers that had crossed the Aegean to the coast of Asia Minor in the face of the Dorian invasions of the eleventh to ninth centuries, but this time they went further afield, to the central and western Mediterranean, and northwards through the Hellespont to the coasts of the Black Sea. Most of their colonies were sited (following the prudent advice of the Delphic Oracle) on major trade routes.

Early colonists set out from Euboea and Dorian Corinth to southern Italy and Sicily, founding amongst others the cities of Cumae (near Naples, soon after 750 BC) and Syracuse in Sicily (733 BC), while later ones from Ionian Asia Minor founded Massilia (Marseilles, 600 BC) and opened up the eastern coast of Spain (previously dominated by the Phoenicians) to trade with Greece. Some colonies then established daughter-colonies of their own: Syracuse founded Camarina (599 BC) and Gela founded Acragas (modern Agrigento, 580 BC), all in southern Sicily. Colonies to the north-east of Greece included numerous eighth- and seventh-century Euboean and Corinthian foundations in Chalcidice (the three-armed peninsula south of Thessaloníki, so called after the Euboean city of Chalcis); Byzantium (modern Istanbul, founded by people from Megara, c.660 BC); a dozen more colonies, mostly founded from Asia Minor, round the shores of the Black Sea in the seventh and sixth centuries BC; and the Athenian colony of Amphipolis, a city of great strategic and economic importance in Thrace (437 BC).

The colonists' reasons for going were various, but some certainly went in response to population increases and food shortages in Greece, often with the firm encouragement of their home governments, as well as simply in order to seek a better or more exciting life abroad. The colonies usually revered and co-operated with their founding cities, but most of them were soon fully independent states, Syracuse, for instance, becoming for a while the richest and most powerful city in the western Mediterranean. Their importance to the transmission and diffusion of Greek culture throughout the ancient world was immense. In particular, the Greeks of southern Italy and Sicily (*Magna Graecia*, Great Greece, as it came to be called) were crucial to the cultural development of the Roman civilisation that was to absorb them.

5 Religion, the arts, education, and books

Religious beliefs and practices

Homer and Hesiod may not have been the first to give the Greek gods their names and qualities, but their writings offered a systematic account of a pantheon, similar in many ways to a human family, that was generally accepted throughout the Greek world (pp. 26, 40–1 above). In fact the Greeks did not have a word for 'religion', but used a word meaning 'piety' or 'observance' instead; and it was in the careful performance of prayer and ritual, and in the respect paid to oracular pronouncements and to the great Delphic maxims ('know yourself' and 'nothing in excess'), that Greek religious beliefs were chiefly expressed. The spirituality and mysticism of later periods probably played a part in the religious life of some Greeks, but it would normally have been a private matter, not one to be displayed in public religious activities; and transcendental experiences were rarely mentioned in works of literature.

Besides the Olympians, the Greek supernatural world included nature spirits (nymphs) and ghosts; and it was considered wise as well as pious to propitiate them when the occasion arose. There were also the cults of particular gods, heroes, and ancestors, celebrated in temples and sanctuaries, at wayside shrines, and in the home. The chief method of propitiation was sacrifice, either bloodless (fruit or corn offered at a shrine, for instance) or blood sacrifice, accompanied by appropriate prayers. At a blood sacrifice, following the purification from pollution of the celebrants, a live domestic animal was slaughtered in such a way that its blood fell on the appropriate altar. It was then skinned and butchered. The bones, with some fat and flesh, were burned on the altar (which was consequently located outside the sanctuary or temple building, not inside); and finally the greater part of the flesh and some of the entrails were eaten by the participants. Apart from formal sacrifice of this sort, small portions of food at a meal might be set aside for a god, or a few drops of wine poured out as a libation before drinking.

Oracles, such as those of Zeus at Dodona in Epirus and of Apollo at Delphi, were consulted for guidance in both public and private affairs. The enquiries might concern religious practice; whether to declare war, or when and whither a group of colonists should sail; personal matters such as whether to get married, how to choose a career, and the legitimacy of children; and problems concerning health. At Dodona, answers were given in the form of interpretations of the rustling of the leaves of a sacred oak tree; at Delphi the priestess of Apollo went into an oracular trance, and gave verbal pronouncements which might need interpretation. Simple, personal questions might be answered 'yes' or 'no'; but the answers to questions of public importance were frequently ambiguous. Oracles were important in the ancient world because their pronouncements were believed and acted upon.

Architecture

The temple architecture of the Archaic and Classical periods is the most visible artistic legacy of the Greeks, having had – and indeed still having – a marked influence on the architecture of the modern world, either directly or through the mediation of Roman imitations of Greek buildings. Being built as houses for the gods, not for religious services, temples could have an extraordinary sublimity; and the Parthenon, seen on the Acropolis in the early-morning light from the hill where the Athenian assembly used to meet, can still be a deeply moving sight.

By the sixth century BC, Greek temple architecture in stone had reached an extraordinarily high standard. Temples of the Classical period, which could be very large (the fourth-century Artemisium at Ephesus was 15m longer than the Parthenon), were rectangular in plan, with a pitched, pedimented roof running the length of the building, supported by a colonnade running right round the outside; there was then an inner colonnade surrounding the room which housed the image of the god. There were conventional designs, or 'orders', for the fluted columns, known to us as 'Doric' (with plain tops) and 'Ionic' (with curlicues at the top); and temples might be adorned with sculptured friezes in bas relief, and painted in bright colours. Architectural features deriving ultimately from this temple style can be seen in the public buildings of nearly every major western city, and even in such things as the window-surrounds and porches of small private houses.

Other Greek public buildings included the 'stoa', a long colonnaded porch, and the circular 'tholos' for meetings; buildings which had later architectural and functional parallels in the cloisters and chapter-houses of Christian monasteries and cathedrals.

Painting

There was once a great deal of early Greek painting on walls and on wooden panels, but very nearly all of it is lost, or is known only from a few Roman copies. From the fragments that do survive we can tell that it progressed from the flat, outlined images (similar to Egyptian painting) of the Archaic period to attempts at giving depth to figures by means of shading; but there was not yet much understanding of perspective.

Where Greek painting does survive in quantity is on pottery, notably on the beautiful painted vases that were produced from Minoan times onwards, especially in Corinth and Athens. Again the drawing – mostly of mythological subjects – was flat, but in their progress from the outline drawing to 'black-figure' painting (in which white lines were scratched on black) during the Archaic period, and then to 'red-figure' painting (black lines drawn on red) at its end, the vase painters produced a vivid body of work, for the most part illustrating mythological subjects.

Sculpture

Small statuette images for votive or other religious purposes had been carved from very early times in bone, wood, and stone, but life-size sculptures of human figures in stone (deriving from Egyptian models) began to be made in Greece in the mid-seventh century BC. Initially these were rather stiff statues of young men and women (known as 'kouros' and 'koré' respectively), but anatomical accuracy of the modelling gradually increased, and by the end of the sixth century the 'new sculpture' was producing works of great beauty. It was mostly intended for use in and about religious centres and as funerary monuments, but portrait statues and busts (usually idealised) also became quite common; and, surprisingly to us who are used to seeing white originals and plaster casts, stone statues were (like temples) painted in bright colours. Besides sculpture in stone, there was a flourishing tradition of sculpture in cast bronze, made from clay models, often ornamented with inlays of other metals. Few actual bronzes survive – they were commonly melted down in later ages for the sake of their valuable metal – but many are known from Roman copies of them made in stone.

Music

Music, often accompanied by dancing, was an essential part of many Greek activities, especially religious ceremonies, of social gatherings, and at public games where music competitions were held. Much poetry was designed to be sung to the accompaniment of the lyre – hence 'lyric' poetry – and instrumental music was played on various sorts of lyre (stringed instruments that were plucked) and of pipe (which were not flutes but reed instruments like the oboe). Ancient Greek music was seldom written down, and hardly any written music has survived, so we know very little about what it sounded like, though we do know something about the 'modes' (or scales) that were used. Music was held to have an ethical and educational value, both Plato and Aristotle (following Pythagoras) believing that it could have a beneficial effect on a man's soul.

Education, literacy, and books

In fifth-century Athens education tended to be an informal, ad hoc affair, not at all like the intensive military training that was mandatory for Spartan boys from the age of seven. It was concerned as much with gymnastics, and with music and poetry, as it was with reading and writing and arithmetic; it was private and fee-paying; and it was chiefly restricted to the sons of citizens and, in a few cases, of resident foreigners. Homer figured largely in the literary part of the curriculum, pupils having to learn key passages of the *Iliad* by heart, together with lists of the words peculiar to the epic dialect. Citizens' daughters might have a scaled-down version of the same schooling, but in different places.

In the absence of statistics it is impossible to judge the effectiveness of Greek education in terms of literacy. We know that the Greek alphabet was invented in the late eighth century BC, and that it was used thereafter by professional scribes and bureaucrats; but we do not know how far ordinary citizens could read and write. There are, besides, varying degrees of literacy, from the mere ability to scratch the letters of one's name, through the functional ability to read simple documents, to the full literacy needed for reading and writing complex documents and literary texts. At a guess, perhaps 20–30 per cent of Athenian citizens were functionally literate in the mid-fifth century BC, but a smaller proportion of women and resident foreigners, and of slaves only the handful of state-owned clerks who worked in the law courts and government offices. It was not of course necessary to be literate to appreciate the epic, lyric, or dramatic poetry that was commonly sung or declaimed aloud. For those who could read them, books were available, but not yet in large quantities; small numbers of copies were made, and were subject to the inevitable errors that are accumulated by repeated transcription. These books were written in columns on sheets of papyrus, a paper-like material prepared from the pithy stem of an Egyptian water reed and imported from Egypt. A number of written sheets were glued end to end, and the beginning and end of the resulting book were attached to thin rolling pins, so that it could be rolled off one pin, read, and rolled onto the other. These fragile rolls were inconvenient compared to the robust codex on paper that we are used to: the reader cannot move quickly from place to place in the text of a roll as can be done by flipping forwards and backwards through the pages of a codex. A papyrus roll would contain from c.750 to 1,500 lines of poetry (two or three books of Homer), or an equivalent block of prose (one book of Thucydides). It is rolls of this length that were referred to when so many 'books' of a poet's work were mentioned by ancient editors and librarians; but there were scarcely any libraries to speak of in the fifth century BC. The first recorded private collection of learned books belonged to Aristotle in the early fourth century BC; and most Greek public libraries were founded in the Hellenistic period.

6 Lyric poetry: Pindar and his predecessors

The lyric

There is evidence that Greek lyric poetry – 'lyric' meaning sung to the accompaniment of a lyre – was flourishing in the seventh and sixth centuries BC; the form was already well developed technically, and had probably been in use for some time. But the surviving verse of the four most notable early lyricists – Alcman, Sappho, Alcaeus, and Anacreon – is so scanty, consisting of a small handful of short poems, collections of odd lines quoted by the literary critics of later centuries, and other short passages found on scraps of papyrus, that it is hard to get a clear view of it. It is as if the early work of Wordsworth, Coleridge, Keats, and Shelley were represented for us only by one or two short poems each, a few hundred odd lines quoted in textbooks, and a few other incomplete passages on bits of torn-up paper recovered from their waste paper baskets. It is not until we get to Pindar, writing in the fifth century BC, that we have a substantial portion of the work of a major lyric poet.

There was a special dialect of Greek used for lyric poetry, as there was for epic poetry, that was not in ordinary spoken use, and individual lyric poets combined it with their own regional dialects of the language (Aeolian, Ionian, Dorian, and so on). There were then two main branches of lyric poetry, choral and monodic. Choral poetry, at least partly sung by a choir and accompanied by instrumental music and dancing, was written for public functions such as religious ceremonies, games, processions, and weddings. An early choral poet was Alcman, a Spartan who was writing in the Dorian dialect around 625 BC; of his poetry about 100 lines plus fragments survive out of six books (papyrus rolls). The greatest exponent of the choral lyric was Pindar, whom we shall be discussing in the second part of this chapter.

Sappho and Anacreon

The other branch, monodic or solo lyric, was performed without a choir; but, although it tended to be more personal in its approach than choral lyric, there was still a greater tendency to generalise than is found in, say, the love poetry of later times. Sappho, a contemporary of Alcman from the large island of Lesbos on the Aegean coast of Asia Minor, is the only major woman writer of the ancient world that we know of, and we know little enough of her. It is the sad fact that Sappho's surviving work from the late seventh century BC is represented by two short love poems (one complete of 28 lines, one not quite complete of 17 lines), and about 200 fragments, some of them extracts of 15–20 lines from longer poems but mostly disconnected single lines or parts of lines, from nine books of lyrics which probably ran originally to at least 7,000 lines.

This is a pity, because the two surviving poems in the Aeolian dialect are extraordinarily powerful love lyrics. Here is the second of them, an unsurpassed account of the physical effects of falling in love, in a literal prose translation:

> He seems as fortunate as the gods to me, the man who sits opposite you and listens nearby to your sweet voice and lovely laughter. Truly that sets my heart trembling in my breast. For when I look at you for a moment, then it is no longer possible for me to speak; my tongue has snapped, at once a subtle fire has stolen beneath my flesh, I see nothing with my eyes, my ears hum, sweat pours from me, a trembling seizes me all over, I am greener than grass, and it seems to me that I am little short of dying. But all can be endured, since ... even a poor man ... [1]

Sappho, who had a homosexual disposition though she is also said to have been married with a young daughter, appears to have been a leader and perhaps a teacher in a circle of intelligent, like-minded women and girls at a time when social custom on Lesbos allowed women greater freedom of activity and association than was normal in ancient Greece. Nothing is known about her later life.

Sappho's contemporary Alcaeus, who also came from Lesbos though he spent much of his life in exile, was another solo lyricist writing in the Aeolian dialect who was much admired in the ancient world. His vigorous verse (originally in at least ten books) covered a wide range of subjects, including love poetry, but its remains are even more fragmentary than Sappho's.

---

[1] *Greek Lyric*, trs. by David A. Campbell, Loeb 1982, vol. 1, pp. 79–81. The ellipses represent missing passages.

The next major monodic lyricist was Anacreon, an Ionian Greek from the city of Teos on the south-western coast of Asia Minor. He may have been born c.570 BC, and have died aged 80+ in about 490–485 BC in Athens, where he spent the later part of his life; he is said to have admired the early plays of Aeschylus, which were staged in 499–496 BC. His poems, in five books, were chiefly concerned with love and wine, but again only fragments survive. Here are prose translations of two of them:

> Come, boy, bring me a bowl, so that I may drink without stopping for breath; pour in ten ladles of water and five of wine, that I may once again play the Bacchant with decorum.

> Once again golden-haired Love strikes me with his purple ball and summons me to play with the girl in the fancy sandals; but she – she comes from Lesbos with its fine cities – finds fault with my hair because it is white, and gapes after another – girl.[2]

The Greeks normally drank their wine watered, but in the proportion 3:1 or 4:1, not Anacreon's 2:1 – which would be 'decorous' only for a Bacchant (a male version of the 'Bacchantes', wild women inspired to ecstasy by the wine-god Dionysus). In the second fragment Anacreon is making fun both of his own white hair – inappropriate on the head of the lover of a young girl – and of the supposed sexual preferences of girls from Lesbos.

Pindar

Pindar is the first Greek lyricist whose poems have come down to us in any quantity. The four books of the choral Epinician Odes totalling about 3,450 lines (c.850 lines per book) – out of the original total of seventeen books of his works – were especially admired in antiquity, and have survived virtually complete. But despite his early popularity we know little about Pindar's life. He was born near Thebes around 518 BC and died in Argos at the age of about 80, that is in c.438 BC, after the defeat of the Persian invasion but before the outbreak of the main Peloponnesian War. He received a musical education in Athens, and was already well enough known as a poet by the time he was twenty to be commissioned to write an Ode (*Pythian* 10) for a victor in the Pythian Games of 498 BC. This poem survives, being the earliest of the forty-four Epinician Odes

---

[2] *Greek Lyric*, trs. by David A. Campbell, Loeb 1982, vol. 2, pp. 55, 57.

commissioned to celebrate the feats of individual aristocratic win-
ners at the Olympian, Pythian, Nemean, and Isthmian Games.[3]

Most of these Odes, written in the Dorian dialect, follow a three-
part arrangement, in which praise of the victor's triumph is followed by a supportive story from mythology and a return to further
praise of the victor and his family and country. Within this overall
pattern the verse is in most of the poems 'triadic', that is arranged in
groups of three stanzas, a 'strophe' and 'antistrophe' that are met-
rically identical being followed by an 'epode' in a different metre.
Most remarkably, the metrical pattern of each one of Pindar's Odes
is different from that of the others. (Most of his metrical subtlety is
lost, of course, in translation.)

Let us look at the longest of the Odes, *Pythian* 4, which celebrates
the victory in the chariot race at Delphi in 462 BC of King Arcesilaus
(or Arkesilas) IV of Cyrene in North Africa. It may have been
commissioned by an exiled kinsman of the king called Damophilus
who wanted to use it to plead for his restoration. There is a total of
299 lines in twenty-three triads of eight, eight, and seven lines each.
It begins (in the spirited but faithful free-verse translation of Sir
Maurice Bowra):

> Today, Muse, you must stand by the side of a friend,
> By the King of Kyrene, the land of good horses:
> And when Arkesilas holds his triumph
> Swell the gale of your songs,
> Paying your debt to Lato's[4] Twins, and to Pytho,
> Where once, when Apollo was in his land,
> The priestess – she who sits by the gold eagles of Zeus –
> Ordained Battos a leader of men
> Into fruitful Libya.
> He must straightway leave his holy island
> And build a city
> Of charioteers
> On a silver breast of the earth.

At first glance this invocation is obscure, for we have to be told that
'Lato's Twins' are Artemis and her twin brother Apollo, the patron
god of Delphi (Pytho), and that Battos was Arcesilaus's ancestor, the
first King of Cyrene, who had been instructed by the oracle to leave

---

[3] These Games were held at Olympia in Elis, Delphi, Nemea in Argolis, and
Corinth respectively, arranged so that Games were held somewhere in each year of
the four-year cycle of the most important of them, the Olympian Games.
[4] Usually spelled 'Leto's'.

Thera (his holy island) to found a colony on the white cliffs of Cyrenaica (Libya). Pindar then recalls a prophecy of Medea (the sorceress daughter of King Aeëtes of Colchis where the Golden Fleece of Zeus was detained) which explained why North Africa had not been colonised long before the time of Battos; and this leads into a lengthy narrative of the legend of how Jason and the Argonauts sailed to Colchis to retrieve the Fleece. It is told as a short epic in 254 lines, and it is in fact the first substantial version of this wonderful story to have come down to us.[5] Pindar tells how King Pelias of Iolcus in Thessaly, who has usurped the throne from King Aeson, is warned by the Delphic oracle to beware of a man wearing one sandal. A godlike man wearing one sandal duly comes to Iolcus and, revealing himself as Jason, son of Aeson, demands restitution from Pelias, not of property but of his father's crown. Pelias calmly responds that he will give it up, but that he has been told by the oracle at Delphi that the ghost of Phrixus, who carried off the Golden Fleece to Colchis, must first be brought back to Greece from the far end of the Black Sea, together with the Fleece itself, and that he is obliged to provide Jason with a ship and provisions to carry out this difficult task. Jason agrees, gathers together a crew of heroes, and sets off for Colchis:

> The Captain at the stern
> Held in his hands a golden cup, and called
> On the Father of the Sons of Heaven,
> Zeus, whose spear is the lightning,
> On the swift rushing of the waves, the winds,
> On the nights and the paths of the sea;
> For days of kind weather, and the sweet road home at last.
> From the clouds answered back to him
> The assenting voice of thunder,
> And the lightnings flashed and tore the sky.
> The heroes found fresh breath of courage,
> For they believed
> The Omens of God.
> The Seer of Signs called to them
> To fall to the oars,

[5] The fullest version of the legend is given in the *Argonautica* of the Hellenistic epic poet Apollonius Rhodius (295–215 BC, p. 118 below). The most exciting of Robert Graves's historical novels of the ancient world, *The Golden Fleece* (1944), is also recommended. While Graves may over-emphasise the cult of the mother-goddess, and may be too eager to believe in matriarchal societies, his novel makes the most of its stirring plot, and relates Greek myth to an anthropological account of Bronze-Age culture.

And he put sweet hopes into them: under their rapid hands
The oars insatiably fell and rose.
A south wind blew, and before it
They reached the Unwelcoming Sea.[6]

Negotiating the Clashing Rocks, the *Argo* reaches Colchis. There
the Fleece is strongly guarded, but Aphrodite provides Jason with a
love-charm that persuades Medea the daughter of King Aeëtes
(whose prophecy was recalled at the beginning of the Ode), to help
him to steal it:

But from Olympos the Queen of sharpest arrows
Bound past loosing
The dappled wryneck
To the four spokes of a wheel:
She, the Kypros-born, for the first time brought
The maddening bird to men.
She taught Aison's wise son
What sorceries he must chant, and Medeia forget
To honour those who begot her,
And her heart be all on fire for lovely Hellas
And tremble under the lash of love.
She showed him at once
How to achieve his father's tasks:
With olive-oil she made an enchantment against hard pains
And gave it to him for anointing.
And they swore to make a sweet marriage one with another.[7]

With Medea's disloyal help Jason overcomes Aeëtes, kills the
serpent that guards the Fleece, and brings his prize back to Greece.
On the way home the Argonauts sleep with the women of Lemnos;
and from the resulting offspring the ancestors of Arcesilaus go first
to Thera and thence to Cyrene, the kingdom of Arcesilaus – who is
to carry his triumph at the Games back to his people just as Jason
carried the Fleece back to the Greeks.

Finally the poet offers a riddle: even if an oak tree is stripped of its
branches it can still serve as firewood or as a house-timber. He is
referring to Damophilus, the exile from Cyrene, who can be useful
at home if he is granted his wish and is allowed to return, but must
otherwise pine abroad. The Ode ends:

[6] 'The Seer of Signs' is Mopsus, the augur; and 'the Unwelcoming Sea' is the Black
Sea, which the Greeks usually called euphemistically the 'Euxine' or friendly sea.
[7] 'Lovely Hellas' is Jason; and it is Medea, not Aphrodite, who shows him what to
do.

– But now, he cries,
He has done with foul illness at last, and he sees home.
Near Apollo's fountain
He shall lie at the feast, and yield his heart to youth
Often, and playing his painted harp,
Where men know music, shall touch the hands of peace:
Giving sorrow to none, and having
No wrong from his fellow-townsmen.
And perhaps he will tell, Arkesilas,
What a well of immortal words he found
When lately a guest at Thebes.

> (Pindar, *Odes*, trs. by C.M. Bowra, 1969, Penguin
> Classics pp. 188–203)

And thus Pindar, Damophilus's host at Thebes, brings his great Ode to a graceful conclusion in which he foresees its immortality. (But if Damophilus was allowed home by Arcesilaus, he may not have found much comfort there, for two years later there was a revolution in which Arcesilaus was overthrown and a republic was established.)

Although the celebratory material of the Odes necessarily involves some repetition, this is not obvious to the reader because of the variety of the details and the interest of the mythological parallels. They are moreover written from an essentially religious point of view – sometimes more obviously so than in *Pythian* 4 – from which the gods are seen lending their divinity to human beings, especially at the special moments of victory in which a transcendental state may be reached. Here, perhaps, Pindar comes as close as any ancient writer to evoking the transcendental experience in which colours are brighter, forms are grander and more vibrant with meaning, than they ever are in the ordinary world.

Translations

The Oxford World's Classics *Greek Lyric Poetry*, selected and translated into English verse by M.L. West (1993), includes poems and fragments from some thirty-five named poets from the seventh to the fifth century BC (excluding Pindar), plus anonymous fragments of various dates, together with a good introduction and notes. This is the handiest collection, but there is much to be said for the excellent prose translation by D.A. Campbell (1982, 1988) in volumes I and II of the inclusive Loeb *Greek Lyric*, which also have valuable introductions and notes.

A collection of sixty-two poems written in the style of Anacreon in late antiquity came to be called the *Anacreontea*; from the mid-sixteenth to the early-nineteenth century these 'Odes of Ana-creon' were wrongly ascribed to Anacreon himself. The Penguin Classics *Pindar: The Odes* translated into English verse by C.M. Bowra (1969) is superb: exact, readable, and well annotated.

7 Sophocles and Athenian drama

Tragedy

Greek drama is the most valuable and influential of the literary legacies bequeathed to us by the ancient Athenians. But although the extraordinary plays of the fifth century BC can still be performed and can still move us, they were originally performed for reasons, and in ways, that differed greatly from those of western theatre as it has developed since the Renaissance.

Attic drama appears to have derived – at least in part – from the performances of choral lyric in the religious processions and other ceremonies that were mentioned in the last chapter; and it continued to be connected solely with religious festivals, and to include choral singing and dancing, throughout its greatest period. The most important of these festivals was the Great Dionysia, the annual spring celebration of Dionysus the god of wine and ecstasy and transformation, which took place over five days at the end of March, when the sailing season had begun and there were visitors in the city. Besides processions, sacrifices, libations, and other rites, the Dionysia included competitive performances of choral songs (dithyrambs) and of plays held in the theatre of Dionysus on the southern slope of the Acropolis. Three tragedians each presented three tragedies and a satyr-play, and five comic poets presented a single comedy each; the choruses and playwrights (who were usually the producers of their own plays, and sometimes acted in them as well) were then judged and awarded prizes. There was also a series of lesser Dionysian festivals held in different localities on several days in December at which plays were performed. Plays were not performed at other times of the year, and the revival of these Dionysian plays, which were performed only *once* at each Dionysia, was allowed only in exceptional circumstances before the fourth century BC.

The plots of the tragedies, which were intimately concerned with religion and the gods, were nearly all taken from Greek mythology; tales of passion and of the power of the gods, which suggested practical and moral problems without necessarily solving them. (Though, as it happens, the earliest play of which we have the text – Aeschylus's *Persae*, 472 BC – concerned the recent Persian Wars in which the Greeks had been victorious, seen from the point of view of the Persian court.) The plays were also designed to celebrate and promote the greatness of Athens and Athenian civilisation.

A Greek theatre, which was unroofed, consisted of an arc, of slightly more than a semicircle, of tiers of stone benches rising up from and partly surrounding an 'orchestra' (or 'dancing place', usually circular), behind which was a narrow acting area and a 'scene' building with changing rooms. Its orientation probably depended primarily on the natural features of the site, but a surprising number of Greek theatres were oriented so that the central seats faced between south-east and south-west, which would have kept the spectators warm in the chilly Greek winter and spring, even though it also meant having the sun in their eyes and backlighting the performers. The audience – enormous by our standards, the theatre of Dionysus seating at least 14,000 spectators – may have been accommodated in blocks of seats according to the Athenian 'tribe' to which each group belonged; and it probably included a number of women and non-citizens.

The earliest plays, of which we have no texts, were probably staged with a chorus of singers and dancers exchanging chanted dialogue with a single actor, perhaps the poet himself. Aeschylus added a second actor, so that two actors and the chorus could be on stage at the same time; Sophocles added a third actor (a development taken up by Aeschylus at the end of his career, and adopted as a matter of course by Euripides), allowing for three actors and the chorus to perform in the same scene; and in the comedies of Aristophanes there might be as many as four actors. The chorus normally numbered twelve or fifteen in tragedy and up to twenty-four in comedy (when it was sometimes split into two choruses). Deaths and the more violent actions usually took place off-stage, and were reported by messengers.

The function of the chorus was to comment, from a particular point of view, on the action of the play, usually in lyric song. In tragedy the chorus frequently repesented a group of ordinary people who were related in some way to the action, often against their will;

while in comedy it sometimes represented groups of animals or inanimate objects rather than people.

Actors and chorus were all men, playing both male and female parts; and they all wore masks as well as costumes. The masks, probably made of painted cloth and plaster complete with wigs and – where appropriate – beards, were fairly realistic in tragedy, unlike the conventional tragic masks of later decorative schemes. Masks enabled a single actor to play more than one part, and also allowed one part to be played by different actors if the production required it. In any case, an actor's facial expressions would not have been visible from the more distant seats of the huge theatres. Very little is known about the style of chanting and acting, though we can guess that, for the same reason, the actors' movements and gestures were broad and obvious. The earliest texts of the plays contain no stage directions, though they have been added by later editors and translators.

The three tragedians

Virtually all our knowledge of Athenian tragedy comes from the surviving work of three playwrights, Aeschylus (c.525–c.456 BC), Sophocles (c.496–406/5 BC), and Euripides (c.485–406 BC). There were many other tragedians working in Athens in the fifth century BC, but these three were recognised, then and later, as being the most eminent, and it is because they and not the others were especially admired that their works were revived, some of them becoming part of the ancient literary canon. Aeschylus wrote 80–90 plays, of which seven[1] survive, and won thirteen victories in the tragedy competitions. Sophocles wrote 120–30 plays, of which again seven survive, and won eighteen victories at the Dionysia. Euripides wrote 90–95 plays, of which eighteen survive (the larger number of his surviving plays being largely a matter of chance), and won four victories.

Aeschylus was the first great master of the form, producing his plays from the 490s; his first surviving work, *Persae*, dates from 472, and his last and greatest, the *Oresteia* trilogy, from 458, two years before his death. Although Sophocles was ten or eleven years older than Euripides, and started producing plays before him, it turns out that the plays for which they are chiefly celebrated were written at very much the same times. The dates are as follows: first surviving play: Sophocles, *Antigone*, c.441; Euripides, *Alcestis*, 438:

---

[1] Or six if *Prometheus Bound* is inauthentic.

most admired surviving play: Sophocles, *Oedipus Tyrannus*, soon after 430; Euripides, *Medea*, 431: last play: Sophocles, *Oedipus Coloneus*, before 406; Euripides, *Bacchae*, c.407. In other words, Sophocles and Euripides were colleagues and competitors working in the same theatre, producing their best-known (and probably best) work during the same thirty-five-year period which began about seventeen years after the death of Aeschylus: c.441–406 BC.

It is conventional to treat Sophocles as Euripides's predecessor, mainly because he was the older of the two and had starting writing plays from c.468 BC, when he competed with Aeschylus; whereas Euripides did not start writing until c.455 and did not compete directly with Aeschylus (though he was old enough to have seen Aeschylus's later plays, and was certainly familiar with the *Oresteia*). There may also be the feeling that, because some of Euripides's characters are more starkly drawn – the word often used for them is 'realistic' – and do not all come from the higher social classes, and because he appears to disdain religious convention, he is not only less orthodox but also somehow more 'modern' than Sophocles. But because their major work appears to have been done at the same time, it makes more sense to see Euripides as the contemporary and rival rather than as the successor of Sophocles, and we should not expect to find Euripides's techniques and approach more developed than those of the older man. What we do find is that they are different from each other in their approach to character and to dramatic technique, and that in some respects Sophocles is the more 'advanced' of the two. Plays by all three tragedians are still performed, but the Sophoclean approach to drama is probably the most accessible to modern readers and theatre-goers, and more will be said here about Sophocles than about Aeschylus or Euripides.

Aeschylus

Aeschylus was born at Eleusis in Attica c.525 BC. He took the first prize in the tragedy competition in 499 BC, and won for the last time with the *Oresteia* in 458. He died in Sicily c.456, aged about 69, having fought as a soldier at the battle of Marathon (490) and perhaps at Salamis (480) as well. Although we have examples from only the last fifteen years of his work (472–458 BC) – and only seven out of his eighty or ninety plays – they show his great powers of imagination and originality, and the quality and beauty of his verse. His plays – and especially the final trilogy of the *Oresteia* –

are strongly religious in their approach, and they deal primarily with situations and events, ideas and beliefs, rather than with character.

The *Oresteia*, the only complete trilogy from fifth-century Athenian tragedy that we have (the satyr-play *Proteus* that was originally attached to it is lost), consists of *Agamemnon*; *Choephori* ('Women Bearing Drink-offerings', or 'The Libation Bearers'); and *Eumenides* ('The Kindly Ones', the Greeks' euphemism for the Furies or spirits of punishment). Totalling 3,796 lines (very nearly the same length as *Hamlet*) the three plays develop a single plot, and can be read as a single three-act play. The story, which was of course already well known to the Athenian audience, told of a series of atrocities committed in the house of Atreus, of their consequences, and of their divine resolution. The first atrocity, which took place before the trilogy begins, was the crime of Agamemnon's father Atreus, who punished his brother Thyestes for having seduced Atreus's wife by feeding Thyestes the flesh of his own children at a banquet. The second was the crime of Agamemnon who was required by Artemis to sacrifice his daughter Iphigeneia in order to get a fair wind for the expedition to Troy. Now, in the first of the three plays, a third atrocity takes place: Agamemnon, on returning home to Argos having led the Greeks in their successful war against Troy, is murdered by his wife Clytemnestra (the mother of Iphigeneia) and her lover Aegisthus (Agamemnon's first cousin and the surviving son of the wronged Thyestes). This murder of a husband is followed by a fourth atrocity in the second play: matricide, when Orestes and Electra, the surviving children of Agamemnon and Clytemnestra, return secretly to Argos at the instance of Apollo, and Orestes kills Clytemnestra and Aegisthus in revenge for the murder of their father. In the third play Orestes is purified of his blood-guilt by Apollo; despite this, he is threatened with pursuit to the death by the implacable Furies, urged on by Clytemnestra's ghost. He calls on Athena for help, and a trial takes place to decide whether or not he was justified under the circumstances in killing his mother. The Athenian judges are evenly split, half for him, half against; but Athena declares that in all even judgements the defendant shall be acquitted (or, in another interpretation of the passage, she gives him her casting vote). The goddess finally conciliates the Furies by promising them a permanent home in Athens, where they may become in truth the city's 'kindly ones'; and *Eumenides* ends with the women of Athens celebrating their city's good fortune.

The great strength of the plot of the *Oresteia* lies first in the dramatic tension and suppressed excitement of the build-up to a series of electrifying climaxes; and secondly in the sense of the power of the gods and the awe in which they are held that ultimately controls the characters and their action. An underlying implication of the trilogy is that the Athenians – and especially the Athenian politicians – should not attract the envy of the gods by the sin of pride, but should live modestly and peaceably with their neighbours. The sense of doom in the *Oresteia* is almost palpable, and the murders, even though the audience knows that they are coming, raise the hairs on the back of the neck. Apart from Clytemnestra, whose language is idiosyncratic and who decides for herself to kill her husband, the individual characters are not strongly personalised, for they are mostly at the mercy of fate or circumstance. Each chorus – of old men, slave-women, and Furies respectively – plays the part of a character, who helps the plot forward as well as commenting upon its development.

Sophocles

Sophocles, who was born at Colonus near Athens in c.496 BC, began his career as a dancer, singer, and actor – a useful background for a playwright[2] – but he soon started writing his own plays, gaining his first victory in the tragedy competition at the Dionysia of 468. He took a fairly prominent part in Athenian life, not in politics directly, but including service as a general at the suppression of the Samian revolt in 440, and as a commissioner following the débâcle of the Sicilian Expedition in 413 (when he was already eighty-three).[3] Only seven of his more than 120 tragedies have survived, which are: *Trachiniae* ('The Women of Trachis', about the death of Hercules) and *Ajax* (the death of Ajax), both of which probably date from before 441, soon after the *Oresteia* of Aeschylus; *Antigone* (about the tragic end of Oedipus's daughter, c.441); *Oedipus Tyrannus* ('Oedipus the King', to be discussed shortly, soon after 430); *Electra* (of which the plot is similar to, but treated differently from, that of Aeschylus's *Choephori*, 418–410); *Philoctetes* (the attempt of Philoctetes to keep the bow of Hercules from Neoptolemus and

---

[2] Aeschylus, too, probably acted in his own plays.
[3] The islanders of Samos revolted agianst Athenian dominion, and were defeated in an eight-month campaign by Pericles; the Athenians themselves were defeated in Sicily during the second Peloponnesian War (see pp. 91–2 below).

Odysseus who need it to win the Trojan War, 409); and *Oedipus Coloneus* ('Oedipus at Colonus', also to be discussed shortly, produced posthumously following Sophocles's death in 406). There is also the incomplete text of one of Sophocles's satyr-plays, *Ichneutae* ('Trackers', date unknown). Although no complete trilogy of Sophoclean tragedies survives – he may have used the trilogy form only rarely – the Theban plays make a subject trilogy if they are considered in the chronological order of the myth: *Oedipus Tyrannus*, *Oedipus Coloneus*, and *Antigone*.

Sophocles's greatest strengths as a playwright lay in the depth and convincing humanity of his characters and the technical virtuosity of his plots; he was also one of the greatest of Greek poets, the aspect of his work that is lost in translation. Let us look first at what is probably his finest surviving tragedy, *Oedipus Tyrannus*. It failed to win the prize when Sophocles was in competition with Aeschylus's nephew Philocles (whose plays have not survived), but it was later referred to by Aristotle as a model of dramatic tragedy.[4]

Sophocles took as his subject the denouement of a well-known myth. When Laius, King of Thebes, and Jocasta, had a baby boy, the Delphic Oracle warned Laius that he would kill his father. In order to avoid this, the baby, who was Oedipus, was exposed on Mount Cithaeron with his ankles pinned together, so that he would die there or be eaten by wild beasts. Although lamed, Oedipus was rescued by a shepherd, and was then taken away to be brought up as the son of the king and queen of Corinth. As a young man, Oedipus himself was told by the oracle that he would kill his father and marry his mother and, in another effort to avoid this fate, he left Corinth for Thebes where he unwittingly fulfilled both predictions; he killed Laius in an affray at a place where three roads met; and then, having destroyed the murderous sphinx that was terrorising the city, he married the widowed Jocasta and became King of Thebes himself. He proved to be a good king, with the Athenian virtues of being swift and strong to act, and if he had been content with that, he might never have found out what he had done.

It is at this point that the play of *Oedipus Tyrannus* begins; and as usual Sophocles plunges straight into the action, without the explanatory prologue-speech favoured by Aeschylus and Euripides. Oedipus learns from Delphi that Thebes can only be saved from a plague that has fallen on the city by the discovery and exile of

---

[4] *Poetics* 11, 13, 15, 26.

Laius's murderer. Teiresias, the blind seer, is summoned to reveal the truth; at first he refuses, but is then forced to give a true but riddling answer. Still suspecting only that Creon, Jocasta's brother, is plotting against him with Teiresias as his accomplice, Oedipus learns from a messenger that he is not in fact the son of the king and queen of Corinth, for it was the same messenger who had brought him as a baby from Mount Cithaeron to Corinth. Against advice, Oedipus sends for the shepherd from whom the messenger had received the baby, and who also happened to have been present at the death of Laius; and he forces the old man to reveal the truth about him. Appalled to discover that he is himself his father's murderer and his mother's husband, he rushes frantically off-stage, only to learn that Jocasta has hanged herself. Putting out his own eyes with her brooch, he returns to be confronted by Creon, who now succeeds him as King of Thebes and accedes to his wish that he shall be sent into perpetual exile if the Delphic Oracle agrees.

It is a gripping and intricately constructed plot, in which the protagonist brings about his own downfall as a result of his excessive self-confidence (though he has of course tried to avoid harming his parents), precipitates the catastrophe, and suffers a complete reversal of fortune. With *Oedipus Tyrannus* in mind as a good example, Aristotle was to propose in his *Poetics* that tragedy should deal with serious themes and end in the suffering or death of one or more of the principal characters, and that the tragic hero should be of high worth or standing, but not perfect. A tragic flaw, weakness, or transgression (*hamartia*),[5] should lead to the reversal (*peripeteia*) of the protagonist's position, bringing him down. The effect of the inevitable disaster (*catastrophe*) on the spectators would be to excite pity and fear, emotions which would be purged (*catharsis*) or understood by seeing them acted out.[6]

The dialogue is realistic, the character of Oedipus is convincingly presented, and the minor persons in the play are well distinguished from each other. If we cannot respond to it in quite the same way as could its ancient Athenian audience, it is partly because we do not see it in the same religious light as they did, and partly because not only did they know the whole story in advance, but most of them also firmly believed that oracular predictions were bound to be fulfilled. They knew, too, that the oracle had said nothing more

---

[5] Or, in other circumstances, an excess of arrogant ambition (*hubris*).
[6] Aristotle, *Poetics* 6–16, esp. 11.

about what would happen to Oedipus than that he would kill his father and marry his mother, as did indeed happen; and that it was therefore chiefly owing to his own over-confident detective work that he and Jocasta ultimately came to realise what they had done. All this indicates Sophocles's pious but perhaps uneasy acceptance of the divine order, the sin of Oedipus and Jocasta having been committed unwittingly and their punishment being in this sense undeserved. For, while his plays are more about people than about the gods, he takes it for granted that the gods are there, that oracles are to be treated seriously, and that proper attention must be paid to the Olympian pantheon. Here is part of the climactic scene in which Oedipus forces the shepherd to tell him who he is:

MESSENGER (*to the shepherd*)　　　　　Come, tell me,
　　　you gave me a child back then, a boy, remember?
　　　A little fellow to rear, my very own.

SHEPHERD　What? Why rake that up again?

MESSENGER　Look, here he is, my fine old friend –
　　　the same man who was just a baby then.

SHEPHERD　Damn you, shut your mouth – quiet!

OEDIPUS　Don't lash out at him, old man –
　　　you need lashing more than he does.

SHEPHERD　　　　　　　　　　　　　　Why,
　　　master, majesty – what have I done wrong?

OEDIPUS　You won't answer his question about the boy.

SHEPHERD　He's talking nonsense, wasting his breath.

OEDIPUS　So, you won't talk willingly –
　　　then you'll talk with pain.　　(*the guards seize the shepherd*)

SHEPHERD　No, dear god, don't torture an old man!

OEDIPUS　Twist his arms back quickly!

SHEPHERD　　　　　　　　　　　　　God help us, why? –
　　　what more do you need to know?

OEDIPUS　Did you give him that child? He's asking.

SHEPHERD　I did ... I wish to god I'd died that day.

OEDIPUS　You've got your wish if you don't tell the truth.

SHEPHERD　The more I tell, the worse the death I'll die.

OEDIPUS　Our friend here wants to stretch things out, does he?
　　　　　　　　　　　(*motioning to his men for torture*)

SHEPHERD　No, no, I gave it to him – I just said so.

OEDIPUS　Where did you get it? Your house? Someone else's?

SHEPHERD　It wasn't mine, no, I got it from ... someone.

OEDIPUS　Which one of them?
　　　(*looking at the citizens*) Whose house?

SHEPHERD   No –
    god's sake, master, no more questions!

OEDIPUS   You're a dead man if I have to ask again.

SHEPHERD   Then – the child came from the house …
    of Laius.

OEDIPUS   A slave? or born of his own blood

SHEPHERD   Oh no,
    I'm right at the edge, the horrible truth – I've got to say
    it!

OEDIPUS   And I'm at the edge of hearing horrors, yes, but I must
    hear!

SHEPHERD   All right! His son, they said it was – his son!
    But the one inside, your wife,
    she'd tell it best.

OEDIPUS   My wife –
    she gave it to you?

SHEPHERD   Yes, yes, my king.

OEDIPUS   Why, what for?

SHEPHERD   To kill it.

OEDIPUS   Her own child,
    how could she?

SHEPHERD   She was afraid –
    frightening prophecies.

OEDIPUS   What?

SHEPHERD   They said –
    he'd kill his parents.

OEDIPUS   But you gave him to the old man – why?

SHEPHERD   I pitied the little baby, master,
    hoped he'd take him off to his own country,
    far away, but he saved him for this, this fate.
    If you are the man he says you are, believe me,
    you were born for pain.

OEDIPUS   Oh god –
    all come true, all burst to light!
    O light – now let me look my last on you!
    I stand revealed at last –
    cursed in my birth, cursed in marriage,
    cursed in the lives I cut down with these hands! (*rushing through the
    doors with a great cry*)
            (*Oedipus the King*, trs. by Robert Fagles, 1982, Penguin
            Classics pp. 227–32)

This scene – which leads straight into the terrible conclusion of the
play in which the chorus is told of Jocasta's suicide, and Oedipus
returns, blind and powerless, pleading for exile – remains a thrilling

piece of dramatic writing even two-and-a-half millennia after it was composed, and it works wonderfully well on stage. If evidence is needed of the modernity – that is, the timelessness – of Sophocles's dramatic mastery, here it is.

It seems hardly possible that Sophocles could write another play as extraordinary and gripping as *Oedipus Tyrannus*, but he did. Almost twenty-five years later, when he was nearly ninety, Sophocles wrote *Oedipus Coloneus* – it was produced posthumously by his grandson – and it is perhaps the most moving and beautiful of all these wonderful Athenian tragedies. The audience knows that Oedipus had four children by Jocasta (who are, appallingly, his siblings as well as his sons and daughters): two sons, Eteocles and Polyneices, and two daughters, Antigone and Ismene; that, after Oedipus was banished, Eteocles and Polyneices were supposed to rule Thebes in alternate years, their uncle Creon (Jocasta's brother) acting as regent; but that Eteocles then refused to give up the crown to Polyneices at the end of the first year.

When the play begins, Oedipus – old, blind, and in rags – is wandering though Attica, led by his devoted elder daughter Antigone, when they come to a holy place by the village of Colonus (where Sophocles himself had been born), just outside Athens. Here Oedipus decides to stay, despite the dismay of the old men of Colonus when they discover who he is. Oedipus's younger daughter Ismene joins him, and he learns from her that an expedition of seven champions is being led against Thebes by Polyneices. Good King Theseus of Athens, appealed to, assures Oedipus of his protection. Next comes Creon, regent of Thebes, who tries to persuade Oedipus to return to the vicinity of Thebes where his presence will give the city protection. Oedipus angrily refuses to go, so Creon – in a scene of almost unbearable tension – kidnaps Antigone and Ismene, and is only prevented at the last moment by Theseus from getting them out of the country. Polyneices now appears, seeking his father's help for his expedition, but Oedipus will have nothing to do with him because both Polyneices and Eteocles had connived at his banishment; and Polyneices goes off with a father's curse to the battle where he and Eteocles will kill each other. At last, when Oedipus and his daughters have realised that their love for each other is their most valuable possession, peals of thunder announce that Oedipus's end is near. He leads Theseus to a sanctuary where, a messenger reports, the gods miraculously remove him from the face of the earth, an event that will prove to be of lasting benefit for Athens. Distraught at the loss of their father, and deprived even of a tomb at which they may mourn and pour libations to his spirit, the two girls set off for Thebes where (as the audience knows) they will meet violent ends.

The characters – especially the pathetic yet still powerful Oedipus, the evil Creon, loving Antigone, and resentful Polyneices – are superbly presented and developed; and the odes of the chorus of the old men of Colonus are outstandingly moving and beautiful. It is an old man's play, about ageing and loss, and the inevitable approach of death, which must be accepted and endured with as much assurance and strength as any other event in a man's life; about the death that Sophocles himself was about to meet. So let us end this account with the chorus of the old men, lamenting the onset of old age:

> Show me a man who longs to live a day beyond his time
>   who turns his back on a decent length of life,
> I'll show the world a man who clings to folly.
> For the long, looming days lay up a thousand things
> closer to pain than pleasure, and the pleasures disappear,
>   you look and know not where
> when a man's outlived his limit, plunged in age
> and the good comrade comes who comes at last to all,
> not with a wedding-song, no lyre, no singers dancing –
> the doom of the Deathgod comes like lightning
>   always death at the last.
>
>   Not to be born is best
> when all is reckoned in, but once a man has seen the light
>   the next best thing by far, is to go back
> back where he came from, quickly as he can.
> For once his youth slips by, light on the wing
> lightheaded ... what mortal blows can he escape
>   what griefs won't stalk his days?
> Envy and enemies, rage and battles, bloodshed
> and last of all despised old age overtakes him,
> stripped of power, companions, stripped of love –
> the worst this life of pain can offer,
>   old age our mate at last.
>
> This is the grief he faces – I am not alone –
> like some great headland fronting the north
> hit by the winter breakers beating down
> from every quarter – so he suffers,
> terrible blows crashing over him
> head to foot, over and over
> down from every quarter –
> now from the west, the dying sun

now from the first light rising
now from the blazing beams of noon
now from the north engulfed in endless night.
> (*Oedipus Coloneus*, trs. by Robert Fagles, 1982, Penguin
> Classics pp. 358–9)

Euripides

Euripides began his career as an Athenian playwright in 455 BC, soon after the death of Aeschylus, when he was about thirty; little is known of his background and early life. He is said to have been personally unsociable and reclusive – though ancient biographical traditions of this sort are of doubtful authenticity – and his sharp intelligence was parodied and ridiculed as a determination to be clever in the *Frogs* (see below), a black comedy by Aristophanes that was produced at about the time of Euripides's death in 406 BC at the age of nearly eighty.[7] His eighteen surviving plays cover a variety of subjects; what they have in common is unconventional social values, sceptical religious views, and acute psychological observation, especially of women. Technically they are uneven, Aristotle criticising him for faults such as failing (unlike Sophocles) to involve the chorus in the action of the play;[8] and Sophocles was indeed the greater master of dramatic structure.

Sophocles is quoted by Aristotle as saying that 'he drew men as they ought to be, whereas Euripides drew them as they are', but he was doing less than justice to himself, for Sophocles's characters are every bit as realistically drawn as those of Euripides, but seen differently.[9] For instance, the *Electra* of Sophocles may be compared with the *Electra* of Euripides, two plays which may have been written at about the same time, c.413 BC, on the theme of the *Choephori* of Aeschylus.[10] The two heroines – who, unlike Electra in the *Choephori*, have stayed with their mother and Aegisthus following the murder of Agamemnon – have almost nothing in common. The Electra of Sophocles, who is on stage for practically the whole of the play, is a fury for whom hatred of her mother Clytemnestra, and to a lesser extent of Aegisthus, has become the grand passion of her

---

[7] The great Athenian tragedians lived remarkably long lives, Aeschylus, Sophocles, and Euripides dying at about seventy, ninety, and eighty years old respectively.

[8] *Poetics* 18.

[9] *Poetics* 25. Aristotle, writing when Euripides was more acclaimed than Sophocles, may have been expressing his own view here.

[10] In both these plays both Sophocles and Euripides conflate Argos and Mycenae.

life, her lust for revenge (a trait doubtless inherited from her mother) being her sole reason for going on living until the arrival of Orestes enables her to express it in violent action; she has no regrets and there is to be no divine retribution. This powerful, terrifying Electra has been called 'the finest female role, perhaps the finest role, in Greek tragedy'.[11] The Electra of Euripides, on the other hand, is a less single-minded, more self-pitying creature, a moaner who has been abused by Aegisthus and married to a peasant (a former aristocrat who has restrained himself from sleeping with her); being ambiguous and weak in her actions and reactions, she cannot admit the sacrilegious, unheroic aspects of her mother's murder. Her lack of positive characteristics is of course intentional, adding an ironical note to the parody of Aeschylus that was part of the point of the play.

Aristotle also called Euripides the most tragic of the poets in arousing pity and fear, and his strength in this respect can be seen in one of his finest plays, the *Medea* of 431 BC. Medea was the sorceress who had been charmed, with the help of Aphrodite, into falling in love with Jason and had helped him to recover the Golden Fleece of Zeus from her father Aeëtes (see p. 61 above). She had then contrived the death of Pelias of Iolcus by tricking his daughters into boiling him alive; and now she and Jason are living in exile in Corinth with their two children. When the play begins Jason has got tired of her, and – perhaps stimulated by political ambition as well as by the prospect of a young bride – has arranged to marry the young daughter of their host King Creon,[12] while pretending to Medea that he is doing so for diplomatic reasons. Creon, rightly fearing Medea's anger, pronounces her banishment from Corinth, but Medea, wild with suppressed fury, is determined to have her revenge first. Begging successfully for a day's grace before she leaves, she sends the princess the present of a poisoned diadem and robe, which kills both her and Creon; and she then murders her own two children, partly in order to save them from death by other hands and partly to deprive Jason of them. Finally she escapes, taking the children's bodies for burial on her way to Athens, jeering at Jason's despair. This overpowering Medea, torn by conflicting emotions, is another of the greatest characters in Greek tragedy, the classic manifestation of the fury of a woman scorned: for she is not just an evil foreign sorceress, she is even more a vigorous, whole-hearted woman who has been

---

[11] J. Michael Walton in *Sophocles: Plays* II, Methuen Drama 1990, p. xxiii.
[12] He is a different Creon from Jocasta's brother, the regent of Thebes.

tricked into love and marriage with an inadequate, self-satisfied man who has now insulted and selfishly dismissed her in favour of a frivolous young girl; a situation guaranteed – as many in the audience, men as well as women, would have recognised – to cause extreme pain and anger. It is an overwhelming play.

Aristophanes and comedy

It has already been mentioned that the Dionysia included competitions for comedy as well as for tragedy; but our evidence for the 'Old Comedy' (as the comedy of late-fifth-century Athens is known) comes from a single main source – the surviving plays of Aristophanes – and fragments of work by other poets. Some form of broadly humorous choral singing was probably known in very early times, perhaps at an earlier date than the processional singing that preceded tragedy, but its development into comic drama is obscure. When we come to the earliest survivor (*Acharnians*, 425 BC), the Old Comedy is a fully fledged form of comic opera, involving ribald jokes, lavatory humour, sexual innuendo, and the ridicule of eminent people and serious subjects. The closest modern parallels are the Savoy Operas of Gilbert and Sullivan, if one can imagine extremely rude versions of *Iolanthe* (1882, ridiculing the House of Lords) and *Princess Ida* (1884, parodying Tennyson, and probably influenced by the *Lysistrata* of Aristophanes). Like W.S. Gilbert, Aristophanes aimed to satirise not only the sillier institutions and individuals of his time, but also the more pompous ones, often with political motives; and his plays were parodic reflections of – as well as comic relief from – the weighty tragedies with which they alternated at the Dionysia.

Comedies had a larger number of speaking parts than the tragedies (though still only three or four main actors), and their choruses, of which there were usually two in a play, might represent people, or animals (birds, wasps, frogs), or even inanimate things (clouds). The masks used by the players were grotesque, as were the robes and tunics, with plenty of padding and monstrous leather phalluses attached to the front of the male costumes.

Aristophanes was probably born in the 450s BC, and died in the 380s; practically nothing is known about his life but that he wrote some thirty-two comedies, of which eleven survive. They are crudely and outrageously funny. In *Clouds* (423 BC, but known only in a revised version), Socrates is ridiculed as the corrupt principal of a school which instructs gullible pupils in a bogus philosophy – teaching which turns the city's traditional religious and social values upside down, encouraging children to attack their parents. (This spoof may have had the unfortunate – and unintentional – effect of lending weight to the prosecution and condemnation of Socrates twenty-four years later for traducing traditional values; see pp. 102–3 below.) *Lysistrata* (411), in which the women of Greece go on a successful sex-strike to force their husbands to stop making war on the Spartans, is hilariously bawdy; the randiest of the sex-striking women are restrained only with difficulty from escaping from their redoubt on the Acropolis to seek sexual partners, and the male characters are eventually incapacited by immense, frustrated erections which cause them to walk about all bent over. In the end the men agree to end the war and the wives return to their husbands' beds. In *Frogs* (405) Dionysus goes to Hades to fetch Euripides to help the Athenians, who badly need good political advice. There (having at first been mistaken for Hercules) Dionysus is asked to be the judge in a competition for best tragedian between Euripides and Aeschylus (Sophocles having modestly given up his claim in favour of Aeschylus). Both tragedians agree that the moral value of poetry is what matters most, Aeschylus arguing that his plays made men better and Euripides replying that his made them think. They then attack each other's poetic and dramatic techniques, but in the end Aeschylus is found to be the 'weightier' poet (on a literal scales), and it is he, the traditionalist, who is finally chosen to advise Athens on its problems.

Translations

Some translators of Greek plays aim at preparing the best reading texts, others are more interested in preparing texts for the stage. The Penguin Classics and Oxford World's Classics volumes are equipped with valuable introductions and notes; see especially the essays on Greek theatre in Sommerstein's *Aristophanes* and on the survival of play texts in Fagles's *Sophocles: The Theban Plays* (see below).

Aeschylus

The Penguin Classics *Oresteia* in irregular blank verse by Robert Fagles (1975) is outstandingly good, and has a valuable introduction by Fagles and W.B. Stanford. The other four surviving plays of Aeschylus are also available in Penguin Classics as *Prometheus Bound and Other Plays*, translated by Philip Vellacott (1961). All these are primarily reading texts.

Sophocles

There is a wide choice. For the *Three Theban Plays* (*Antigone*, *Oedipus the King*, and *Oedipus at Colonus*) the translation by Robert Fagles in Penguin Classics (1982) is again the recommended reading version; as with his *Iliad* and *Oresteia*, it is hard to see how they could be better done in modern blank verse. The Oxford World's Classics *Sophocles* (containing *Antigone*, *Oedipus the King*, and *Electra*) has texts translated for the stage by H.D.F. Kitto (1962); they include cuts and alterations for student productions which are not best suited to reading texts. The translations of all the plays by Don Taylor and others in the two volumes of the Methuen Drama *Sophocles* (1986, 1990) are intended for the stage but nevertheless make lively, uncut reading texts; particularly recommended are Kenneth McLeish's sprightly versions of *Electra* and *Philoctetes* in volume II.

Euripides

The Penguin Classics *Euripides: Alcestis and Other Plays* (which includes *Medea*, *The Children of Hercules*, and *Hippolytus*), translated by John Davie (1996) in what the publishers call 'dignified English prose', is the only one of all these translations of Greek plays that is not at least partly rendered in verse, but it still makes a very readable version of Euripides. The Penguin Classics *Euripides: Medea and Other Plays* (including *Hecabe*, *Electra*, and *Heracles*) is well translated by Philip Vellacott (1963). Both are intended as reading texts.

Aristophanes

Alan Sommerstein's Penguin Classics translation of *Aristophanes: Lysistrata, The Achannians*, and *The Clouds* (1973) is an appropriately rumbustious version of these outrageous plays; the *Lysistrata*, which makes the Spartans speak in a strong Scottish dialect (to indicate the difference between the Greek spoken by the Spartans and that spoken in Athens) and gives the choruses Gilbert and Sullivan tunes to sing, would work especially well on stage. The Penguin Classics *Aristophanes: The Wasps, The Poet and the Women, The Frogs*) translated by David Barrett (1964) is slightly more restrained but still renders Aristophanes in lively colloquial English, and (like the Sommerstein) has a good Introduction to Aristophanes's theatre.

8 Herodotus and Greek history

Greek historians

Late sixth- and early fifth-century Greek prose histories, short and local rather than general in scope, survive in a few fragments, but it is not until we come to Herodotus (born c.490 BC) that history as we understand it begins. He is followed a generation later by a second major historian, Thucydides (born c.460–55 BC); and we shall also be looking at an account of a particular military campaign in which the author had taken part, written by Xenophon, a historian born another generation on (c.428 BC) who was also a soldier and a disciple of Socrates.

In fact the great histories of Herodotus and Thucydides, too, were chiefly concerned with warfare: Herodotus's purpose, for all his digressions, being essentially to tell the encouraging story of the invasions of Greece by the Persian kings Darius and Xerxes, and their ultimate defeat by the joint efforts of the Athenians and the Spartans; while Thucydides's history is the story of the Peloponnesian War, the later conflict between the Athenians and the Spartans which ended with the victory of Sparta. The chronological table lists the major events of the fifth century BC.

The histories of Herodotus, Thucydides, and Xenophon were, like most ancient history, 'anecdotal': not so much on account of their diverting tales (of which Herodotus was particularly fond), but because they were made up of mixtures of personal observation, the reminiscences of others, and oral tradition. They were not histories in the modern sense of the term, meaning accounts based primarily on documents or other hard (such as archaeological) evidence. This does not mean that their authors were not good and reliable historians – on the whole they were – but that their method of writing history differed from ours. (As we shall see, they also differed from each other in their approach to their work.)

82

BC

499	Ionian revolt
496	Sophocles b.
495	Pericles b.
490	Persians invade Greece and are defeated at Marathon; Herodotus b.
485	Euripides b.
484	Aeschylus's first victory in the tragedy competition
480	Persians invade Greece; battles of Thermopylae and Salamis
479	Persians defeated at Plataea
469	Socrates b.
468	Sophocles's first victory in the tragedy competition
464	Spartan helots revolt
461–429	Age of Pericles
461–456	Long walls of Athens built
460–446	First Peloponnesian war between Athens and Sparta
458	Aeschylus, *Oresteia*
450s	Thucydides b.; Aristophanes b. (d. c.385)
456	Aeschylus d.
447	Parthenon begun
431–404	Second Peloponnesian war
431	Euripides, *Medea*
430	Plague in Athens
430+	Sophocles, *Oedipus Tyrannus*
429	Pericles d.; Plato b. (d. 347)
428	Xenophon b. (d. c.354)
425	Herodotus d.
423	Aristophanes, *Clouds*
415–413	Sicilian Expedition
411	Oligarchic revolution in Athens
406	Euripides d.
406/5	Sophocles d.
404	Thucydides d.; Athens capitulates to Sparta; Thirty Tyrants
404–371	Sparta supreme
403	Restoration of Athenian democracy
401	Expedition of the Ten Thousand
400–386	Sparta at war with Persia
399	Trial and death of Socrates

For instance, one of the favourite ways in which all three of them explained complex political and military situations was by presenting 'speeches', sometimes of considerable length, supposedly delivered at the time to various assemblies by particular politicians, ambassadors, and soldiers. Rhetoric of this sort was indeed a means, much used in antiquity, of informing and persuading groups of friends and foes, and no doubt speeches were made by many of the people and on many of the occasions quoted by the historians. But the historians themselves were rarely present when the speeches – delivered without scripts and without the presence of shorthand reporters – were made, so that they cannot be giving us exact accounts of the actual words spoken, even if they supply the gist of the arguments used at the time. Thucydides – of our three historians the one most obsessed with accuracy – realises that such 'speeches' cannot be accurate; but then compounds the problem by saying that, since neither he nor his informants could remember the exact words of the speeches he reports, 'my method has been, while keeping as closely as possible to the general sense of the words used, to make the speakers say what, in my opinion, was called for by each situation' (*History* I.22).

Certainly all three historians wanted to be – and to be considered – accurate in what they wrote. Herodotus was always careful to say that he had been told such and such a thing by this person or that, and equally willing to admit that he himself did not necessarily believe it to be true. Thucydides made a point of not trusting second-hand tales and claimed to have checked other sources as far as he could; Xenophon had been personally involved in practically all the events he described. There is no reason to doubt that they did their best; but their books, written in the absence of documents and in the light of their own attitudes and prejudices, inevitably contained inaccuracies and special pleading.

Before discussing the work of these three historians, a word should be said about the nature of the Greek warfare of the fifth and early-fourth century BC that is the background of their histories. Although some of the Greek city-states were able to combine forces to defend Greece from the barbarian[1] invaders (though others joined the Persians), at most other times they were quarrelsome, ambitious,

---

[1] The Greeks called foreigners barbarians (because they said *bar-bar* instead of speaking Greek), and tended to look down on them; but the term did not necessarily mean savage or uncultured.

and jealous of each other, ready and generally eager to fight for the sake of gaining territory, trade advantage, money tribute, and influence. The frequent wars, large and small, that resulted were viciously and vigorously fought. One reason for this was that the losers, even if they survived a battle, were likely to be slaughtered or enslaved; only in inconclusive engagements could prisoners of war hope to be exchanged. Certain conventions might be respected – the enemy's heralds, for instance, normally went unmolested – but warfare was generally unrestricted by rules. Enemy lands were laid waste, crops and herds destroyed, cities plundered and razed, sanctuaries polluted, old men killed, women and children carried off into concubinage and slavery – and all this at the time when the bellicose and expansionist Athenians were sublimely rebuilding the Parthenon, commissioning the sculpture and architecture of Pheidias, discussing the teaching of Socrates, and watching the plays of Sophocles. States and individuals might speak of acting honourably, and of upholding or defending their honour; but, in general, warfare – even between fellow-Greeks – was a merciless and ignoble business.

Herodotus and the Persian Wars

Herodotus was a native of Halicarnassus, an Ionian city on the south-west coast of Asia Minor, probably being born in the 490s BC and dying in a colony which he helped to found in the south of Italy in the 420s. It appears that he was exiled by the tyrant of Halicarnassus in the 460s, and that he travelled widely thereafter, from mainland and Aegean Greece to Phoenicia and Italy, to Egypt and the Black Sea. His *Histories* (the Greek word *historié* means 'enquiries' or 'researches'), which were perhaps given first as readings, cover a huge range of subject matter, mostly related in the third person but with much authorial comment: large-scale accounts of the political history of the Persian Empire up to the early fifth century BC; geographical and cultural descriptions of interesting foreign countries; the military history of the Persian invasions of 490–479 BC; and large numbers of individual stories about a wide variety of things that Herodotus thought were illustrative and interesting, and was anxious to preserve. He believed that causes had effects that balanced them, that good deeds were rewarded and bad ones punished, by the gods if not by men; so that to understand a particular situation you might have to look back several generations to see how it had come about. Like Homer, who had also written of conflict between west and east, Herodotus believed that the gods took an active part in human affairs, but that they remained invisible, and that even they could not overcome fate (or destiny); and he believed, as did most of the ancients, in divination, both the sort that foretold the future and the sort that decided whether a certain thing was lucky or unlucky, whether it should or should not be done.

The Histories was divided by later editors into nine 'books', of which 1.1–6.41, the rise of the Persian Empire, serve essentially as background to 6.42–9.122, which deal with the Persian invasions of the Greek mainland; but, within this large scheme, Herodotus dodged about chronologically, and set off on side tracks which often took him far from the main subjects. One of his favourite digressions was to describe, at length and with amiable sympathy, the customs of the foreign peoples who appeared in the main story. For instance, 2.2–182 is a fascinating account of the geography of Egypt and of the history and customs of the ancient Egyptians, an invaluable commentary which includes accounts of Egyptian religious beliefs and practices, mummification of the dead, attitudes towards animals, and so on, which could hardly be derived in such vivid detail even from archaeological remains as rich as those of Egypt. Herodotus is endlessly and genially inquisitive, interested in everything, and eager to tell us all about it.

Even the main story of the Persian Wars is interrupted by major flashbacks: the history of the double monarchy in Sparta, earlier troubles between Athens and Aegina, how Athens came to protect Plataea, the rise of Gelon as tyrant in Sicily, the origin of the Macedonians, and so on. There are also many stories, some more relevant than others, inserted in the main narratives because Herodotus felt that they illustrated something, or simply because he found them interesting; digressions that generally result in three-part structures in the form narrative/insertion/narrative resumed. To take one of the irrelevant examples, he mentions a eunuch called Hermotimus, sent by King Xerxes to escort the female warrior Artemisia and his children from the failing campaign in mainland Greece to safety in Ephesus; and he then pauses in his main narrative of the campaign to tell Hermotimus's story:

> No one we know of has ever exacted a more total retribution for a wrong done to him than Hermotimus. He was taken prisoner in a war, put up for sale, and bought by a man from Chios called Panionius. Now, Panionius made a living in the most atrocious way imaginable. What he used to do was acquire good-looking boys, castrate them, and take them to Sardis and

Ephesus, where he would offer them for sale at very high prices; in foreign countries eunuchs command higher prices than whole men on account of their complete reliability. One of Panionius' victims – one among a great many, because this was the way he made a living – was Hermotimus. In fact, however, Hermotimus' luck was not all bad: he was sent from Sardis to Xerxes' court as one of a number of gifts, and eventually became the king's most valued eunuch.

Now, when Xerxes was in Sardis, in the course of setting out with his army against Athens, Hermotimus went down on some business or other to the part of Mysia called Atarneus, where people from Chios live, and he met Panionius there. He entered into a long, friendly conversation with him, first listing all the benefits that had come his way thanks to Panionius, and then offering to do as much good to him in return; all he had to do, he said, was move his family to Atarneus and live there. Panionius gladly accepted Hermotimus' offer and moved his wife and children there. So when Hermotimus had Panionius and his whole family where he wanted, he said, 'Panionius, there is no one in the world who makes a living in as foul a way as you do. What harm did I or any of my family do to you or any of yours? Why did you make me a nothing instead of a man? You expected the gods not to notice what you used to do in those days, but the law they follow is one of justice, and for your crimes they have delivered you into my hands. As a result, then, you should have no grounds for complaint about the payment I am going to exact from you.' When he had finished this rebuke, he had Panionius' sons brought into the room and proceeded to force him to castrate all four of them. The deed was done, under compulsion, and afterwards Hermotimus forced the sons to castrate their father. And that is how vengeance and Hermotimus caught up with Panionius.

> (*Histories* 8.105–6, trs. by Robin Waterfield, 1998, Oxford World's Classics pp. 523–4)

And back Herodotus goes to the campaign in Greece. Of course this story has very little to do with the main narrative, but it is typical of Herodotus: a gripping tale of cruelty and vengeance in which the good end (fairly) happily and the bad unhappily, and in which the sins of the father are ruthlessly visited on his sons.

Then there is Herodotus's revisionist account of the abduction of Helen and the Trojan War – revisionist not in the way of the modern historian who doubts whether the Trojan War ever happened, but a revision resulting from Herodotus's feeling that Homer's story does not make sense, which incidentally makes a point about his own historical outlook. How could Priam, Herodotus asks, have fought a destructive ten-years' war with the Greeks, resulting in the death of one after another of his bravest sons, when he could easily have stopped the whole thing by handing Helen back to Menelaus? The answer, he believes, lies in an old story, confirmed by some Egyptian priests, that Paris escaped from Greece with Helen, not to Troy, but to Egypt, where Helen was detained; that the Greeks refused to believe the Trojans when they said that they had not got Helen, and continued the war until Troy fell and they found that she really was not there; and that Menelaus finally had to collect Helen from Egypt. Herodotus believes that this version of the story is what really happened because it makes more sense than the traditional one, and that Homer, although he knew about it, rejected it as unsuitable for his epic.[2]

It might be thought that all these anecdotes and more substantial subsections spoil the main story by diverting the reader's attention from it, but in fact they do not: Herodotus never lets us forget for long how the small forces of the Greeks defeated the large ones of the Persian invaders. And, since he tells the story from the point of view of the Greeks, the reader identifies with them in their struggle against the barbarians, feeling at first that they are bound to lose, and then cheering them on to final victory. It has the same heartening effect as reading about the allies' crucial victories in the Second World War; and we can be tempted to see parallels between the battle of Marathon (490 BC, *Histories* 6.102–20, when the Athenians, fighting alone, threw back the invading forces of Darius) and the Battle of Britain (1940); between the naval battle of Salamis (480 BC, 8.83–96) and the American defeat of the Japanese carriers at Midway (1942); and between the battle of Plataea (479 BC, 9.31–85), in which the Spartans and their allies defeated the Persian army, and the Russians' decisive defeat of the German army at Kursk (1943).

Let us look at part of the account of the Spartans' heroic defence of the pass of Thermopylae (480 BC, 7.198–239), which took place at an early stage in the second Persian invasion. Xerxes was marching south with a large army – Herodotus says that it numbered 1,700,000 soldiers, but a more realistic figure would be 200,000–250,000 – and the Greeks decided to try to hold him at a narrow pass on the road he was obliged to take; they had a total force of about 4,000, mostly hoplites (heavy infantry), led by the Spartan king Leonidas. The Greeks took up position, and the Spartans prepared for the coming battle:

> [...] Xerxes sent a man on horseback to ascertain the strength of the Greek force and to observe what the troops were doing. He had heard before he left Thessaly that a small force was concentrated here, led by the

[2] *Histories* 2.113–20.

Lacedaemonians [Spartans] under Leonidas of the house of Heracles. The
Persian rider approached the camp and took a thorough survey of all he could
see – which was not, however, the whole Greek army; for the men on the
further side of the wall[3] which, after its reconstruction, was now guarded,
were out of sight. He did, none the less, carefully observe the troops who were
stationed on the outside of the wall. At that moment these happened to be the
Spartans, and some of them were stripped for exercise, while others were
combing their hair. The Persian spy watched them in astonishment; nevertheless he made sure of their numbers, and of everything else he needed to
know, as accurately as he could, and then rode quietly off. [...] Back in his
own camp he told Xerxes what he had seen. Xerxes was bewildered; the
truth, namely that the Spartans were preparing themselves to die and deal
death with all their strength, was beyond his comprehension, and what they
were doing seemed to him merely absurd.

> (*Histories* 7.208–9, trs. by Aubrey de Sélincourt, rev. John Mar-
> incola, 1996, Penguin Classics pp. 439–40)

Once battle was joined, the Greeks held the Persians at the pass, and
seemed likely to be able to go on holding them off indefinitely:

On the Spartan side it was a memorable fight; they were men who understood war pitted against an inexperienced enemy, and amongst the feints
they employed was to turn their backs in a body and pretend to be retreating
in confusion, whereupon the enemy would pursue with a great clatter and
roar; but the Spartans, just as the Persians were on them, would wheel and
face them and inflict in the new struggle innumerable casualties. The
Spartans had their losses too, but not many. At last the Persians, finding
that their assaults upon the pass, whether by divisions or by any other way
they could think of, were all useless, broke off the engagement and withdrew. Xerxes was watching the battle from where he sat; and it is said that in
the course of the attacks three times, in terror for his army, he leapt to his
feet. [...] How to deal with the situation Xerxes had no idea; but just then, a
man from Malis, Ephialtes, the son of Eurydemus, came, in hope of a rich
reward, to tell the king about the track which led over the hills to Thermopylae – and thus he was to prove the death of the Greeks who held the pass.[4]

> (*Histories* 7.211–13, trs. by Aubrey de Sélincourt, rev. John
> Marincola, 1996, Penguin Classics p. 441)

When the Greeks learned that they were being outflanked and that
the pass would inevitably be lost, most of their units retreated
southwards, leaving only 300 Spartans and 700 Thespians (plus
400 unwilling Thebans who were held by the Spartans as hostages)

---

[3] An old defensive wall across the pass, now rebuilt.
[4] Malis was the Greek territory north of Thermopylae, occupied by Xerxes's
troops; Herodotus says that Ephialtes was eventually murdered for some reason
unconnected with his betrayal of Thermopylae.

to face the Persian hordes. They fought it out with spears and swords, and in the end with their bare hands, until all were killed. Among the inscriptions at the site of the battle quoted by Herodotus was a famous verse commemorating the Spartan dead:

> Go, tell the Spartans, thou who passest by,
> That here obedient to their laws we lie.[5]

It is clear, even from these brief extracts, that Herodotus wrote his *Histories* in a clear, racy narrative style that is essentially timeless; it is also the case that almost everything that he has to say remains immediately interesting, with remarkably little matter that is at all tedious, even today; and true, too, that we are dependent on him alone for much of the history of Greece and Persia in the sixth and fifth centuries BC. He was called in antiquity 'the father of history', and rightly so; but we have to ask, how good a historian was he, really? How far can we rely on what he says, granting that he was dependent on personal observation, the reminiscences of his sources, and oral tradition, not on documentary evidence? And how did he influence the writing of history by those who followed him?

We have seen that Herodotus looked at the history of the past and of his own time from a personal point of view – as every historian must – which included beliefs about how fate, the gods, and reciprocity (the balancing of one thing by another) exerted their influence on the world. We have also seen that he wanted to be accurate and to tell the truth as far as he could ascertain it. He mentions at one point a report that Phoenician ships had sailed round Africa in about 600 BC from the Red Sea to Gibraltar (4.42), and that, as they sailed westward round the Cape, the midday sun was seen to be in the north. Herodotus says that he cannot believe the part about the direction of the sun, but he tells us anyway, which shows that the report was true and that the Phoenician sailors had indeed circumnavigated the continent.

Accuracy is a prime virtue in a historian; just as important, Herodotus aimed to tell his story without giving undue favour or disfavour to particular people or states, even though he wrote as a Greek who believed in the superiority of Greek politics and culture, and was inclined to interpret the Persian Wars as a struggle between barbarism and culture, slavery and freedom. Nevertheless, his book

---

[5] Attributed (though not by Herodotus, 7.228) to the Greek poet Simonides of Ceos, c.556–468 BC.

implies, people are what they are, not who they are; Greeks can behave badly and Persians well, just as much as vice versa.

Having said all this, there are inaccuracies in the *Histories*, especially in Herodotus's second-hand accounts of the customs of distant foreign lands which he had not visited (we should remember that his title meant 'enquiries' or 'researches'). The semen of dark-skinned Indians, he tells us, 'is as black as their skin, not white like that of other men'; and the Indians, moreover, can collect unlimited quantities of gold dust from the sand which is dug up into ant-hills by 'ants which are bigger than foxes, although they never reach the size of dogs' (3.101–2). In the ancient world he was sometimes called 'the father of lies' as well as 'the father of history', but we are better placed to interpret and value his folk tales and fantastic wonders than were his immediate successors. Certainly we need no longer be put off by them; and the real wonder is how much he got right.

Herodotus, as the first major western historian, established the full scope of history, including in his enquiries not only 'history' in its more restricted sense, but also what later came to be called geography, anthropology, ethnography, and archaeology. He combined boundless curiosity – the first requirement of any historian – with a serious attempt to evaluate his sources of information; he wrote clearly and effectively; and he gave his narrative a formal structure based on cause and effect. In these essentials Herodotus set the course of western historical writing that it follows still.

Thucydides and the Peloponnesian War

In the middle years of the fifth century BC – the great age of Attic culture – the Athenians quickly recovered their pre-eminence in mainland Greece north of Corinth following the ravages of the Persian Wars; and they strengthened their hold on a tributary empire (politely called the Delian League) that encompassed most of the islands and periphery of the Aegean Sea. They had a fine navy – probably the best in the world at the time – but they were challenged on land by the militarily formidable Spartans, who controlled most of the Peloponnese (the Peloponnesian League). There was intermittent but inconclusive fighting between these two major powers in 460–446 BC (the first Peloponnesian War); but by 431 Sparta was sufficiently alarmed by Athenian expansion to undertake a second and more vigorous war against Athens, in which the Spartans were finally victorious – to a considerable extent as the result of over-confident mistakes made by the Athenians – in 404 BC. Following this defeat, Athens never recovered its leading position in Greece.

Thucydides, an Athenian born c.460–455 BC, believed that the second Peloponnesian War, which occurred during his lifetime and in which he took some part, was an event of unique importance; and he decided to write an accurate history of it while it was still going on, a book that would be more reliable than the *Histories* of Herodotus, and which would keep strictly to the main subject. In both these aims he succeeded very well, writing from personal experience about the parts of the war in which he himself had taken part, and carefully collecting evidence – confirmed from other sources wherever he could find them – about the parts in which he had not. His work was still based on reminiscence and oral tradition, and he still employed the device of using invented 'speeches' to make certain points, but the result was certainly more 'historical' and focused than the *Histories* of Herodotus; it was also less fun.

This was partly because, with few exceptions, Thucydides did not allow himself the intriguing digressions and anecdotes which had enlivened the *Histories* of Herodotus, and partly because Thucydides himself comes across to us as a more obsessive, disbelieving, less optimistic and genial man than Herodotus. There is also the disadvantage for the reader of Thucydides that, unlike Herodotus, he wrote the story of a war which his own side was losing to a relatively unattractive enemy; and one likes the side with which one identifies – the good guys – to win, not to lose.

That said, the *History of the Peloponnesian War* is an astonishing achievement. Thucydides's decision to tell the story of one particular historical event accurately and without digression was without precedent, and he had to invent for himself the necessary techniques: how to collect dependable information, how to select from a disordered collection of information what was essential, how to order the selection so that it told a story clearly and without undue bias, how to see the typical in the particular, how to distinguish between the real and apparent causes of events. All these things presented Thucydides with new challenges, and he met them with extraordinary skill, presenting a clear, logical narrative told in the third person. It is a narrative, moreover, in which his understanding of the tragic nature of human affairs and the grim realities of power politics can still touch us today.

His chief technical shortcoming was his failure to identify his sources – apart from his own experiences in the war – by naming his informants, for instance, or by referring to such documents as existed. We cannot reasonably blame Thucydides for not working like a modern historian, but the omission is a serious one, because there is no other history of the period with which his work may be compared, and which might contain alternative judgements, material which he mistakenly discarded on grounds of irrelevance, and so on. Nearly everything that we know about the Peloponnesian War comes from Thucydides, and we have to take him on trust.

Besides striving for accuracy and focus in writing his history, Thucydides allowed himself set-piece speeches and descriptions that save the work from becoming too dry and unemotional. Two of them, which complement each other at the beginning of the history proper, are especially notable: the oration of Pericles at the public funeral of the Athenians who had died in the first year of the war, 431–430 BC, and the account of the plague that devastated Athens shortly afterwards.

The aristocratic Pericles was an elected general – and the un-official ruler – of Athens in the mid-fifth century BC: the leading politician, law-maker, empire-builder, military commander, and art-patron of what is often called 'Periclean Athens'. A man of great probity as well as ability, it was natural that he should give the public funeral oration; and natural too that he should choose to speak on this occasion, at the start of a war, of the peculiar greatness of Athens. Here are two extracts from the lengthy speech that Thucydides put into his mouth:

> Let me say that our system of government does not copy the institutions of our neighbours. It is more a case of our being a model to others, than of our imitating anyone else. Our constitution is called a democracy because power is in the hands not of a minority but of the whole people. When it is a question of settling private disputes, everyone is equal before the law; when it is a question of putting one person before another in positions of public responsibility, what counts is not membership of a particular class, but the actual ability which the man possesses. No one, so long as he has it in him to be of service to the state, is kept in political obscurity because of poverty. And, just as our political life is free and open, so is our day-to-day life in our relations with each other. We do not get into a state with our next-door neighbour if he enjoys himself in his own way, nor do we give him the kind of black looks which, though they do no real harm, still do hurt people's feelings. We are free and tolerant in our private lives; but in public affairs we keep to the law. This is because it commands our deep respect. [...]

Our love of what is beautiful does not lead to extravagance; our love of the things of the mind does not make us soft. We regard wealth as something to be properly used, rather than as something to boast about. As for poverty, no one need be ashamed to admit it: the real shame is in not taking practical measures to escape from it. Here each individual is interested not only in his own affairs but in the affairs of the state as well: even those who are mostly occupied with their own business are extremely well-informed on general politics – this is a peculiarity of ours: we do not say that a man who takes no interest in politics is a man who minds his own business; we say that he has no business here at all.

(*History* 2.37, 40, trs. by Rex Warner, rev. M.I. Finley, 1972, Penguin Classics pp. 145, 147)

The nobility of Pericles's sentiments, and the virtuosity of the rhetoric in which they are expressed, take us to a high point of classical Greek civilisation; it is easy to forget that its benefits were enjoyed by a small minority of the population, the adult male citizens. But there was more than one view to be seen from the top, and Thucydides has not finished. Immediately after recounting these lofty words, he plunges us into a harrowing description of the plague that struck Athens soon afterwards, and of the terrible effects that it had on the numbers and morale of the Athenians. Just as the Spartans invaded Attica in the spring of 430 BC, and the people were crowded together for safety inside the city walls, a lethal and highly infectious disease broke out among them.[6] Huge numbers died; and those who survived suffered a moral collapse. What happened then mocks the high-flown sentiments attributed to Pericles in the immediately preceding section:

[. . .] Athens owed to the plague the beginnings of a state of unprecedented lawlessness. Seeing how quick and abrupt were the changes of fortune which came to the rich who suddenly died and to those who had previously been penniless but now inherited their wealth, people now began openly to venture on acts of self- indulgence which before then they used to keep dark. Thus they resolved to spend their money quickly and to spend it on pleasure, since money and life alike seemed equally ephemeral. As for what is called honour, no one showed himself willing to abide by its laws, so doubtful was it whether one would survive to enjoy the name for it. It was generally agreed that what was both honourable and valuable was the pleasure of the moment and everything that might conceivably contribute to that pleasure. No fear of god or law of man had a restraining influence. As

---

[6] We do not know what the disease was, even though Thucydides – who contracted it himself but survived – describes its symptoms. Typhus and smallpox are possible candidates; but it could have been a disease that has since mutated out of recognition.

for the gods, it seemed to be the same thing whether one worshipped them or not, when one saw the good and the bad dying indiscriminately. As for offences against human law, no one expected to live long enough to be brought to trial and punished.

(*History* 2.53, trs. by Rex Warner, rev. M.I. Finley, 1972, Penguin Classics p. 155)

There was, Thucydides implies, a hollowness at the centre of the culture celebrated by Pericles which both brought his leadership to an end and foreshadowed the collapse of Athenian power in the war against Sparta. But Thucydides goes doggedly on with his history, knowing of the woe that is to follow the ill-advised Sicilian Expedition of 415 BC, and the final defeat of the Athenians in 404; soon after which he died.

Xenophon and the Persian Expedition

Born in c.428 BC, Xenophon was an Athenian aristocrat who became a disciple of Socrates and an enemy of democracy. Finding the political atmosphere of Athens in the aftermath of the Peloponnesian War uncongenial – he was known to have been a supporter of the oligarchy and an admirer of Sparta, as well as an associate of Socrates, at a time when these tendencies were unsafe – he left the city in 401 BC to enrol as a mercenary officer in a military expedition being mounted by Cyrus the Younger of Persia. Later in his life – he died in his seventies, c.354 BC – Xenophon wrote a number of books, including memoirs and dialogues of Socrates (see pp. 102–3 below), a general history of Greece, and various other didactic works. His writings were unassuming and pleasing in their tone; and he remained throughout his life an unquestioning believer in the power of the gods and in the efficacy of sacrifice and divination. But he did not really understand Plato's Socrates; and his *Hellenica* – an attempt to complete and continue the *History* of Thucydides – is a disorganised though useful source of miscellaneous information. As a soldier, however, and as a writer of engaging military reminiscence – which he narrated in the third person from 'Xenophon's' point of view – he was outstanding.

Cyrus was the younger brother of King Artaxerxes of Persia, and a man, according to Xenophon, of great talent and charm. The purpose of his expedition, however, was hardly a creditable one: it was to assemble an army of Persian troops with a core of Greek mercenaries (including both hoplites and peltasts, heavy and light

infantry respectively) and march it from Sardis in western Asia
Minor to Mesopotamia, where Cyrus proposed to kill his elder
brother Artaxerxes and become the 'great king' in his place. Greek
hoplites, supported by lightly armed peltasts, were the most formidable troops available, especially if they were led by Spartan officers,
and mercenary units recruited in Greece had been employed in
Persia more than once during the fifth century BC. For them soldier-
ing was a job; they were not much concerned with the politics of
their employers providing that they were paid; and it offered an
attractive way of life, with plenty of adventure and loot, for young
men with some military training who chose or were obliged to
leave home.

For his expedition Cyrus employed an army of 10,000 Greek
mercenaries, initially with a Spartan officer in overall command;
but it was an army without a fixed military hierarchy. These Greek
soldiers organised themselves like a small city-state on the move. The
hoplites and peltasts, like two middle classes of 'citizens', elected
their own upper-class officers, and expected to be consulted on
matters of policy that affected them; while there was also a train
of 'non-citizens', suppliers, cooks, drivers, and camp-followers of all
sorts, who had to be accommodated and protected on the march.
The baggage train carried equipment and plunder, but the army lived
on the land, taking food and drink from the locals – with or without
payment, according to circumstances – wherever they pitched camp.
The Spartan commander-in-chief was Clearchus; Xenophon, then
aged about twenty-seven, was one of his senior officers.

The army set off from Sardis in the early summer of 401 BC, and
marched by easy stages to Cunaxa, a town on the Euphrates about
50km north of Babylon, which they reached in September. Here
they were met by the army of Artaxerxes and, in an otherwise
inconclusive battle, Cyrus was killed. With its head cut off, the
expedition no longer had any purpose or will, and the Greek contin-
gent was faced with the problem of avoiding capture and enslave-
ment by Artaxerxes and getting back safely to Asia Minor or Greece
itself. The story of how this was achieved is the main subject of
Xenophon's exciting *Anabasis* (the word means something like
'journey up country'), a memoir which he wrote in c.370 BC, some
thirty years after the event.

Harassed by the Persian army, the ten thousand Greeks set off
northwards and marched without serious incident until they
reached the hill country inhabited by the Kurds (who resented

foreign domination then as much as they do now), through which they passed with some difficulty. The subsequent crossing of the mountains of Armenia to the Black Sea coast, molested by hostile tribesmen and in atrocious weather conditions – it was now early winter, with heavy, freezing snow – is a tale of astonishing endurance and military skill; some of the soldiers and many of the camp-followers perished, but the main body reached a Greek colony on the sea-coast and eventually made its way back to the Bosporus.

Xenophon's book is the first masterpiece of western military history, the dispassionate account of a notable campaign written by a soldier who took part in it and who was sufficiently senior to understand the problems of command. He was a general in the Greek army throughout the campaign, and was elected commander-in-chief towards the end of it. No one was better placed to write about it, and he did so exceedingly well: the reader's attention and excitement never flag.

The *Anabasis* does have some shortcomings, connected chiefly with the length of time that appears to have elapsed between the events and the writing about them, and with the author's occasional exaggeration of his own importance and popularity. There is no evidence that Xenophon was writing with the aid of a diary kept at the time of the expedition, and he had inevitably forgotten details concerning places and dates – generally of minor importance – thirty years later. More serious, perhaps, is the feeling we have that Xenophon was inclined to improve on his own part in the events of 401 BC, diminishing that played by the Spartan commander; but again such self-serving is not uncommon in the memoirs of old soldiers, allowance can be made for it, and in this case it does not detract from Xenophon's overall credibility or from the excitement of his story.

Here is part of the account of a night march through the icy hills of Armenia. Some of the soldiers were straggling, sitting down in the snow and refusing to go any further:

As soon as Xenophon, who was with the rearguard, heard of this, he begged them, using every argument he could think of, not to get left behind. He told them that there were large numbers of the enemy, formed into bands, who were coming up in the rear, and in the end he got angry. They told him to kill them on the spot, for they could not possibly go on. Under the circumstances the best thing to do seemed to be to scare, if possible, the enemy who were coming up and so prevent them from falling upon the soldiers in their exhausted condition. By this time it was already dark, and the enemy were

making a lot of noise as they advanced, quarrelling over the plunder which
they had. Then the rearguard, since they had the use of their limbs, jumped
up and charged the enemy at the double, while the sick men shouted as hard
as they could and clashed their shields against their spears. The enemy were
panic-stricken and threw themselves down through the snow into the
wooded hollows, and not a sound was heard from them afterwards. Xenophon and his troops told the sick men that a detachment would come to help
them on the next day, and he then proceeded with the march. However,
before they had gone half a mile they came across some more soldiers resting
by the road in the snow, all covered up, with no guard posted. Xenophon's
men roused them up, but they said that the troops in front were not going
forward. Xenophon then went past them and sent on the more able-bodied
of the peltasts to find out what was holding them up. They reported back
that the whole army was resting in this way; so Xenophon's men posted what
guards they could, and also spent the night there, without fire and without
supper. When it was near daybreak Xenophon sent the youngest of his men
back to the sick with instructions to make them get up and force them to
march on.

(*Anabasis* 4.5, trs. by Rex Warner, 1949, Penguin Classics pp. 198–9)

Anyone who has been a soldier on active service will recognise the
authenticity of Xenophon's account: the exhausted stragglers and
the officer who drives them on, the threat of enemy harassment, the
confusion in front, the missing rations: this is the real thing.

Translations

Herodotus

The translations of the *Histories* in Penguin Classics by Aubrey de
Sélincourt (1954, revised and annotated by John Marincola 1996),
and in Oxford World's Classics by Robin Waterfield (1998), are
both excellent; extracts from each of them are given above. The
introductions, notes, and other apparatus in both editions are full
and convenient.

Thucydides

The translation of the *History of the Peloponnesian War* in Penguin
Classics by Rex Warner (1954, revised with a new apparatus by
M.I. Finley 1972) is very readable, though short on annotation. The
work is not yet included in Oxford World's Classics.

Xenophon

Rex Warner is again the translator of the *Anabasis* in Penguin
Classics (1949, reprinted with introduction and notes by George

Cawkwell 1972), and he does it very well.[7] Penguin Classics also include Xenophon's *Conversations of Socrates* (see pp. 103–4 below), *Hiero the Tyrant and Other Treatises*, and *History of My Times (Hellenica)*. Xenophon is not yet included in Oxford World's Classics.

---

[7] The *Anabasis* was once used as a first text for learning ancient Greek at school, and – as with the use of Caesar's *Gallic War* (see p. 193 below) as a first text for learning Latin – it put a lot of schoolchildren off Xenophon.

9 Plato and philosophy

The Pre-Socratics

Philosophy – literally 'the love of wisdom' or 'knowledge' – has always involved the search for what is the real nature of things and what is not; for what is permanent rather than transitory; for what is good and what is bad. Several early Greek philosophers working in the century and a half before Socrates became active, that is from about 600 to about 450 BC, began to ask questions about these things in terms that we can recognise, even if we have to reject many of their answers. Some of them were inclined to what we should call a 'mystical' approach, being particularly concerned with the nature of divinity and of the soul; some to a more 'scientific' one, involving cosmology and speculation about the nature and stability of matter; though neither group was exclusively mystical or scientific. Our knowledge of them is patchy at best. A few fragments of their teachings survive in quotations by later authors, and there are biographical details (some of questionable authenticity) in such works as the *Lives and Opinions of Eminent Philosophers* of Diogenes Laertius (third century AD), which was itself compiled from earlier collections.

Thales, who was working at the beginning of the sixth century BC, and *Anaximander* and *Anaximenes* who followed him later in the sixth century BC, were 'scientific' philosophers from the city of Miletus in south-west Asia Minor. Thales, whom Aristotle considered to have been the first 'natural philosopher', had some skill in geometry and astronomy, and proposed the scientific hypothesis that everything in the world was made of water. Anaximander held that everything came from a single, primal substance, not water but something other than any of the substances we know; while Anaximenes thought that the fundamental substance of matter was air.

100

Pythagoras, a native of the island of Samos who lived and worked in southern Italy in the later sixth century BC, was a philosopher of a strongly mystical tendency, who founded a contemplative religious order. He may – the evidence is uncertain – have combined mysticism and a belief in the transmigration of souls with developing the most abstract of the sciences, mathematics, concentrating in particular on geometry. 'All things', he may have said, 'are numbers'; and for him numbers existed outside the world of sense, where they connected with the eternal. *Parmenides*, an early-fifth-century BC philosopher from Elea in southern Italy, went further and proposed that everything apprehended through the senses was an illusion (an idea that was developed by Plato) but that the essential matter of the universe was single, indivisible, and unchanging.

Heraclitus of Ephesus (c.500 BC) was another mystic, who believed that fire was the fundamental substance and that unity in the world was achieved by the combination of opposites, so that change in one thing leads to change in another. He is chiefly remembered for his conclusion that everything in the world was in a state of endless combination and recombination, that 'all is flux', and for saying that it is not possible to step twice into the same river.

Xenophanes, a near-contemporary of Heraclitus, was another Ionian who lived most of his life in southern Italy. He was a rationalist and empiricist who thought that all things were made of earth and water. He was especially notorious for his attacks on the Olympian pantheon (if animals could draw, he said, they would draw the gods in their own images), and his belief in a single God who controlled everything by the strength of his mind.

Three other early philosophers are usually grouped with the pre-Socratics, though they overlapped chronologically with Socrates. *Empedocles* (c.495–c.435 BC) was a Sicilian aristocrat and statesman only about twenty-five years older than Socrates, a Pythagorean who followed Parmenides in believing that all matter is eternal. Having decided that air is a separate substance, he proposed that all matter consisted of different (and differing) mixtures of four 'elements': earth, air, fire, and water, a belief that persisted until medieval times. Empedocles appears to have been a polymath: a philosopher who believed in cycles of history, a mystic who was also a rationalist, a physician, a cosmologist who believed (following Heraclitus) that the earth was a sphere, an experimental physicist, and a transcendental biologist who hinted at theories of evolution and the survival of the fittest. *Anaxagoras* (c.500–c.428 BC), the first philosopher to live in Athens, was chiefly interested in cosmology and physics, but the remains of his work are fragmentary. *Democritus* (460–c.357 BC, actually younger than Socrates), whose work again survives only in fragmentary quotations, was the founder of Greek atomic theory besides writing on a wide range of other subjects, and was frequently referred to by Aristotle.

What chiefly matters about the pre-Socratic philosophers is not so much the answers they proposed to their questions about the nature and permanence of reality, of the soul, of substance, of the good life, and so on, as the fact that they asked these questions; that they attempted to answer them rationally; and that their questions turned out to be the basic problems of philosophy which were to concern Socrates, Plato, Aristotle, and all their successors.

Socrates

Who was Socrates? In one respect we know a great deal about this most extraordinary and charismatic of philosophers, but in another we find that we can be certain about rather little. It appears that he was born near Athens in 469 BC; that he served as a hoplite in the Peloponnesian War, which means that his family was reasonably well off; that he was attracted sexually by young men, though he had a wife and children as well; that he discussed philosophy with anyone who would argue with him; that he charged no fees as a teacher and cared little for his personal comfort or appearance; that he had a number of devoted followers; that by the end of the fifth century his views and personality had become politically and socially unacceptable to many of his fellow-citizens; and that he was tried, condemned, and executed for blasphemy and corrupting the young in 399 BC.

But Socrates wrote nothing himself, so that what we know about his ideas and teaching comes to us through the writings of others, and is to a greater or lesser extent affected by their ideas and attitudes. We have the surviving accounts of three major authors who knew him well: Aristophanes, Plato, and Xenophon; and Aristotle is another source of information, though he did not know Socrates personally. There are a few other early writings about Socrates; they are slight and fragmentary, but they do not importantly contradict the writings of Plato and Xenophon.

Although the *Clouds* of Aristophanes (which came last in the comedy competition of 423 BC, see pp. 79–80 above) was produced in Socrates's lifetime, its portrait of the philosopher is so different from the composite portrait given by Plato and Xenophon that they cannot both be accurate.[1] The Socrates of *Clouds* is a shifty, dishonest, trivial charlatan, whose only point of contact with the ascetic Socrates of Plato and Xenophon is his unkempt appearance. It seems likely that Aristophanes took Socrates as the visible example of a type of philosopher who could be ridiculed in Athenian comedy, deservedly or not; and Plato suggests later on that Aristophanes and Socrates remained friends despite *Clouds*, though it probably damaged Socrates's reputation in Athens.

The evidence for a very different Socrates described by Plato, Xenophon, and the fragments is so overwhelming in its scope and detail that Aristophanes's burlesque account has to be rejected. But this utterly different portrait, though it presents a consistent personality – a Socrates of outstanding charm, curiosity, honesty, and intelligence – is not entirely consistent philosophically.

Plato appears to have started by using the character of 'Socrates' to record the work of his old teacher, a philosopher who asked how we should live and what was the nature of this or that virtue, who claimed not to know or understand things in order to draw the answers from his interlocutors. But then Plato seems to have gone on to expound his own later philosophical ideas using 'Socrates' as his mouthpiece; and the 'Socrates' of the later dialogues does not hold all the views he did in the early ones. Xenophon, more conventional and shallower than Plato, gives us yet another 'Socrates', a portrait of the teacher he loved and learned from, who is not grossly dissimilar from the 'Socrates' of Plato, but who is also partly a reflection of himself, just as Plato's changing Socrates was partly a reflection of Plato.

Plato

Born to an aristocratic Athenian family in c.429 BC, Plato may not have met Socrates until c.407, when he was twenty-two and the philosopher was sixty-three, but the effect on him of the teaching of the old man during the last few years of his life, and equally of the

---

[1] The text we have is of a version of *Clouds* – which was never performed – revised by Aristophanes in about 415 BC.

manner of his death, was profound, and set Plato on his course as philosopher and writer. He lived to the age of eighty, first travelling abroad and then settling down at home to teach, dying at Athens in 347 BC.

A few of Plato's philosophical ideas came from the pre-Socratics, but he was the first to combine them, together with the teaching of Socrates and his own original thinking, into a coherent system. He believed in the immortality of the soul; and he believed that all objects of knowledge are eternal and timeless (the theory of Ideas), but that there is nothing real or permanent in the sensory world. He believed, therefore, that knowledge (and wisdom gained through knowledge) could be approached only through the intellect, not through the senses; that pursuit of 'the good' through knowledge was the proper object of the philosopher; and that the legislators of mankind should be philosophers – certainly not poets (as Johnson and Shelley were to propose), for whom he had little respect. He continued to develop these ideas during his lifetime, and he explained them as he went along in his major works.

The form Plato chose for most of his writings was the 'dialogue', in which, typically, Socrates seeks solutions to philosophical problems by means of question and answer with the interlocutors by whose names most of the dialogues are known; and they were cast either in narrative ('Socrates said', 'he answered', and so on) or in dramatic form (with speech headings). The method chiefly used was the *elenchus*, a form of questioning to prove the negative, what something is not (though it could also lead on occasion to a positive conclusion). Socrates did not always find the answers he sought, especially in the early dialogues, but had to be content with identifying the questions. What is courage (he asked), what is justice? Is virtue the same thing as wisdom? Can virtue be taught? Will men do the right thing if they know what it is? Can men achieve happiness by living rightly?

We do not know when Plato's twenty-six or so books were written except that they probably belong to the middle and later periods of his life; but they can be put in a rough chronological order on grounds of subject and style (see the list under 'Translations', below). We shall be looking here at three of the works – considering them as works of literature as much as of philosophy – concerned with the trial and death of Socrates (the early *Apology*, Socrates's speech at his trial; the *Crito*, an early dialogue; and the

Phaedo, a middle-period dialogue); and at the *Symposium* (Plato's middle-period literary masterpiece).[2]

The setting of the *Apology* is an assembly of perhaps 500 Athenian citizens, who are to act as both jury and judge in the case of Socrates, who is accused, first, of failing to acknowledge the gods of the state religion (he also claims to be guided by a 'sign' divinely accorded to him – one is reminded of Joan of Arc's 'voices'); and secondly of corrupting young men. Apart from a brief cross-examination of Socrates's chief accuser, Meletus, the work consists almost entirely of three monologues by Socrates, which – as with the orations in the histories mentioned in the last chapter – are given in direct speech but which cannot represent exactly what Socrates said. Plato may or may not have been present at the trial, but there is in any case no way in which such a long speech – the *Apology* runs to about 11,000 words in translation and would have taken the best part of three hours to deliver – could have been recorded at the time, or remembered verbatim afterwards. However, there is reason to suppose that the *Apology* does give the gist of what Socrates said, for Xenophon, writing perhaps at roughly the same time in the mid-390s BC, gave his version of the same speech.[3] Xenophon's account, while not agreeing in detail with Plato's, has enough in common with it to suggest that both derived from an actual event which neither of them grossly distorted.

The *Apology* is in three parts. The first and longest of them contains Socrates's speech for the defence, in which he explains the reasons for his unpopularity as he sees them, and describes his actual practice as a teacher of young men; undertakes a hostile cross-examination of Meletus, his main accuser; and self-confidently justifies his activities. As a result the jury finds him guilty, though not by a large margin. Now Socrates is invited to propose his own penalty; and in the second part of his speech, having remarked that the city ought to reward him, not penalise him, he rejects prison or exile and proposes a trivial fine. This is too much for the jurors, who sentence him to death by a larger margin than before. In the third

[2] The *Republic*, Plato's major philosophical work, is not included in this discussion because it is long and technical, though – like all Plato's dialogues – it can be approached as a work of literature as much as one of philosophy, history, social history, and so on. *Republic* Book 1 is a good introduction to Plato as a philosopher.
[3] Usually known as *Socrates' Defence*; there is some disagreement as to whether the *Apology* and the *Defence* were written independently of each other.

and final part of his speech Socrates berates the jurors for their injustice, and prophesies that they will come to regret it.

Far from attempting to ingratiate himself with the court in this speech, Socrates treats both it and the whole trial with disdain, and it comes as no great surprise to the reader that he is found guilty, even if death seems an excessive sentence. In any case it is reasonable to suppose that, by the standards of the Athenian state, he actually was guilty. To withhold respect for the state religion was to attack the fabric of the state itself, which required its people to worship the gods who held it together. To teach people – especially influential young men – to think for themselves was to encourage them to defy the common morality and will of the state. And Socrates did question the state religion, he did teach young men to think in original and untraditional ways.

Plato's Socrates could not have done other than what he did. For him, honest enquiry and telling the truth mattered more than anything else, and if pursuing the truth resulted in his death, so be it. Besides, he was seventy years old and was nearing death in any case; better to meet it now than drag out his days in prison or exile; and, as we shall see in the *Phaedo*, the third of these pieces about his end, Socrates believed that death would come as a welcome release from life.

Meanwhile, his old friend Crito comes to visit Socrates in prison and implores him to escape now while his supporters can still help him to get away, arguing that not only will they be distressed if he refuses and is executed, but they will also be blamed for letting him down. Socrates answers that by accepting citizenship of Athens he has contracted to obey its laws, whatever their merits, and that one may not act unlawfully and therefore unjustly (unless obeying the law leads to wrongdoing), either to oblige one's friends or to harm one's enemies. Here is an extract from the dramatic dialogue known as the *Crito* which encapsulates the central argument:

CRITO: I agree with what you say, Socrates; now consider what we are to do.

SOCRATES: Let us look at it together, Crito; and if you can challenge any of my arguments, do so and I will listen to you; but if you can't, be a good fellow and stop telling me over and over again that I ought to leave this place without official permission. I am very anxious to obtain your approval before I adopt the course which I have in mind; I don't want to act against your convictions. Now give your attention to the starting point of this inquiry if you are happy with the way I've put it, and try to answer my questions to the best of your judgement.

CRITO: Well, I will try.

SOCRATES: Do we say that there is no way that one must ever willingly commit injustice, or does it depend upon circumstance? Is it true, as we have often agreed before, that there is no sense in which an act of injustice is good or honourable? Or have we jettisoned all our former convictions in these last few days? Can you and I at our age, Crito, have spent all these years in serious discussions without realizing that we were no better than a pair of children? Surely the truth is just what we have always said. Whatever the popular view is, and whether the consequence is pleasanter than this or even tougher, the fact remains that to commit injustice is in every case bad and dishonourable for the person who does it. Is that our view, or not?

CRITO: Yes, it is.

SOCRATES: Then in no circumstance must one do wrong.

CRITO: No.

SOCRATES: In that case one must not even return injustice when one is wronged, which most people regard as the natural course.[4]

CRITO: Apparently not.

SOCRATES: Tell me another thing, Crito: ought one to inflict injuries or not?

CRITO: Surely not, Socrates.

SOCRATES: And tell me: is it right to inflict injury in retaliation, as most people believe, or not?

CRITO: No, never.

SOCRATES: Because, I suppose, there is no difference between injuring people and doing them an injustice?

CRITO: Exactly.

SOCRATES: So one ought not to return an injustice or an injury to any person, whatever the provocation. [...]

SOCRATES: Well, here is my next point, or rather question. Ought one to fulfil all one's agreements, provided that they are just, or break them?

CRITO: One ought to fulfil them.

SOCRATES: Then consider the logical consequence. If we leave this place without first persuading the state to let us go, are we or are we not doing an injury, and doing it to those we've least excuse for injuring? Are we or are we not abiding by our just agreements?

CRITO: I can't answer your question, Socrates; I am not clear in my mind.

> (*The Last Days of Socrates*, trs. by Hugh Tredennick and
> Harold Tarrant, 1993, Penguin Classics pp. 84–5)

So Socrates accepts his sentence with a serenity very different from his emotional outburst in the courtroom; and he remains calm on the day of his execution, while the friends who come to be with him

---

[4] The idea that one should not harm one's enemies was contrary to the common Greek belief of the time, and was abandoned by Plato himself in his later writings.

– not including Plato, who was unwell – are in tears. On that evening he has to drink the executioner's cup of hemlock, but he spends the day with the group of sixteen friends 'and some other local people' who are in the jail with him calmly discussing the nature and probable immortality of his soul, and the pleasure he feels at the prospect of its departure from his body. As Plato tells the story in the longish narrated dialogue called the *Phaedo*, Socrates says to Simmias:

'Is not what we call death a freeing and a separation of soul from body?'

'Certainly,' he said.

'And the desire to free the soul is found chiefly, or rather only, in the true philosopher; in fact the philosopher's occupation consists precisely in the freeing and separation of soul from body. Isn't that so?'

'Apparently.'

'Well then, as I said at the beginning, if a man has trained himself throughout his life to live in a state as close as possible to death, would it not be ridiculous for him to be distressed when death comes to him?'

'It would, of course.'

'Then it is a fact, Simmias, that true philosophers make dying their profession, and that to them of all men death is the least alarming. Look at it in this way. If they are thoroughly dissatisfied with the body, and long to have their souls in isolation, when this happens would it not be entirely unreasonable to panic and be annoyed? Would they not naturally be glad to set out for the place where there is a prospect of attaining the object of their lifelong desire, which is wisdom, and of escaping from an association of which they disapproved? [...] We must suppose so, my comrade; that is, if he is a genuine "philosopher" [i.e. a 'lover of wisdom']; because then he will be of the firm belief that he will never find wisdom in all its purity in any other place. If this is so, would it not be quite unreasonable (as I said just now) for such a man to be afraid of death?'

'It would, indeed.'

'So if you see anyone distressed at the prospect of dying,' said Socrates, 'it will be proof enough that he is a lover not of wisdom but of the body (this man would presumably be a lover of money) and prestige, one or the other, or both.'

'Yes, you are quite right.'

(*The Last Days of Socrates*, trs. by Hugh Tredennick and Harold Tarrant, 1993, Penguin Classics pp. 120–1)

It is not difficult to see, both in this and in the quotation from the *Crito*, themes that were to recur in the Christian gospels.

The *Symposium*, written c.384 BC, is the story of a dinner-party given by the young playwright Agathon to celebrate his victory in the tragedy competition of 416. It is agreed that each of the guests shall deliver a short speech in honour of love – personified as Eros, god of erotic love – and entertaining but fairly lightweight addresses are given by Phaedrus, Pausanias, Eryximachus, Aristophanes (the playwright), and Agathon, divided by narrative interludes. Then Socrates speaks and carries the discussion onto a more serious level; and Plato allows himself to use his favourite dialogue form by having Socrates first argue with Agathon and then narrate a conversation about love that he once had with a wise woman called Diotima. The evening is then interrupted by a group of revellers including the young politician Alcibiades, very drunk, who is invited to join the party and bring the event to an end by giving his own speech about love.

The love that is discussed in the *Symposium* is love between men; and it is not really so surprising that homosexuality was a normal and approved form of love amongst intellectuals in a male-dominated society which was contemptuous of women and their role in reproduction (see pp. 49–50 above). Besides, the ancient Greeks categorised sexual relationships not so much by the degree of sameness or difference of sex between the partners as by their relative status; and they had no word for 'homosexuality'.

The type of homosexual relationship particularly sought was that between an adolescent and an older man who would assist in his young friend's development and education; whereby the young man would mature, and eventually acquire young male friends of his own, as well as getting married and having children. Relationships of this sort were not normally 'platonic' in the sense of being spiritual, not sexual, but had a strong homoerotic content. This is given dramatic expression in the speech of Alcibiades, which recalls an occasion on which he lay down with Socrates and attempted to seduce him, but was unsuccessful because Socrates – despite being bisexual – had the character and self-control to refrain from sex, even with the attractive and disreputable Alcibiades.

The greatest satisfaction in love (it is implied in Socrates's speech) will come from perpetuating goodness in the world by mating ideas with beauty. Here is part of Diotima's explanation:

> "'Now, when men are *physically* pregnant," she continued, "they're more likely to be attracted to women; their love manifests in trying to gain immortality, renown, and what they take to be happiness by producing children. Those who are *mentally* pregnant, however ... I mean, there are people whose minds are far more pregnant than their bodies; they're filled with the offspring you might expect a mind to bear and produce. What offspring?

Virtue, and especially wisdom. [...] when someone's mind has been pregnant with virtue from an early age and he's never had a partner, then once he reaches adulthood, he longs to procreate and give birth [...] Since he's pregnant, he prefers physical beauty to ugliness, and he's particularly pleased if he comes across a mind which is attractive, upright, and gifted at the same time. This is a person he immediately finds he can talk fluently to about virtue and about what qualities and practices it takes for a man to be good. In short, he takes on this person's education.

"What I'm saying, in other words, is that once he's come into contact with an attractive person and become intimate with him, he produces and gives birth to the offspring he's been pregnant with for so long. He thinks of his partner all the time, whether or not he's there, and together they share in raising their offspring. Consequently, this kind of relationship involves a far stronger bond and far more constant affection than is experienced by people who are united by ordinary children, because the offspring of this relationship are particularly attractive and are closer to immortality than ordinary children.'"

(*Symposium*, trs. by Robin Waterfield, 1994, Oxford World's Classics pp. 52–3)

There is also a *Symposium* by Xenophon (probably written a few years after Plato's), in which Socrates makes a speech about a love between men in which each partner educates the other; and it is clear that he is attracted to his young male friends although he condemns physical homosexuality as 'debauchery'.

Plato's influence on the subsequent development of philosophical and religious thought has been profound, partly through his theory of an eternal world of Ideas, referring to abstract and concrete objects of knowledge which are unavailable to the senses; partly through the application of some of his philosophical methods by his pupil Aristotle (see the next section); and partly as a result of the superlative literary quality of his writings, which has ensured both their survival and the intense interest that they have continued to arouse in readers of later periods.

Aristotle

With Aristotle, born in Chalcidice in 384 BC, we come to a bridge between the classical fifth century and the Hellenistic period which is the subject of the following Interchapter, for he links the two periods by having been Plato's pupil in 367–347 BC, and by becoming the tutor in 342–335 BC of the teenage prince Alexander of Macedon (356–323 BC), later known as Alexander the Great. The other periods of his life were spent in teaching, chiefly at Athens; and he died in Euboea in 322 BC.

Aristotle is said to have written some 400 works, but only about thirty-five of them survive, mostly in the form of notes and summaries of lectures given in his later years. His early philosophical writings, which are nearly all lost, appear to have been Platonic in tone; but most of his later thought, which diverged considerably from Plato's, was applied to works on logic (in the *Organon*); metaphysics (what Aristotle called 'primary philosophy', on the nature of existence); natural science (astronomy, physics, biology, psychology, but including *De Anima*, 'concerning the soul'); ethics (the *Nicomachean Ethics* is a particularly good introduction to his work); politics; rhetoric; and poetry. He differed fundamentally from Plato in believing that 'form', the nature of a thing, was inherent in the object, rather than existing apart from it as Plato proposed in his Theory of Ideas; and consequently that investigation, in natural science for instance, could not be pursued by means of the intellect alone but must involve observation. He also differed from Plato in his attitude to poetry, as we shall see in a moment.

Aristotle was a polymath of prodigious scope and erudition – and the owner, incidentally, of the first known library of works of learning – whose teaching and influence remained strong in many of these areas of knowledge for more than two thousand years. His observations and discoveries in biology were unsurpassed until the seventeenth century AD, and his work on logic was still used in the twentieth. On the other hand Aristotle accepted the geocentric model of the universe proposed by Eudoxus of Cnidus (c.400–350 BC), and his immense authority ensured that the erroneous belief in an earth surrounded by moving spheres (refined by Ptolemy of Alexandria in the second century AD) was not seriously challenged until the sixteenth century AD, even though Aristarchus of Samos had correctly postulated, in the third century BC, a heliocentric universe with fixed stars and the earth going round the sun.

Aristotle's *Poetics*, which has been called the most influential work of literary criticism ever written, is of particular relevance here. It has been mentioned that Plato proposed that philosophers should rule the world; and he disapproved of the influence of poetry, especially in education, because he believed that it stimulated emotions that a good man should learn to suppress. Aristotle disagreed, arguing that the experience of the emotions resulting from reading an epic or going to the theatre were beneficial, enabling the reader or listener to be purged of them (probably in the sense of balancing and making use of them).

Poetics (probably a late work) is a treatise on aesthetic theory which uses works of poetry – chiefly dramatic tragedy – as examples. Aristotle accepts the general belief that all art is representational; and he argues that aesthetic pleasure arises from the fact that people enjoy learning and understanding things, in this case from what is represented ('imitated') by poetry or drama – a theory that favours realistic representations, rather than those that are fantastic or irrational. Aristotle comes to the conclusion that dramatic tragedy is the form of poetry best able to realise its potential to please, instruct, and purge, because it can act on a consciousness made more intense by emotion. *Poetics* proceeds to a definition of tragedy, descriptions of its constituent parts, explanations of their effect on the audience, and a comparison of tragedy and epic. Aristotle's theory of tragedy can be followed in its application to a particular play in the section on Sophocles, pp. 71–3 above.

The *Poetics* continued to exert an influence on drama into the modern period, especially in the sixteenth and seventeenth centuries AD. Parts of it were misunderstood: by French dramatists of the seventeenth century, for instance, who wrongly believed that Aristotle had decreed that the three unities (of time, place, and action) should be strictly observed in dramatic tragedy.

Translations

The Pre-Socratics

The best collection is without doubt the Penguin Classics *Early Greek Philosophy*, edited and translated by Jonathan Barnes (1987). This volume, which is a model of how difficult ancient texts can be presented and explained to non-specialist readers, contains translations of *all* the surviving fragments of the pre-Socratics, from Thales down to Democritus and Diogenes of Apollonia, who were near-contemporaries of Socrates. They are given in context, with a lucid introduction and explanations of the textual and exegetical problems involved.

Plato

It may be helpful to give a list here of Plato's main works in groups arranged in approximately chronological order – scholars disagree about the precise chronology – showing which ones are available in translation in Penguin Classics (PC) and Oxford World's Classics (OWC):

Early Period

> *Apology* (PC in *Last Days*, OWC in *Defence*)[5]
> *Charmides* (PC in *Early Socratic Dialogues*)
> *Crito* (PC in *Last Days*, OWC in *Defence*) *Euthydemus* (PC in *Early Socratic Dialogues*)
> *Euthyphro* (PC in *Last Days*, OWC in *Defence*)
> *Hippias Major* and *Minor* (PC in *Early Socratic Dialogues*)
> *Ion* (PC in *Early Socratic Dialogues*)
> *Laches* (PC in *Early Socratic Dialogues*)
> *Lysis* (PC in *Early Socratic Dialogues*)
> *Menexenus*
> *Protagoras* (PC in *Protagoras and Meno*, OWC)

Between Early and Middle Periods

> *Gorgias* (OWC)
> *Meno* (PC in *Protagoras and Meno*)

Middle Period

> *Phaedo* (PC in *Last Days*, OWC)
> *Phaedrus* (PC in *Phaedrus and Letters*)
> *Republic* (PC, OWC)
> *Symposium* (PC, OWC)

Late Period

> *Cratylus*
> *Critias* (PC in *Timaeus and Critias*)
> *Laws* (PC)
> *Letters* 7 and 8 (PC in *Phaedrus and Letters*)
> *Parmenides*
> *Philebus* (PC)
> *Statesman*
> *Sophist*
> *Theaetetus* (PC)
> *Timaeus* (PC in *Timaeus and Critias*)

The three works discussed in this chapter concerned with the trial and death of Socrates (*Apology*, *Crito*, and *Phaedo*) are collected in *The Last Days of Socrates*, translated by Hugh Tredennick and Harold Tarrant (1954, 1993) in Penguin Classics, together with *Euthyphro*; two of them are in *Defence of Socrates, Euthyphro,*

---

[5] *Last Days* = *The Last Days of Socrates*; *Defence* = *Defence of Socrates, Euthyphro, Crito*.

Crito, translated by David Gallop (1997) in Oxford World's Classics; and *Phaedo* translated by David Gallop (1993) is in a separate Oxford World's Classics volume. All of them are very readable and have good introductions and notes. The Penguin Classics *Symposium* is well translated by Walter Hamilton (1951); but the Oxford World's Classics version translated by Robin Waterfield (1994) is just as good, and is preferred for its excellent introduction and notes.

Aristotle

Poetics is included in the Penguin Classics *Classical Literary Criticism*, translated by T.S. Dorsch (1965), together with Horace *On the Art of Poetry* and Longinus *On the Sublime*. Oxford World's Classics has a volume with the same title (1989) that includes *Poetics* along with relevant works by Plato, Horace, Tacitus, Longinus, Dio, and Plutarch, edited by D.A. Russell and M. Winterbottom (the *Poetics* being translated by M.E. Hubbard); this is a more extensive collection than the Penguin one, and has fuller notes. Other works by Aristotle in these series are: in Penguin Classics, *The Art of Rhetoric*; *The Athenian Constitution*; *De Anima*; *The Nicomachean Ethics*; *Metaphysics*; and *Politics*; and in Oxford World's Classics, *The Nicomachean Ethics*; *Physics*; and *Politics*.

Interchapter: The Hellenistic age

Greek culture did not come to an end when the extraordinary fifth- and fourth-century BC city-states were superseded by large Greek kingdoms as the predominant political form following the reign of Alexander the Great (336–323 BC). Indeed, it continued to flourish and to have an even wider influence on the civilised world until the power of Rome began to spread into what we now call the Hellenistic world in the mid-second century BC, nearly two hundred years after Alexander. Even after that, Greek influence, linguistic and cultural, remained a powerful force in the expanding territories of the eastern parts of the Roman Empire; and continued to affect educated Romans everywhere.

Alexander's empire and its successors

Alexander of Macedon, who was only thirty-two when he died, was the most sucessful military conqueror who has ever lived. His father, Philip II of Macedon, had already taken control of the Athenian outposts in the north-west Aegean. Alexander first subdued the rest of mainland Greece, and then, with an army of 40,000–50,000 troops (including a high proportion of mercenaries), he set off to conquer the east. In a mere seven years' campaigning he extended his empire to include the areas now known as Asia Minor, Syria, Palestine, Egypt, Iraq, Iran, Pakistan, Afghanistan, Tajikistan, Uzbekistan, and Turkmenistan, founding cities (many of which were called Alexandria) as he went. On the way home he fell ill and died,[1] and the new empire broke up into a number of large and fairly stable kingdoms; many of the old city-states – including those in mainland Greece – were allowed some degree of self-government within these

---

[1] Some of his contemporaries ascribed his illness to poison.

kingdoms. Substantial provinces changed hands in the endemic warfare of the third century BC, but at the beginning of the second century the kingdoms that remained under predominantly Greek rule were those of Macedonia plus the confederations of the city-states of the Greek mainland; Pergamum in western Asia Minor; Egypt, including Palestine and Syria; and the Seleucid kingdom in modern Iraq and western Iran.

Language and society

The most striking feature of this enlarged Greek world was its homogeneity. The native populations differed from each other, of course, but the ruling Greeks spoke and wrote a common language – the *koiné*, a derivative of Attic – in place of the old dialects; and everyone except the Greeks had to be bilingual if they wanted to get on in the world. The ruling classes shared a culture that characterised not only the lavish royal courts and the administration, but also social life, the arts and sciences, and scholarship. The rich became richer, fewer in number, and more given to display; and the position of women improved somewhat (in some cities they could own property and divorce husbands who behaved more than ordinarily badly, though society was still dominated by men, and for the most part women were still excluded and despised). Great public buildings, including theatres and libraries, were erected in the cities; and more Games were held all over the Greek world, for which men prepared in *gymnasia*, which were exclusive social clubs as well as places for exercise. Slavery continued as one of the bases of the economy and there was a flourishing slave trade, with as many as 10,000 slaves a day being bought and sold in the central slave market of Delos.

The visual arts

There were considerable advances in town planning, but types of architecture, such as temples, did not change much from those of the Classical period; one minor innovation was the increasing use of the Corinthian column with its extravagant capital of acanthus leaves. The wealthy patrons of the Hellenistic world, however, subsidised a rich proliferation of art, most notably in the third century BC. Sumptuous jewellery was crafted in precious stones and gold; and large numbers of beautiful and realistic bronze statues of notabilities – now known chiefly from Roman copies in marble – adorned the streets and public buildings of the cities. The art of mosaic in *tessarae*, small cubes of coloured stone and glass, was introduced in the Hellenistic period, and was used to decorate floors with still lifes and mythological scenes. Important technical advances were made in painting on flat surfaces, using fresco (water-colour on wet plaster) and tempera (pigments in an emulsion) on plastered walls, and tempera and encaustic (wax paint burnt in) on wood and marble surfaces. The painters of the Classical period had discovered foreshortening, shading, and so on; but now Hellenistic artists were mastering more sophisticated perspective and were giving naturalistic settings to their subjects, including landscape, as well as making their portraits more realistic. Again nearly all the original works are lost, but copies of celebrated and vivid examples from the Hellenistic cities were made for Roman interiors, and have been preserved as murals in the houses of Pompeii and Herculaneum.

Literature

About 130 tragedians of the Hellenistic period are known by name but not by their works, which have survived only in fragments. This was partly because play texts were always more likely to be lost than other forms of literature, but also because they were written in the *koiné*, which from the mid-first century BC was felt to be an inferior form of Greek compared with the Attic of the fifth and fourth centuries. Similarly we have only one complete example of Menander's entertaining situation comedies (*Dyskolos*, 316 BC), which has survived accidentally on an early papyrus, although he is known to have written about 100 plays.[2] This 'New Comedy', as it was called, was urbane and and witty, favouring bourgeois love stories with happy endings, and was a long way from the boisterous, hard-hitting 'Old Comedy' of Aristophanes.

We are somewhat better off for surviving texts with the three major poets of the early third century: Theocritus (who will be dis-cussed in Chapter 15, pp. 154–5 below), Callimachus, and Apollo-nius Rhodius. Callimachus (c.305–c.240 BC), who came from Cyrene in north Africa, was employed as chief cataloguer at the Alexandrian library (see below), and is said to have written 800 books, though

---

[2] A second play by Menander survives which is nearly complete, and several substantial fragments of other plays by him.

only half a dozen hymns and sixty epigrams have survived from his verse apart from fragments. He was a scholar-poet who incorporated the results of his bibliographical researches into his poems, and wrote verse of great technical virtuosity. His best-known poem is the epigram which found new life in William Cory Johnson's moving adaptation of 1858 ('They told me, Heraclitus, they told me you were dead [...]'). Here is a literal prose translation of the original:

> One told me, Heracleitus, of thy death and brought me to tears, and I rem-
> embered how often we two in talking put the sun to rest. Thou, methinks,
> Halicarnassian friend, art ashes long and long ago; but thy nightingales live
> still, whereon Hades, snatcher of all things, shall not lay his hand.
>   (*Callimachus, Lycophron, Aratus*, trs. by A.W. and G.R. Mair, 2nd
>   ed., 1955, Loeb, p. 139)

Apollonius Rhodius (c.295–215 BC), who will appear again as Librarian of Alexandria from c.270 to 245 BC, is alleged to have quarrelled with Callimachus because their approach to poetry was so different, though there is probably little to the story. But it is true that, where Callimachus wrote brilliant, polished iambic epigrams, Apollonius produced an apparently old-fashioned epic poem in hexameters, the *Argonautica*, which retells the myth of Jason's quest for the Golden Fleece. But, for all its Homeric surface, the *Argonautica* is very much a poem of the Hellenistic period: witty, sophisticated, and an engrossing read: what we should call a novel in verse.[3]

History

A number of probably reliable and interesting historians were writ-ing Greek history in the Hellenistic period, such as Ephorus, Theo-pompus, and Hieronymus, but their texts are lost except for a few small fragments. We know about them chiefly because their books were among the sources consulted by later historians of Greece such as Diodorus Siculus (late first century BC). An exception is Polybius (second century BC), the Greek historian of the rise to power of Rome in the fifty-three years from 220 to 168 BC, five of whose forty books survive complete.

---

[3] For Pindar's version of the story, and for a modern version which relies heavily on Apollonius, see pp. 61–2, and p. 61 n. 5 above (see also the note on Theocritus, p. 154 below). For Hellenistic Greek novels in prose, see pp. 184–5.

Philosophy and science

The philosophical schools of Plato and Aristotle were carried on by their followers into the later fourth and third centuries BC, but there were changes: Plato's teaching was gradually transmuted into Scepticism, which held that knowledge of the true nature of things was unattainable; while the teaching of Aristotle, which continued for a while under Theophrastus and then Strato, came to an end of its development by the mid-third century BC. Two new schools now became prominent: the Epicureans and the Stoics. Epicurus of Samos (341–270 BC) founded a community in Athens in c.307 which included women and slaves, and which lived austerely in spite of the hedonistic beliefs of its members. Epicurus was an 'atomist' who taught that human beings were chance assemblages of elementary particles suspended in a void, which were dispersed again at death; and that their aim should be to seek the good (which he identified as pleasure) through a proper understanding of nature in order to live in happy tranquillity, withdrawn from the distractions of society. By contrast Stoicism, founded at Athens by Zeno of Cyprus (335–263 BC), held that the universe was controlled by the *logos* (divine reason, identified with fate or providence); so that the Stoic aimed to live in harmony with this ruling principle and to accept whatever happens to him in the world with willing acquiescence, knowing that the *logos*, not pleasure, was the ultimate good.

The Hellenistic period was also a golden age of scientific achievement, which included the discoveries of three outstanding mathematicians – Euclid, Archimedes, and Apollonius of Perge – and the medical tradition of Hippocrates. Euclid (c.325–250 BC) may have produced his great textbook, the *Elements*, in Alexandria. It included a rigorous exposition of geometry by means of a series of propositions and their logical development; astonishingly, it continued to be used as a fundamental teaching aid until the end of the nineteenth century. Archimedes of Syracuse (c.287–212 BC), who also studied at Alexandria, was one of the greatest mathematicians of all time; amongst other things he worked out the value of pi and the area of a parabola, and he invented a system for expressing very large numbers. Archimedes was also an outstanding astronomer, and a theoretical and applied physicist, solving problems of specific gravity and inventing a screw for raising water. Much of the work of Apollonius of Perge in Asia Minor (fl. c.225 BC) is lost, but as a mathematician he was second only to Archimedes: he established the geometry and mathematics of cones, and he was a powerful theoretical astronomer.

The most celebrated name in early Greek medicine was that of Hippocrates of Cos (fl. late fifth century BC), but nothing is known of his life and he may not have written anything himself. The treatises attributed to him were probably written by other physicians in the fourth and third centuries BC, and are best known to us through the commentaries of, amongst others, Galen of Pergamum (late second century AD). However, their insistence that the effects of diseases have specific causes, and that successful treatment begins with careful observation – beliefs which have remained at the heart of all subsequent medical teaching – may well have derived originally from Hippocrates himself.

Scholarship and libraries

The disciplines of philology (the study of language) and bibliographical scholarship emerged in the fourth century BC, and were fostered by the establishment of public libraries in the major cities. These became large and wealthy institutions, eager to collect, collate, and annotate every work of Greek literature, history, philosophy, and science that they could get hold of. The greatest library of them all, that of Egyptian Alexandria, was probably founded by Ptolemy I Soter of Egypt (ruled 323–283 BC). It was variously stated to have contained from 100,00 to 700,000 papyrus rolls; a likely figure is about half a million, equivalent to perhaps 100,000 modern books, stored on shelves and in boxes and buckets. The Alexandrian Library, which also served as a copying centre for collectors and other libraries, numbered amongst its distinguished librarians Apollonius Rhodius, the epic poet (librarian c.270–245 BC); Eratosthenes, the polymath who calculated the circumference of the earth with amazing precision (librarian 245–194 BC); Aristophanes of Byzantium, a distinguished editor of Homer and Pindar (librarian 194–180 BC); and Aristarchus of Samothrace, the first great textual critic (librarian 153–144 BC). There were also many private book-collectors who accumulated substantial private libraries.

III Late-Republican and early-Imperial Rome

10 The expansion of Rome

From city-state to superstate[1]

Occupation of the site of Rome in Latium – by a group of hill-top villages on the left bank of the Tiber, about 22km from the sea – may have begun as early as the middle of the second millennium BC, but it was not until about the mid-eighth century that the villages appear to have coalesced into a single, larger trading centre; that is to say, at about the time when the Homeric poems were reaching their final form, and when the Greeks were beginning to colonise Sicily. The date of the foundation of Rome by the legendary Romulus and Remus, supposedly the descendants of Trojan Aeneas, was believed in later tradition to have been 753 BC, which agrees more or less with the archaeological evidence for its growth.

At the time Latium was inhabited by several groups of Italic-speaking people, their dialect being the ancestor of what was to become Latin. There were other Italic-speaking tribes in central Italy, but beyond them both to north and south were foreigners: to the north the Etruscans, a numerous and culturally advanced people who spoke a non-Indo-European language; further north still were Celtic tribes which were later to invade and control the Po valley (and to give their name to Cisalpine Gaul, 'Gaul this side of the Alps'). To the south were an increasing number of Greek colonies in the foot of Italy and eastern Sicily; and beyond them again the powerful Phoenician colony of Carthage (near Tunis in North Africa), founded in the ninth century BC, which held the western half of Sicily.

In its earliest years, from the eighth to the end of the sixth century BC, Rome was a monarchy, in constant conflict with its neighbours, gradually extending its influence over the other tribes of Latium.

---

[1] See the chronological chart on pp. 191–2 below.

The monarchy was finally overthrown in 510 BC and succeeded by a form of oligarchic republic, dominated by a limited number of patrician families from which pairs of magistrates (consuls) were annually elected; other elected officials were soon added, and there was a powerful senate made up of patricians and former officials. The Republic, later modified as the mass of Roman citizens (the plebeians) got an increasing say in politics, proved to be an efficient form of government for an expansionist city-state, and a solid basis for its military organisation.

In two hundred and fifty years of almost non-stop warfare, from the late sixth to the early third century BC, Rome took control of most of Italy south of the Po valley. There were setbacks – Rome itself was occupied by Celts (or Gauls) from the north in 390 BC – but in the long run no other tribe or state could stand up to the Roman army (pp. 135–7 below). With most of Italy in its power, Rome then absorbed the remaining Greek colonies in the south (280–275 BC); fought three hard but eventually successful wars against the Carthaginians;[2] and suppressed the Celtic tribes in northern Italy (202–190 BC), which became a Roman province.[3] Masters of all Italy, the Romans were now unstoppable and, as we shall see in the next chapter, they used their great military and economic strength to build an empire hitherto unparalleled in the west. One of its central and most cohesive institutions was the Latin language.

The Latin language

Latin is an Indo-European language related only distantly to Greek, but sharing with Greek the characteristic of being a heavily inflected tongue, in which variable suffixes of nouns, adjectives, and verbs could override word-order in determining the meaning of a sentence (see pp. 20–1 above). It developed into what we now call Classical Latin, which was an artificial language of literature and rhetoric,

---

[2] The first Punic War of 264–241 BC, which gained Sicily; the second Punic War of 218–201 BC which ended with the defeat of the great Carthaginian general Hannibal in North Africa; and the third Punic War, 149–146 BC, at the end of which Carthage was destroyed and the population sold into slavery.

[3] A province was a territory subject to Rome ruled by a Roman magistrate; the name survives in Provence, the Gaulish province on the other side of the Alps ('Transalpine Gaul') which was the first part of modern France to come under Roman control. The Po valley province of Cisalpine Gaul was incorporated into Roman Italy in 42 BC.

and Vulgar Latin, the everyday speech of ordinary people which varied a good deal from place to place.

To show how far inflection could replace word-order to convey meaning in Latin poetry, here are two lines from Virgil (*Eclogue* 4.46–7), with a literal word-for-word English translation, followed by the same words rearranged as an English sentence, and three other translations in a footnote (the *Parcae* are the Fates):

> *'Talia saecla' suis dixerunt 'currite' fusis*
> *concordes stabili fatorum numine Parcae*

'Talia	*saecla'*	*suis*	*dixerunt*	*'currite'*	*fusis*
Such	ages	to their	said	run on	spindles
concordes	*stabili*	*fatorum*		*numine*	*Parcae*
in harmony	fixed	of destiny		with the will	the Parcae

> 'Run on, such ages', said the Parcae to their spindles
> in harmony with the fixed will of destiny[4]

The vocabulary of Latin has a familiar sound to us because a good deal of the word stock of English derives from Latin forebears (having come to us through Norman French as well as directly); but the grammar is anything but familiar. In Classical Latin nouns were assigned to five groups called declensions (with stems ending in -*a*, -*us* [or -*um*], ...), in which there were up to eight cases (nominative, accusative, genitive ...). As in Greek, there were three genders (masculine, feminine, and neuter), and two numbers, singular and plural. The verbs, in five groups called conjugations, were similar to Greek verbs in having special suffixes to indicate action, time, mood, voice, and person (see p. 21 above). Again, Latin is not an easy language for us to learn but, expertly used, it has both beauty and precision. Anyone with the most basic knowledge of how it works, a summary of its grammar, and an adequate Latin–English dictionary can make good use of parallel-text translations of the major Latin authors.

Here is an example of high Classical Latin prose, a complex

---

[4] 'Ages such as these, glide on!' cried to their spindles the Fates, voicing in unison the fixed will of Destiny! (H. Rushton Fairclough, Loeb 1916)

> 'Run, looms, and weave this future!' – thus have the Fates spoken
> In unison with the unshakeable intent of Destiny.
> (C. Day Lewis, Oxford World's Classics 1963)

> 'Speed on those centuries', said the Parcae to their spindles,
> Concordant with the steadfast nod of Destiny.
> (Guy Lee, Penguin Classics 1980)

sentence written by Cicero, which illustrates the familiar sound of the language's vocabulary; the unfamiliarity of its syntax; the dependence of its meaning on suffixes, not word-order; a play on the words *scio*, *scientia*, and *nescio* (which have a common root); and the euphony and balance of the whole. A literal translation is given under each word, followed by a translation of the whole sentence into ordinary English, with changes to a few of the words of the literal translation:

> *Ars earum rerum est quae sciuntur, oratoris autem omnis actio*
> *opinionibus non scientia continetur, nam et apud eos dicimus qui*
> *nesciunt, et ea dicimus quae nescimus ipsi.*[5]

Ars	*earum*	*rerum*	*est*	*quae*	*sciuntur,*	
Art	of those	things	is	which	are known,	
oratoris	*autem*		*omnis*		*actio*	*opinionibus*
of an orator	but		whole		the activity	with opinions
non	*scientia*	*continetur,*	*nam*	*et*		*apud*
not	knowledge	deals,	for	both		in the presence of
eos	*dicimus*	*qui*	*nesciunt,*	*et*	*ea*	*dicimus*
those	we speak	who	do not know,	and of	that	we speak
quae	*nescimus*	*ipsi.*				
which	we do not know	ourselves.				

Art consists of those things which are known, but the whole activity of an orator deals with opinions, not knowledge; for we speak in the presence of those who do not know, and we speak of that which we ourselves do not know.

The Vulgar Latin of everyday speech is best known through its descendants: Italian, French, Spanish, Portuguese, Romanian, and their subsidiary dialects. There are few written examples of demotic Latin from the time of Republican or Imperial Rome, though we can guess at what it may have sounded like from slangy speeches in the plays of Plautus and Terence (early second century BC) and in Petronius's novel *Satyricon* (first century AD, see pp. 138–40 and 185–6 below). Its chief and increasing difference from Classical Latin was that meaning came to rely more on word-order than on grammatical suffixes, using first the early Indo-European word-order subject–object–verb ('the man the woman loves', which survives in complex German sentences), and later the word-order that is used in English, French, and so on, subject–verb–object ('the man loves the woman'). The suffixes declined in importance, and were gradually dropped; French, for instance, has no case suffixes for

---

[5] Cicero, *De oratore* 2.30.3–6.

nouns, but retains several tense suffixes for verbs; while English has dropped all but one of the case suffixes, and most of the tense suffixes for regular verbs.

As the power of Rome spread across the ancient world, so did Latin, coming to be spoken as a first language throughout Italy (in various dialects), and then spreading into the conquered provinces with the Roman armies (which used Latin as a common language whatever the ethnic origin of their troops). As the Roman Empire became a world empire, so Latin became a world language, uniquely so in the west, and alongside the *koiné* in the Greek-speaking east. Later on Latin continued to be widely used, as the liturgical language of the western Christian Church until the mid-twentieth century, and as the language of European learning and international scholarship until the seventeenth century (and occasionally later). Latin continued to occupy the centre ground of European secondary education well into the twentieth century.

Roman names

Greeks of the Classical period had only one name, distinguished if necessary by mentioning the father's name as well: thus the grandson of Sophocles the playwright, who was also called Sophocles, was known as Sophocles son of Ariston. The names of Roman men in the late Republic, however, were more complicated, being in three parts – *praenomen* (forename) + *nomen* (name) + *cognomen* (additional name) – and an individual could (and still can) be referred to either by his *nomen* or by his *cognomen* or by both together (or, when related individuals with the same *nomen* are referred to, by *praenomen* and *cognomen*); examples will be given in a moment. Roman women, who did not change their names when they married, were known by the feminine form of their father's *nomen*.

The *praenomen* was a personal name, like John or William; and in late-Republican and early-Empire times there were only about sixteen of them in general use, the commonest being *Gaius* (abbreviated in writing as 'C.'), *Lucius* ('L.'), *Marcus* ('M.'), *Publius* ('P.'), and *Quintus* ('Q.').

The *nomen* was the name of the *gens*, the clan (or group of families of common descent) to which a person belonged, and was inherited from the father: names such as *Julius* (feminine form *Julia*) for members of the Julian *gens*, *Claudius/Claudia* for the Claudian *gens*, and so on.

The *cognomen* originated (very much like some English surnames) as attributes of individuals: names such as *Longus*, tall,
Naso, nosy, *Pulcher*, beautiful, *Felix*, fortunate, *Magnus*, the Great,
Agricola, farmer, *Atticus*, of Attica, and so on. However, they often
became hereditary (as English surnames did), and were passed on
from father to son with the *nomen*, perhaps serving to distinguish
different families of the same *gens*. Later, an extra *cognomen* for a
particular individual could be added at the end, making a four-part
name.

To take as examples some of the Romans considered in this book,
Marcus Tullius Cicero is now known by his *cognomen* as Cicero
(but formerly, by the anglicisation of his *nomen*, as Tully). Cicero's
wife, whose father's *nomen* was Terentius (or Terence in English),
was called Terentia; and his daughter was called Tullia.

Publius Vergilius Maro is known to us by his *nomen* anglicised as
Virgil; Quintus Horatius Flaccus is known by his *nomen* anglicised
as Horace; and Titus Livius (who had no *cognomen*) is known by
his *nomen* anglicised as Livy.

Gaius Julius Caesar is known by his *nomen* and *cognomen* as
Julius Caesar; but his relative Lucius Julius Caesar was called, by his
praenomen and *cognomen*, Lucius Caesar. Julius Caesar's daughter
by his first wife Cornelia, who married Pompey the Great (Gnaeus
Pompeius Magnus), was called Julia. When Julius Caesar's great-
nephew Gaius Octavius (he had no *cognomen*) was adopted as
Caesar's son, he took the name Gaius Julius Caesar Octavianus;
and he was known first by the additional *cognomen* as Octavianus
(anglicised as Octavian), and was later awarded the title Augustus.

11 Republic and Empire

Conquest abroad, strife at home

The late second century BC saw the consolidation of Roman rule round much of the Mediterranean coast, including the territories (to give them their modern names) of eastern Spain, southern France, the Adriatic Balkans, Macedonia and Greece, western Asia Minor, and Tunisia. Added during the next century and a half (c.90 BC to c.60 AD) were the rest of Spain, Portugal, the rest of France, England and Wales, Belgium and Holland up to the Rhine, all the territories south of the Danube, the rest of Asia Minor, Syria, Palestine, Egypt, Libya, Algeria, and Morocco. (The only substantial later additions, in the early second century AD, were Dacia in Transylvania north of the Danube, the lands south of the Caucasus, and Iraq.)

While these astonishing conquests were in progress abroad, things were going less well at home. The last hundred years of the Roman Republic (c.130–30 BC) were a time of intense social and political struggle, with episodes of anarchy and actual civil war in Italy. There was hostility between democrats and patricians; republicans and would-be autocrats; patricians and 'new men'; landowners and peasants; town-dwellers and countrymen; soldiers and civilians; citizens and non-citizens; free men and slaves. At the end of the second century BC two brothers called Gracchus successively attempted agrarian reform in favour of small land-holders, and some alleviation of urban poverty, but they were thwarted by conservative reactionaries determined to protect their property. The Social War of 90–88 BC was fought on the issue of granting Roman citizenship to all Italians. In 87 Marius, the general who had defeated the African king Jugurtha (105 BC) and an attempted Germanic invasion of north Italy (102–101 BC), marched on Rome and set up a repressive government with the politician Cinna. In 82 another successful general, Sulla, marched on Rome in his turn, where he made

himself dictator for three years and attempted to reform the constitution of the state and its laws; he retired voluntarily in 79, after
which most of his reforms were overturned by his successors in
government.

From this time until the end of the Republic in 30 BC, Roman
politics was in constant turmoil, characterised by struggles for
power between leading politicians and – most destructively – generals. Ruthless individuals allowed their ambitions to overcome any
thought for the good of the Republic; and in the end they brought it
down. This was possible because the soldiers in the Roman army
recognised that their rewards in pay and booty depended on the
success of their commanders in war; and they were prepared to
follow a successful commander wherever he led them, if necessary
against Rome itself. In effect the leading generals had private armies;
and they were prepared to use them for their own advancement.

The leading generals after Sulla's retirement were Pompey, Crassus, and Caesar; and, after some sparring in the 70s and 60s, they
agreed in 60 BC to rule the Republic between them, as what is now
known as the 'First Triumvirate'. Caesar felt sufficiently confident
of his position in the 50s to go and increase his prestige by conquering the rest of Gaul; but when Crassus was killed following a defeat
by the Parthians in 53 BC, rivalry between Caesar and Pompey
increased and brought their compact to an end. In 49 Caesar led
his army across the river Rubicon from the north Italian province of
Cisalpine Gaul into Rome's home territory, and defeated Pompey.
Caesar became dictator and instituted a programme of reforms, but
his rule ended with his assassination by republicans in 44 BC.

The murder of Caesar did not result, as the conspirators had
hoped, in the restoration of the Republic, but in another round of
civil war, in which the republicans were defeated. Caesar's former
colleague Mark Antony eventually joined the senator Lepidus and
young Octavian, Caesar's ambitious adopted son, in a second
Triumvirate, but inevitably rivalry flared up between them. Lepidus
was forced out of power in 36 BC; and Antony, having been defeated
by Octavian's forces at the naval battle of Actium in 31 BC,
committed suicide in Alexandria in 30.

So Octavian came out on top. The Republic finally collapsed, and
Octavian was the new Caesar, being named Augustus by the senate
in 27. Thus he became the first and perhaps the greatest of the
Roman emperors, ambitious to recover Rome's traditional virtues
and to rebuild its moral fabric under a paternalistic autocracy.

Politics and society

Or society and politics: the two were more than usually bound up with each other in ancient Rome. The class system was even more important politically in Rome than it had been in the Greek city-states, but it proved to be less rigid and immutable. Throughout the history of the Republic a limited and declining number of aristocratic families – the patricians – formed a privileged class, arranged in clans or groups of related families. In its early years only male patricians could be elected to the governing and religious offices and to the senate, which between them wielded the real power in the state; but during the fifth and fourth centuries BC 'plebeians' – the rest of the male citizens – also became eligible. There was in addition a wealthy class of 'equestrians' defined in the second century BC by a property qualification, the members of which, though called 'knights', were predominantly rich businessmen who were often more concerned with making money in the law, banking, trade, and so on than with warfare or politics. Although patrician influence on government remained disproportionately strong into imperial times, there was some social mobility between the classes; and many of the most powerful politicians of the late Republic were from plebeian families which had joined the senatorial class.

The Roman Republic, though nominally a democracy, was in fact a largely aristocratic oligarchy. Consuls, and later other officials, were elected annually, and exercised considerable power during their terms of office; but they were ultimately responsible to the senate, to which ex-consuls and other officers were appointed for life; in practice most of its members were from patrician backgrounds, and were inclined to support measures which benefited their own class. The emperors continued to claim democratic legitimacy and to make a show of respect for the senate, but Julius Caesar, and later Augustus and his successors, were dictators: absolute monarchs ruling what was supposed to be a commonwealth.

The status of Roman citizen, which carried legal privileges such as voting rights and obligations to the state such as military service, was originally limited to the inhabitants of Rome, but was gradually extended to territories incorporated into the Roman state, either directly or as provinces. All the Italian allies were enfranchised following the Social War of 90–88 BC. Under the empire, when most voting was replaced by direct rule and military service was performed by professional soldiers, citizenship still accorded some privilege and prestige in relation to native peoples who were not citizens, and was given as a reward to old soldiers when they were discharged.

Not only was citizenship given to non-Italians; it might be granted, other things being equal, to people of any race or colour. Another feature of Roman society was that it was possible for slaves, either bred at home or acquired as the result of foreign conquest, to be freed by their masters and eventually to become citizens themselves; a lifelong social stigma and some legal restraints attached to 'freedmen', those who were not born free, but the children of freedmen were full citizens in every sense. Both slaves – who were generally too valuable to be used for unskilled labour to the extent that they had been in Greece – and freedmen could be well educated, and they were frequently appointed to important and responsible posts, especially under the Empire.

Roman women, too, were more privileged than had been the women of Classical Greece. Patrician women might wield considerable political power; while upper- and middle-class women were generally well educated and accorded some dignity. They were not exclusively under their husbands' control, and they did not live in seclusion but were able to go out in public to the shops, the baths, the theatre, or the law courts.

Two interrelated features of Roman politics, especially in republican times, were conspicuous: the constant jockeying for position and power by individual politicians and generals; and the almost perpetual condition of war against one neighbour-state after another. The warfare was self-perpetuating in that each conquest both brought in the wealth required to support further conquests, and was the means whereby its leaders might seek to advance themselves.

Leisure activities included visits to the public baths (which included exercise areas and public toilets as well as men's and women's hot and cold baths); and attendance at the theatre and at 'Games' in the amphitheatre. Games, mounted at considerable expense by wealthy individuals (and later by emperors), were primarily exhibition killings of men and animals in gladiatorial contests and wild beast shows. (For Roman theatres, see p. 138 below.)

Religion

From the earliest times that we know about Roman religion incorporated three main strands. These were worship, with appropriate sacrifices, of individual major deities (Jupiter, Mars, Quirinus, and others); propitiation of the guardian spirits (*lares*) of hearth and countryside; and the practice of divination to learn the will of the gods. The archaic deities of primitive Rome, some of them of Etruscan origin, were later identified with the anthropomorphic Olympian gods that came to Italy with Greek colonists: Jupiter being identified with Zeus, Juno with Hera, Diana with Minerva, Mars with Ares, Vulcan with Hephaestus, and so on. Great stress was laid on the punctilious performance of ritual in religious ceremonies. Guardian spirits were paid particular attention in individual households, often respectfully identified with the ghosts of dead ancestors, and accorded shrines and small images both in and out of doors. The chief forms of divination, also Etruscan in origin, involved interpretation of the behaviour of birds ('augury'); of the state of the entrails of sacrificial animals; and of omens such as monstrous births and lightning. The results of divination were treated very seriously, and even the most powerful and pragmatic rulers, such as the Emperor Augustus, held good and bad omens in superstitious awe.

Various eastern cults were imported in late-Republican times, such as the mystery religion of Indo-Iranian Mithras, late first century BC. A major change that came in with the end of the Republic was the cult, then the deification, of individual emperors. Julius Caesar was deified (that is, worshipped as a god) after his death in 42 BC, and Augustus encouraged his own cult, though again he was not deified until after his death.

12 Maintaining the state

Economics and technology

The expanding Roman Empire had three main economic interests: these were the needs to ensure an adequate supply of food and other goods for Rome itself; to enable the free flow of trade throughout the Empire; and to provide logistical support for its military forces in the form of reinforcements, pay, and services. All three needs were met to a large extent by the process of expansion by conquest. North Africa and parts of Spain became Rome's granary; Italian olive oil, wine, and pottery were traded for foreign goods – especially minerals and luxuries – everywhere from Britain to Mesopotamia; and the Roman armies' conquests provided them with more soldiers, treasure, and supplies.

All this indicates the importance of good communications. Mediterranean trade goods had been carried by sea since archaic times, and shipping remained of prime importance, especially for carrying heavy commodities and moving troops. But Rome began to build fine all-weather roads in Italy from the time of the early Republic – chiefly for military purposes – and this magnificent road system, eventually extended throughout the Empire, was used not only by marching troops, but also by local transport for carrying light-weight trade goods. It was also essential for the official postal service of couriers who normally averaged distances of 80km a day (or up to 200km a day in emergencies), using horses and wheeled vehicles. However, there was no postal service available to the public, and private letters were normally carried between correspondents by their servants.

Great technical skill was also shown in Roman buildings other than roads, as is still to be seen in great public works such as the extraordinary aqueduct bridge of the Pont du Gard in Provence (20–16 BC), and the Pantheon in Rome (117–38 AD) with its vast dome of poured concrete. Their construction too was ultimately paid for out of the spoils of war.

Donkeys, mules, and oxen were used as draught animals, for ploughing, and for powering simple machinery such as grain mills. Horses were reserved for pulling light carriages and for riding (chiefly by cavalrymen), but ancient horses were small (about fourteen hands high, the size of a modern pony), and their use was further limited by the facts that they were seldom shod and that fully efficient horse-collars and stirrups had not yet been invented.

There was in general little powered machinery, and most of what there was took the form of man-powered devices such as levers, block and tackle, and capstans for lifting heavy weights, tensioning military catapults, and so on; and as bucket-chains and screws for raising water from mine shafts. Exceptions were water-powered mills, several of which might be stacked up a hillside to make full use of the fall of the water.

The Roman army[1]

The Roman army had started as a force of the better-off citizens doing military service as a civic duty, but by the end of the fifth century the soldiers were being paid, and from the time of the second Punic War (218–201 BC), when the resources of Roman manpower were plainly overstretched, the army became increasingly a professional force, much of it recruited outside Roman territory; and eventually a standing army.

The largest and most powerful unit of the professional army was the legion of heavy infantry, which recruited physically fit citizens who were engaged for up to twenty-five years' service, after which they were given plots of land to farm, either in Italy or in the territory they had conquered. Originally mustering some 6,000 men, the strength of the legion later settled at about 4,800 in 60 'centuries' of 80 men each – although, like army units of all periods, they were seldom up to full strength. The early tactical structure grouped two centuries into each of thirty 160-man 'maniples', but in the second century BC this arrangement was changed to groups of six centuries in each of ten 480-man 'cohorts' (ten cohorts being easier for a general to manoeuvre than thirty maniples). Besides heavy infantrymen, legions mustered various specialists such as

---

[1] See also pp. 190, 193, about Caesar's campaigns in Gaul.

engineers for organising the building of roads, bridges, and fortifications; and artillerymen using bolt- and stone-throwing 'engines'. Roman armies also included, as essential adjuncts to their strength, smaller units of cavalry and lightly armed auxiliaries recruited locally, who were attached to individual infantry legions, and were usually granted citizenship at the end of their service.

Each century was commanded by a 'centurion', a professional officer who may be thought of in modern terms as both company commander and company sergeant-major; he had probably come up through the ranks, though patronage and influence played their part in all military promotions.[2] Each cohort was led either by its senior centurion or by one of six 'tribunes', usually of equestrian rank; but by late-Republican times the legion came under the overall command of a 'legate' of senatorial rank, and the tribunes were more likely to be his staff officers than cohort commanders. Tribunes and legates were not professional soldiers, but they normally had some previous military experience.

Roman legionaries, who were rigorously trained, were more lightly armed than Greek hoplites, partly for the sake of tactical flexibility, and partly so that in emergencies they could carry their own equipment without having to rely on the baggage train. Even so each man's helmet, body armour, shield, light spear, short sword, entrenching tool, cooking pot, and rations weighed at least 30kg, a serious burden for five-hour forced marches on hard roads of up to 35km per day, ending with the digging and palisading of a temporary fortified camp.[3]

Set-piece battles, with flights of javelins followed by hacking and thrusting with sword and shield, were not very common, but both then and in the more frequent skirmishes, trained Roman soldiers could normally beat any barbarian force that came up against them in the open. When they themselves were beaten – and there were occasions when whole legions were lost – it was usually the result of well-organised barbarian ambushes.

---

[2] By early-Imperial times the first cohort of a legion might be twice the size of the others, when its senior centurion, the *primus pilus*, was an officer of central importance in the affairs of the legion.
[3] Vegetius, writing in the mid-first century AD, said that the Roman army trained on route marches of 32km per day (A.K. Goldsworthy, *The Roman Army at War*, Oxford University Press 1996, p. 110). In 1914 British regular infantry were also expected to march 32km per day in training, though the median distance actually marched by trained German troops was only 20km per day (John Keegan, *The First World War*, Hutchinson 1998, pp. 37–9, 86).

Roman warfare was no kinder than fighting had been in ancient Greece (pp. 84–5 above). When the Romans decided to punish a town, the built-up area would be flattened, the whole population massacred or sold into slavery, and the surrounding countryside pillaged and burned. Enemy soldiers captured in battle were also either killed off or enslaved; and mass crucifixions were carried out for the purpose of subduing and terrorising subject peoples.[4] The Roman soldiers themselves were not so badly off: they belonged to an elite force, complete with medical services for the wounded, that usually won its battles and was rewarded with plunder as well as pay. However, the legionary's conception of the afterlife, while not quite so gloomy as that of the Greek hoplites, offered no hope of heaven to ordinary soldiers unless they displayed exceptional heroism: most of them, they believed, would join the shades in 'Pluto's meagre dwelling'.[5]

[4] Crucifixion was a very common method of executing non-citizens in the first century AD; and part of its point (in the crucifixion of Jesus, for instance) was that it was a humiliating as well as a painful punishment.
[5] *Domus exilis Plutonae*, Horace, *Odes* I.4.

13 The arts

Painting, sculpture, and architecture

The strongest influences on the Roman visual arts were the Etruscan, Classical Greek, and Hellenistic Greek traditions, which can be followed in the copies and original paintings, busts, and statues produced in Italy (see pp. 54–5, 116–17 above), many of which were made by immigrant Greek rather than Roman artists. Although it was also of Greek origin, the form which became especially typical of Roman art was the historical low-relief sculpture, widely used on funerary monuments and such things as columns and arches set up to commemorate Roman achievements.

The most spectacular legacy of Roman visual art is to be found in its architecture. The Romans took over traditional Greek forms for building their temples, roofed colonnades, and porches; but their complex, monumental public works exceeded in size and dignity anything that had been seen before, and perfectly expressed the greatness and self-confidence of Rome. There are many surviving examples. The Pont du Gard and the Pantheon have already been mentioned, and among many other works there are the Colosseum, the Porta Praenestina, and Trajan's column in Rome; Trajan's arch in Benevento (all these of the late first and early second century AD); and numerous provincial theatres, amphitheatres, baths, and so on, which are especially well preserved in Tunisia. Technical innovations were the introduction of the 'composite' order for capitals (a mixture of Ionic and Corinthian); and the use of structural concrete, usually faced with brick or marble.

Drama

The first surviving Roman drama – which was also the first distinctive flowering of Latin literature – came from Plautus and

Terence, who wrote comedies at the beginning of the second century BC. Their plays were derivative in the sense that both of them adapted Hellenistic Greek plays for the Roman stage, but their dramatic and verbal skills were such that their productions were much more than pale imitations of Greek originals. The younger Seneca, who wrote literary tragedies two hundred years later, took the Classical Greek tragedians as his model. All three of these playwrights had a special importance for the later development of western literature because it was the Latin dramatists, not the Greek ones, who chiefly influenced and were in their turn imitated by the playwrights of the Renaissance and Neoclassical periods – notably by Shakespeare, Molière, and Racine.

We have twenty of the 130 plays attributed to Titus Maccius *Plautus* (c.250–184 BC), all of them apparently adaptations of Greek comedies of the Hellenistic period, including works by Menander (see p. 117 above). Plautus wrote in spirited, colloquial Latin and, where comparisons can be made, it may be seen that he altered and tightened up the texts of his Greek originals to make them more accessible to his Roman audiences; and his plays have the additional importance of being almost the only evidence we have of the state of the Latin language at the beginning of the second century BC. There was no chorus, but the plays probably introduced songs and perhaps musical interludes, and they were produced with temporary scenery and seating rather than in permanent theatres. (The first stone theatre in Rome was not built until 55 BC.) These exuberant, near-farcical comedies such as *Amphitruo* and *Menaechmi* (from which Shakespeare took the plot of *The Comedy of Errors*), and *Aulularia*, with their exotic Greek settings, are very funny even in translation, and are still eminently actable on the stage.

The source of *Aulularia* ('The Pot of Gold'), probably one of Plautus's later plays, is unknown, but it must derive from one of the many hundreds of lost Hellenistic plays. Euclio, its central character, is a miser who is obsessed with keeping safe a pot of gold which he has inherited, and Plautus makes him so absurd in his passion as to be almost tragic. The other characters are less fully developed, but the dialogue never loses pace, and is laced all through with outrageous puns and racy jokes. Molière took *Aulularia* as the basis for one of his comic masterpieces, *L'Avare* ('The Miser', 1668), and developed Euclio into Harpagon, the miser who reaches even greater depths of near-tragic misery as a result of his obsession.

Terence (Publius Terentius Afer, 193 [or 183] to 159 BC), working a little later than Plautus in the 160s BC, seems to have written only six plays, all of which survive. Four of them were adapted from Menander, and the other two from Apollodorus of Carystus; and it appears that they follow their originals more closely than did the plays of Plautus, including the original Greek titles. Terence also wrote more seriously and naturalistically than his predecessor had done: he avoided anachronistic Roman intrusions into the Greek plots, and concentrated on character rather than caricature. Again there was no chorus, but probably no music either; and again he wrote plays that still work well on the stage.[1]

Terence's *Phormio* (161 BC) was based on a lost play, *The Claimant*, by Apollodorus of Carystus. Phormio himself, the character who dominates the play that bears his name, is the most formidable creation in surviving Roman comedy: a rascally chancer who lives by his wits, and who is the prototypical adventurer just as Plautus's Euclio is the prototypical miser. The other main characters, too, in this elegant comedy of intrigue are well developed as human beings; and although Terence enjoys farcical humour he does not follow Plautus in his grosser clowning. Again, Molière knew a good comedy when he saw one, and he followed *Phormio* very closely – sometimes line for line – in his hilarious *Les Fourberies de Scapin* ('That Scoundrel Scapin', 1671).

The best-known Roman tragedian was *Seneca the Younger* (Lucius Annaeus Seneca, c.4 BC to 65 AD), whose ten plays – a small fraction of his writings on a variety of subjects (see pp. 150–1 below) – derived not from Hellenistic but from Classical Greek models (especially the tragedies of Euripides). These extravagant, violent, and highly rhetorical tragedies such as *Hercules Furens*, *Medea*, and *Phaedra*, with their prologue and five acts,[2] had a strong influence on later European drama, especially that of the sixteenth and seventeenth centuries; but they seem originally to have been intended to be read or recited rather than acted in the theatre.

---

[1] Terence's plays have also provided the once-familiar tags *hinc illae lacrimae* ('hence those tears', *Andria*); *Quot homines, tot sententiae* ('so many men, so many opinions', *Phormio*); and *Homo sum, humani nil a me alienum puto* ('I am a man, I count nothing human indifferent to me', *Heauton Timorumenos*).

[2] The plays of Plautus and Terence were also divided into five acts by early editors, but these divisions were not made by the playwrights themselves.

The *Phaedra* of Seneca (?c.50 AD) – more a dramatic poem than a play – derives from the *Hippolytus* of Euripides (429 BC).[3] The myth, as retold by Euripides, is that Phaedra, the wife of Theseus, falls in love with her stepson Hippolytus, and approaches him through his servant; he scorns her approach; she hangs herself, and denounces Hippolytus to Theseus in a suicide note; her guilt is then revealed by Artemis to Theseus, so exonerating Hippolytus. While Euripides is chiefly interested in the noble character of Hippolytus, Seneca alters the plot in order to concentrate on Phaedra; she approaches Hippolytus in person, not through an intermediary, and she herself confesses her guilt to Theseus before killing herself in front of him. Seneca's Phaedra is a more sympathetic character – paradoxically both more shameless and more repentant – than the Phaedra of Euripides, and his Hippolytus is more priggish. Seneca's dramatic tone and technique, while he still uses a chorus, can seem eerily familiar to us because of the effect they were to have on English and French dramatic tragedies of the sixteenth and seventeenth centuries. Both *Hippolytus* and *Phaedra* were drawn on by Racine for his masterpiece *Phèdre* (1677), though he took care to make his heroine 'rather less odious than she is in the classical tragedies'.[4]

Translations

Plautus's *Aulularia* is translated with great panache by Erich Segal (1996, along with *Miles Gloriosus, Menaechmi*, and *Mostellaria*) in the Oxford World's Classics *Plautus: Four Comedies*. Terence's *Phormio* is translated by Betty Radice (1965, together with Terence's other five comedies) in the Penguin Classics *Terence: The Comedies*. Seneca's *Phaedra* is translated by E.F. Watling (1966, with *Thyestes, Troades, Oedipus*, and *Octavia*) in the Penguin Classics *Seneca: Four Tragedies and Octavia*.

Education, books, and libraries

In the early Republic the education of children was family-based, but by the third and second centuries BC private schools were increasingly available for both primary and secondary education.

[3] This is the second, and only surviving one, of two plays written by Euripides on this subject.
[4] Racine's Preface to *Phèdre*.

The Greek model of concentration on literary subjects and rhetoric was followed, with the Greek language and Greek literature being studied as well as the Latin language, and Latin literature being added in the later first century BC. Except for potential soldiers, there was less emphasis on physical training; and the education of girls was taken more seriously. Further education might be pursued abroad, especially in Athens or Rhodes. By late Republican times cultivated Romans could read Greek fluently; they were very well read in literature, history, and philosophy in both Greek and Latin, and they could apply their knowledge of the two languages to rhetorical purposes. As to literacy outside the cultured class, what has been said about it in Classical Greece (pp. 55–6 above) is generally applicable to the situation in late-Republican and early-Empire Rome: we have no statistics and can only guess at levels of literacy in the lower classes; but again it seems unlikely that functional literacy was ever achieved by more than 20–30 per cent of the population.

The papyrus roll continued to be the chief form of the book in late-Republican and early-Imperial Rome, copied, collected, and stored in public and private libraries; and by the first century BC the 'publication' of books was taking place, by means of the multiple copying of texts. We have already seen that great deposit libraries, such as that of Alexandria, were also copying centres for other libraries and collectors. Now an individual, such as Cicero's friend Atticus, might act as a 'publisher', employing copyists to produce new books for sale before they could be pirated.[5]

At the same time, in the first century AD, the greatest of all revolutions in book production was quietly taking place: this was the invention and introduction of the codex. A book in the form of a papyrus roll is like a film (or an audio tape or a video tape): to find your place in it you have to scroll backwards or forwards through the roll, which is inconvenient and time-consuming. A codex, on the other hand, in which sheets of parchment or paper are folded into pages attached to each other at the spine, is like a gramophone record or a CD or a computer disk: you can flip the pages (or move the needle or the reading head) rapidly back and forth to find your place easily and quickly; and with a codex you can even have access with your fingers to several places at once. Codices, moreover, are less bulky and more robust than rolls, and parchment is a more

---

[5] On the survival and accuracy of classical texts, see the Appendix, pp. 206–8 below.

durable material than papyrus.[6] Codices can be of various dimensions and capacities, are easy to store and find on library shelves, and can be adapted both to the reading desk and to the pocket.

Proto-codices existed in the second century BC when two or more wooden tablets, faced with wax and written on with a stylus, were connected at the spine with leather thongs (the writing on the wax could be erased and the tablet reused). But parchment codices were being used by the late first century BC as pocket notebooks, and by the first century AD pocket codices of literary works were being copied for sale. Important books continued to be written on rolls for some time after this, but from the second century AD biblical and Christian texts were increasingly written on codices, and the obvious superiority of the new form led to its general adoption. By the fourth century AD three out of four literary texts were copied as codices, not as rolls.

---

[6] Paper, a Chinese invention of the first century AD, did not reach Europe from the east until early in the twelfth century.

14 Cicero: rhetoric and philosophy

The legacy of Greece: (1) rhetoric

Rhetoric – the art of persuasive speaking – although it must have developed originally alongside human speech itself, was systematised by the Greeks in the fifth and fourth centuries BC, and taught under five main headings: Invention, which involved finding the relevant material for the speech; Arrangement, putting the material in the right order; Diction, choosing the right words and style in which to express it; Memory, how to memorise the speech; and Delivery, the technique of speaking in public. Aristotle's *Rhetoric* (fourth century BC) was the best-known treatise on how to compose a good speech, giving practical advice on how to gain the audience's good opinion of the speaker and how to persuade it to accept his arguments. But perhaps a better introduction to classical rhetoric is Plato's *Gorgias*, one of his most stimulating dialogues, in which Socrates discusses the nature and ethical dimensions of rhetoric with Gorgias (who was an actual rhetorical pioneer from Greek Sicily) and some of his fellows.

Demosthenes

The most celebrated of the Athenian orators, whose influence was great and lasting, was Demosthenes (384–322 BC). He was a politician, public figure, and patriot as much as he was an orator, but it is for his speeches, with which he attempted to persuade his fellow-Athenians that his policies were the right ones, that he is chiefly remembered. They were delivered in a pure Attic Greek, very carefully constructed for their persuasive logic, for their verbal harmony, and not least for the impression of informal spontaneity that Demosthenes sought to give. He achieved all these ends, and his oratory usually succeeded in persuading his audience that his advice was right, even when another course might have produced better

144

results for the city. His best-known speeches, which had a strong influence on the technique of his successors, especially Cicero, were the *Philippics* 1–4 (351–341 BC) against the incursions of Philip of Macedon; the *Olynthiacs* 1–3 (349 BC), urging support for the city of Olynthus against Philip; and *On the Crown* (330 BC), in which Demosthenes defended his own record in the public affairs of Athens.

The legacy of Greece: (2) philosophy

Epicureanism and Stoicism have already been mentioned (p. 119 above), but something more must be said about them here because of their influence on Roman thinking. The Romans saw the Epicureans largely in terms of their supposed belief in pleasure as the only aim in life, without taking into account the self-denying conduct of Epicurus and his followers in the fourth and third centuries BC, who had believed that pleasure lies as much in limiting desire as in satisfying it; so that serious Romans tended to agree with the Stoics in despising Epicureanism. Stoicism, with its aim of living in willing acquiescence with whatever fate provided, was in any case more in tune with the qualities admired by sober Romans of *pietas* (dutiful respect for gods, fatherland, and family) and *gravitas* (dignity and moderation).

The Stoics of the second and first centuries BC who had most influence on Roman thought were the Greek philosophers Panaetius and Posidonius, both of them based in Rhodes. Panaetius (c.185–109 BC) was especially influential in emphasising the positive virtue of doing what is right rather than the negative one of not doing what is wrong, and the importance of having high moral standards in private as well as in public life. He wrote a tract *On Duty* (now lost), on which Cicero was to base the first two books of his *De Officiis* (p. 149 below). Posidonius (c.135–c.50 BC), a philosophical pupil of Panaetius but better remembered as a scientist and historian (though his works, too, are lost), both carried on Panaetius's ethical teaching, and believed the all-embracing, all-accepting dominion of Rome to be the ultimate embodiment of Stoicism. But their enthusiasm for Stoicism did not prevent educated Romans of the second century BC and later from being familiar with the earlier classics of Greek philosophy, especially the works of Plato and Aristotle, which were widely read.

Cicero

Of all the writers discussed in this book – of all the eminent people of the ancient world, indeed – we know most about Marcus Tullius Cicero (106–43 BC); which is as much to the disadvantage as to the advantage of his reputation. He was both a major politician in a time of civil strife, and a notable writer whose works survive in quantity. He was outstandingly able – as a pleader in court, as a political orator, as a populariser of Greek philosophy, as a letter writer – but his political achievements, remarkable though they were, were limited by vanity and egotism, and in the end by a lack of common sense that led to his murder by his political enemies. From his own time right up to the late nineteenth century he was one of the most admired and influential of classical writers, but since then his influence has decreased, along with his former reputation as one of the greatest writers and thinkers of antiquity.

Cicero was born in January 106 BC in Arpinum, 100km south-east of Rome, to a family of *equites* ('knights'), which, though old-established and well off, belonged to a class that was despised by aristocratic Roman society; and a feeling of social inferiority troubled Cicero throughout his career. The family moved to Rome when Cicero was ten, where he and his brother Quintus received a first-class education. He served briefly in the army when he was about seventeen, and appears to have kept his head down for most of the next ten years: the violent 80s of the first century BC when the generals Sulla and Marius were slogging it out for supremacy, each side taking bloody revenge on the supporters of the other. In 82 Sulla was victorious, capturing Rome and spending the next three years as dictator, during which time he imposed a new republican constitution on the state and then retired voluntarily into private life. Cicero's career as an orator in the courts controlled by the Senate got under way during Sulla's dictatorship, his first major success being a speech in defence of Roscius of Ameria, *Pro Roscio Amerino*, in 80 BC. From then on he was in constant demand as a legal and political speaker, leading in court (more often for the defence than for the prosecution), speaking frequently in the Senate; and the texts of some thirty-five of his speeches, much admired then and afterwards, have survived. One the most astonishing of his forensic pleadings was his successful defence of Aulus Cluentius Habitus (*Pro Cluentio*, 66 BC), who was charged, probably rightly, with killing his stepfather. This is advocacy at its most ingenious and persuasive, in which defending counsel uses every device – relevant or irrelevant, straightforward or devious – to get his client off. Cicero was to write several treatises on the techniques of oratory, the most finished of them being *De oratore* ('Concerning Oratory', 55 BC) and *Orator* ('The Orator', 46 BC).

Cicero's political career also got off to a smooth start, his sheer ability and his high (if occasionally flexible) principles taking him up through the ranks of the magistracy. Despite his middle-class background, he was successively elected at the youngest legal ages to the public offices of Quaestor, Aedile (69 BC), Praetor (66), and the highest office of all, Consul (63). But this was still a violent time, in which desperate men might plot against the state, private quarrels could end in murder, and the mob, unrestrained by a police force, could be rallied to almost any cause, good or bad. When Cicero was elected Consul, his unsuccessful opponent was a disreputable patrician called Catiline who then actively conspired to raise a revolt on behalf of his own faction against the government. Cicero persuaded the Senate in a series of rousing speeches (*In Catilinam* I–IV, 63 BC) that Catiline should be outlawed. Here he is laying into Catiline at the beginning of *In Catilinam* I, in an unbridled rhetorical style that has been the weapon of demagogues down the ages:

> In the name of heaven, Catilina, how long do you propose to exploit our patience?[1] Do you really suppose that your lunatic activities are going to escape our retaliation for evermore? Are there to be no limits to this audacious, uncontrollable swaggering? Look at the garrison of our Roman nation which guards the Palatine by night, look at the patrols ranging the city, the whole population gripped by terror, the entire body of loyal citizens massing at one single spot! Look at this meeting of our Senate behind strongly fortified defences, see the expressions on the countenances of every one of these men who are here! Have none of these sights made the smallest impact on your heart? You must be well aware that your plot has been detected. Now that every single person in this place knows all about your conspiracy, you cannot fail to realize it is doomed. Do you suppose there is a single individual here who has not got the very fullest information about what you were doing last night and the night before, where you went, the men you summoned, the plans you concocted? What a scandalous commentary on our age and its standards!
>
> (Cicero, *Selected Political Speeches*, trs. by Michael Grant, 1969, Penguin Classics p. 76)

[1] The Latin original of this passage, beginning *Quousque tandem abutere, Catalina, patientia nostra?*, was used by Baskerville and other British typefounders of the eighteenth century as a favourite text for their type specimens.

148   *Landmarks in classical literature*

Catiline was killed soon afterwards in battle; and later Cicero was chiefly responsible for having five prominent conspirators executed without trial. In the short run Cicero was praised for his firmness in the emergency, but in the longer term these executions laid him open to attack by political enemies who claimed that they had been carried out illegally.

Now Cicero's career and prestige began to decline, although he lived for twenty years more. He could have joined the 'First Triumvirate' (see p. 130 above), but did not do so because he saw the combination of Pompey, Crassus, and Caesar as a threat to the Republic. But the Republic, lacking the organisation to administer its growing empire and control its ambitious soldiers, was doomed whatever Cicero did. He was exiled, and then recalled to Rome (58–57 BC); he served a term as an effective Governor of the province of Cilicia in southern Asia Minor (51–50); but he backed the losing side when Pompey and Caesar fell out, and Pompey was decisively defeated at Pharsalia in 48 BC.

When Caesar returned to Italy in 47 he acted generously towards Cicero, but Cicero could see that Caesar as dictator would never restore the Republic. Although Cicero did not take part in the assassination of Caesar in 44 BC, he approved of it, hoping that the Republic could now be restored; and he continued to support the conspirators, attacking Caesar's henchman Mark Antony in fourteen 'Philippics'[2] (*In Marcum Antonium* 1–14, 44–43 BC). This was too much for Antony who, as *triumvir*, placed Cicero's name high on the list of proscriptions[3] of the republicans with whom he had scores to settle. Cicero made an ineffective attempt to escape from Italy in December 43 BC, but was caught and killed, his head and hands being cut off and sent to Rome. He was sixty-three.

So far we have considered Cicero as a writer of powerful forensic and political speeches, but there were two other groups of his writings of at least equal importance: his letters and his philosophical tracts. Well-to-do Romans travelled a good deal – to Rome and back from their country houses, and often abroad, especially to

[2] So called with reference to the *Philippics* of Demosthenes, which had attacked Philip of Macedon. It was an ironical coincidence that Brutus and Cassius were to be defeated at Philippi in Macedonia in 42 BC.
[3] A 'proscription' was a legal declaration, at the instance of a dictator or *triumvir*, that a Roman citizen was an outlaw, that he was to be hunted down and killed, and that his property was to be confiscated by the state. For good measure, Cicero's brother Quintus was also proscribed and killed in 43 BC.

Greece – and they kept in touch with their friends and family by writing letters. Cicero was a keen correspondent, writing many hundreds of personal letters to his old friend Atticus, to his wife and children, to his brother Quintus, to Marcus Brutus, and to other friends; besides more formal letters concerning political and other business. Whether Cicero's correspondence was typical of the period we cannot tell, for it is his letters alone that were preserved and eventually published. We still have over 800 of them – but very few of the replies – in two large groups and two smaller ones: *Epistulae ad Atticum* (letters to Atticus, covering the years 68–44 BC), and *ad familiares* (to his friends and family, 62–43 BC), in sixteen books each; *ad Quintum fratrem* (to his brother Quintus, 60–54 BC, three books); and *ad Brutum* (to Marcus Brutus, of which two books survive, 44–43 BC). Cicero cultivated letter-writing as an art, matching his style and degree of intimacy to particular correspondents, and giving the readers of his collected letters, both early and late, a unique revelation of the mind and personality of one of the leading figures of antiquity. It has even been felt by some readers that Cicero tells us too much about himself in his letters, that he would seem a greater man if we did not have them; but personal revelations work both ways, telling us both about the subject's failings and about the good qualities that are deployed to overcome them. Certainly Cicero had his faults of vanity and egotism, and he often made them plain, but he also had great abilities, and a fundamental honesty that went far towards making up for his shortcomings.

Cicero did not claim to be an original philosopher, but he did a great service in his later years for ordinary readers, both of his own time and afterwards, by expounding the work of the Greek philosophers whom he admired. 'Tully's Offices' (*De officiis*, 44 BC, based on the philosophy of Panaetius) remained the central text of Stoicism until the eighteenth century, and continued as part of the school curriculum for even longer. *De Republica* ('The Republic', 54–51 BC) and *De legibus* ('The Laws', 52+ BC) were dialogues modelled to some extent on Plato's *Republic*. Other philosophical tracts of 45–43 BC included *De finibus bonorum et malorum* ('On the Greatest Degrees of Good and Evil'); translations of Plato's *Timaeus* and *Protagoras*; *Tusculanae disputationes* ('Tusculan Disputations', on the conditions of happiness); *De divinatione* ('On Divination'), *Laelius de amicitia* ('Laelius on Friendship'), and *De natura deorum* ('On the Nature of the Gods'). But perhaps the most attractive of all Cicero's philosophical writings is the *Cato maior de senectute* ('Cato the Elder on Old Age', 44 BC); writing in his early sixties, Cicero takes as his starting point a brief dialogue between Socrates and old Cephalus at the beginning of Plato's *Republic* (329a–c), and goes on – encouragingly – to consider the many advantages and the relatively few and unimportant disadvantages of growing old. Here are some extracts:

> I have known many old men who had no complaints about their age or its liberating release from physical pleasures, and who were by no means treated with contempt by their associates. When you hear protests of this kind, the trouble is due to character, not age. (216)[4] [...] [The old man] may not be doing what the younger men are doing, but his contribution is much more significant and valuable than theirs. Great deeds are not done by strength or speed or physique: they are the products of thought, and character, and judgement. And far from diminishing, such qualities actually increase with age. (220) [...] Provided the old retain their concentration and application, they stay sound of mind. (221) [...] So old age, you see, far from being sluggish and feeble, is really very lively, and perpetually active, and still busy with the pursuits of earlier years. Some people never stop learning, however old they are. (223) [...] For the man whose whole life consists of study and activity of this kind does not notice old age creeping up on him. Instead, he grows old by slow stages, imperceptibly; there is no sudden break-up, only a gradual process of extinction. (228)

Seneca

We have already met Seneca the Younger (Lucius Annaeus Seneca, c.4 BC to 65 AD) as the author of rhetorical closet tragedies (pp. 140–1 above), but he was even better known in antiquity and early modern times for his philosophical writings. Yet Seneca was no more a professional – or an original – philosopher than Cicero had been. Born in Spain to a wealthy family of Italian descent, he was brought to Rome as a child and was educated there, then entered the public service as Quaestor and Senator. He was banished in 41 AD for alleged adultery with Julia Livilla (a member of the imperial family), but Julia's sister Agrippina had him recalled eight years later so that he could become tutor to her twelve-year-old son, the future Emperor Nero. Seneca stayed on as political adviser to Nero following his accession in 54, at first with considerable political and material success, but Nero's extravagant and unstable behaviour made Seneca's position increasingly difficult; and he was eventually forced to commit suicide in 65 because of his supposed involvement in a revolutionary plot.

---

[4] These references are to the pages of the Penguin Classics *Cicero: Selected Works*, trs. and ed. by Michael Grant, 1960.

The younger Seneca's public life is hard to reconcile with the sober philosophical principles that he espoused, for the boy he tutored and the man he advised did terrible things (such as having his wife and his mother killed so that he could marry his mistress); and Seneca also amassed an enormous private fortune. However, the ethical and practical advice derived from the Stoics and compiled in his numerous philosophical treatises is generally admirable, and its value was recognised by the early Fathers of the Christian Church as well as by later writers and thinkers from Petrarch onwards. His most influential works are the ten ethical treatises written in the 50s and known as the *Dialogi* (though they are not true dialogues); the 124 *Epistulae morales*, which are short moral essays, not real correspondence; and *Naturales quaestiones* 1–8, essays on natural phenomena considered philosophically rather than scientifically. All of them are sharply written with engaging metaphors, and contain many quotable apophthegms; for instance:

> Even while they teach, men learn. (*Ep. mor.* 7.8)
> If one does not know to which port one is sailing, no wind is favourable. (*Ep. mor.* 71.3)

> Learning how to live takes a whole life, and, which may surprise you more, it takes a whole life to learn how to die. (*Dial. De brev. vit.* 7)

> Can anything be more idiotic than certain people who boast of their foresight?[5] They keep themselves officiously preoccupied in order to improve their lives; they spend their lives in organising their lives. (*Dial. De brev. vit.* 9)[6]

Yet, however well said, much of Seneca's philosophical teaching lacks depth, and is sometimes obvious to the point of banality. Nevertheless its influence from the twelfth to the eighteenth century was considerable, and Seneca was quoted with approval by writers as disparate as Erasmus, Montaigne, Hume, and Rousseau.

Translations

Plato's *Gorgias* is well translated and introduced by Robin Waterfield (1998) in Oxford World's Classics; and Aristotle's *The Art of*

---

[5] 'How do you make God laugh?' – 'Tell him your future plans' (Woody Allen).
[6] The translations of the two quotations from Seneca's *Dialogi* are by C.D.N. Costa in *Seneca: Dialogues and Letters*, Penguin Classics 1997, pp. 66, 68.

Rhetoric, translated by Hugh Lawson-Tancred (1991), is in Penguin Classics. Speeches by Demosthenes are included in *Greek Political Oratory*, trs. by A.N.W. Saunders (1970), Penguin Classics; but the philosophical works of Panaetius and Posidonius are lost, and what we know of them comes to us through the writings of others, chiefly Cicero and Seneca.

Cicero

There are something like sixty-four works by Cicero (depending on how you count them) which survive in whole or in part, and a few more that are lost; a list of the English titles of the surviving ones is given in chronological order in the Penguin Classics *Selected Works* of Cicero, trs. and ed. by Michael Grant (1960), pp. 251–2. The collections of translations of Cicero's works that are available in Penguin Classics and Oxford World's Classics are:

> *Cicero: Murder Trials*, trs. and ed. by Michael Grant (1975, Penguin Classics) (*Pro Roscio Amerino, Pro Cluentio, Pro Rabinio, Pro Rege Deiotaro*)
>
> *Cicero: The Nature of the Gods*, trs. by H.C.P. McGregor, ed. by J.M. Ross (1972, Penguin Classics); trs. and ed. by P.G. Walsh (1998, Oxford World's Classics) (*De natura deorum*)
>
> *Cicero: On Government*, trs. and ed. by Michael Grant (1993, Penguin Classics) (*In Verrem* 2.5, *Pro Murena, Pro Balbo, De Republica* 3, 5, 6, *De legibus* 3, *Brutus, Philippics* 4, 5, 10.)
>
> *Cicero: On the Good Life*, trs. and ed. by Michael Grant (1971, Penguin Classics) (*Tusculanae disputationes* V, *De officiis* 2, *Laelius de amicitia, De oratore* I, *Somnium Scipionis*)
>
> *Cicero: The Republic and the Laws*, trs. by Niall Rudd, ed. by Jonathan Powell and Niall Rudd (1998, Oxford World's Classics) (*De Republica, De legibus*)
>
> *Cicero: Selected Letters*, trs. and ed. by D.R. Shackleton Bailey (1986, Penguin Classics) (137 *Epistulae ad Atticum, ad Familiares, ad Quintum fratrem, ad Brutum*, etc.)
>
> *Cicero: Selected Political Speeches*, trs. and ed. by Michael Grant (1969, Penguin Classics) (*Pro lege Manilia, In Catalinam* 1-4, *Pro Archia, Pro Caelio, Pro Milone, Pro Marcello, Philippics* 1)
>
> *Cicero: Selected Works*, trs. and ed. by Michael Grant (1960, Penguin Classics) (*In Verrem* I, 23 *Epistulae, Philippics* 2, *De officis* 3, *Cato maior de Senectute*). This is a particularly useful collection for new readers of Cicero, containing as it does two of his most powerful speeches (one forensic and one political), a brief selection from the letters, the introduction to Stoicism, and 'On old Age'.

Seneca

Selections from Seneca's philosophical writings are well translated and edited by C.D.N. Costa (1997) in the Penguin Classics *Seneca: Dialogues and Letters.*

15 Virgil: from pastoral to epic

Theocritus and pastoral poetry

Before considering Virgil and his works, we must look at the poems of Theocritus, the Hellenistic Greek poet who was Virgil's first model. Theocritus, who flourished in the first half of the third century BC, invented a form of poetry that took as its subject the life of herdsmen: the 'bucolic' or 'pastoral'.[1] Born in Sicily, he lived later in the island of Cos, and then in Alexandria; and he and his contemporary Callimachus (see pp. 117–18 above) were the outstanding poets of the Hellenistic period. His twenty-two surviving poems have been known since Roman times as 'Idylls'.[2] They were in various forms, including court poems, a mime, and narratives such as two poems on mythical themes that parallel the *Argonautica* of Apollonius of Rhodes (the lovely *Idyll* 13, 'Hylas'; and 22, 'The Dioscuri').[3] But it was the half-dozen pastoral poems that were to have the greatest influence on later poets, ancient and modern. These were primarily *Idylls* 1, 'The Passion of Daphnis'; 3, 'The Love-songs'; 4, 'The Herdsmen'; 5, 'Goatherd and Shepherd'; 6, 'Damoetas and Daphnis'; and 11, 'The Cyclops'.

> I am going to serenade Amaryllis. My goats
> Graze on the hill. Tityrus is there to guard them.
> Tityrus, do me a favour, look after the goats,
> Drive them to water, Tityrus. Watch out for the billy,
> The yellow one from Libya, or he will butt you.

[1] 'Bucolic' and 'pastoral' derive from the Greek and Latin words respectively for 'herdsman'. 'Pastoral' is sometimes used in English to refer specifically to shepherds, but both Theocritus and Virgil write about herdsmen of cows and goats as well as of sheep.

[2] There were formerly supposed to be thirty idylls of Theocritus, but it is now agreed that eight of them are spurious.

[3] We cannot be certain that these poems were written after the appearance of the *Argonautica*, but this is more likely than that they preceded Apollonius's epic.

I am here, Amaryllis. What has become of your love?
Where is the glance that would call me into your cave?

Tell me what fault you found when you saw me close.
Must I hang for a hairy chin or turned-up nose? [...]

My head aches, my legs give way. As if you cared!
No more songs. I shall lie here, food for the wolves.
May you relish that sweetly as honey in your mouth.
    (*Idylls* 3.1–9, 52–4, trs. by Robert Wells, 1988, Penguin
    Classics p. 66)

In these artfully constructed works Theocritus evokes a stylised
landscape (later located by Virgil both in Italy and in Greek Arca-
dia), in which his herdsmen, aware of the pervasive presence of their
god Pan and of the nymphs of rivers, trees, and mountains, pipe and
sing of the calamity of passionate love, and tell stories to each other:
charming, idealised scenes that were deliberately remote from the
realities of pastoral life. The *Idylls* were imitated by other poets,
most notably by Virgil, as we shall see in a moment; but the essentials
of Theocritean pastoral survived in early Greek novels (see pp. 184–5
below), in much later poems, such as Milton's *Lycidas* (1637), and in
Neoclassical paintings of the seventeenth and eighteenth centuries.

Virgil

Publius Vergilius Maro (70–19 BC) was born near Mantua (Manto-
va), in the middle of the Po valley, about half way between Milan
and Venice. Mantua was in the province of Cisalpine Gaul, so that
Virgil had a partly Celtic background, and did not become a Roman
citizen until the province was incorporated as part of Italy in 42 BC.
Little is known about his family but that they were probably prosperous farmers,[4] well-enough off to send the boy to be educated
successively in Cremona, Milan, and Rome. Following the defeat of
Brutus and Cassius at Philippi in 42 BC, Antony and Octavian confiscated land in the Mantua area for the resettlement of their
veterans, and it is likely that Virgil's family suffered some loss as a
result. It was also around 42 BC that Virgil began to compose his first
cycle of poems, the *Eclogues*, which was completed in 39–38. Its
outstanding quality was recognised by the statesman Gaius Asinius

---

[4] Suetonius, in the best surviving life of Virgil (*Suetonius* II, trs. by J.C. Rolfe, Loeb
1979), says that his parents were 'of humble origin', and that Virgil himself was tall
and portly, 'with a dark complexion and a rustic appearance' (pp. 465, 467).

Pollio (76 BC to 4 AD, Consul in 40 BC and founder of the first public library in Rome), who came to Virgil's assistance over the land confiscations, and saw to it that he was recompensed with property near Naples. Here the poet was to spend most of the rest of his life, from about 37 BC under the patronage of another rich man, Octavian's trusted counsellor Gaius Maecenas, who, together with Octavian himself, made Virgil independently wealthy.

For the next seven years Virgil was engaged in the composition of the four books of his rural poem, the *Georgics*, which was published in 29 BC. This was two years after the final defeat of Antony by Virgil's other patron Octavian at the battle of Actium; and by now Octavian, although he formally restored the Republic in 27 BC, was in fact the sole ruler of the Roman Empire, and was soon to be called Augustus. With the *Georgics* completed, Virgil was encouraged by Augustus to get straight on with writing a Latin epic in the style of Homer, the *Aeneid*, and this occupied the last ten years of his life.

Now Virgil became an active supporter of the Augustan project of rebuilding the moral as well as the physical fabric of Rome, both public and private; and of replacing political freedom, and the anarchy which had resulted from it, with benevolent autocracy. (Horace, the subject of the next chapter, became another supporter of this grand design; Ovid, Chapter 17, did not.)

Although it was largely complete, the *Aeneid* had not been finally revised when Virgil fell ill on a visit to Greece. He died on the way home at Brindisi in 19 BC, when he was not quite fifty-one.[5]

The *Eclogues*

The *Idylls* of Theocritus had been a heterogeneous collection of poems, but Virgil's *Eclogues*,[6] which set out to imitate some aspects of Theocritus's pastorals, was a coherent cycle of ten short poems which embraced more than simple, pastoral themes. The order in which the poems have come down to us – which is probably not the

---

[5] '[Virgil] had arranged with his friend Varius, before leaving Italy, that if anything befell him his friend should burn the "Aeneid"' (Suetonius, *Life* of Virgil 39). Similarly Kafka, who had not revised his unpublished writings (including *The Trial* and *The Castle*), left a note for his friend Max Brod saying that in the event of his death they should be burned unread. We are fortunate that both Varius and Brod disobeyed their friends' instructions.

[6] The *Ecologues*, as they are now known, would be more appropriately called *Bucolica* (from the Greek word for 'pastoral'); the term 'eclogue' originally described any short poem, but it became a synonym for 'pastoral' in the Middle Ages.

order in which they were written – results in a symmetrical pattern of subjects combined with alternations of dialogue and narrative form. The ten poems centre on *Eclogue 5*, which describes the death and deification of Daphnis. *Eclogues* 1 and 9 concern the land confiscations which may have given Virgil the impetus to write the collection; 2 and 8 are laments by frustrated lovers; 3 and 7 are antiphonal[7] exchanges between competing singers; 4 and 6 are 'millennial' poems, the one predicting the coming of a 'messiah', and the other telling of a past Golden Age; and 10, the final poem, winds the collection up in a pastoral Arcady.

The *Eclogues* contain deliberate references to Theocritus – *Eclogue* 4 begins with an invocation to *Sicelidae Musae* ('Sicilian Muses'), and the beginning of *Eclogue* 3 follows the beginning of *Idyll* 4 very closely – but Virgil's pastoral world is not the same as the timeless country of Theocritus. We learn at the start of the first *Eclogue* that the countryside is in turmoil, that Meliboeus is a farmer who is being evicted from his land, and that the herdsman Tityrus was once a slave who went to Rome and gained his freedom; Meliboeus envies Tityrus and deplores his own loss. Meliboeus begins:

> Tityrus, lying back beneath wide beechen cover,
> You meditate the woodland Muse on slender oat;
> We leave the boundaries and sweet ploughlands of home.
> We flee our homeland; you, Tityrus, cool in shade,
> Are teaching woods to echo *Lovely Amaryllis*.
> (trs. by Guy Lee, 1980, Penguin Classics p. 31)

The poem hints at autobiography – Virgil like Meliboeus suffered from the land confiscations, and like Tityrus gained redress in Rome – but it is more a lament for the sufferings endured by all countrymen as a result of civil war. So too with the other poems in the cycle: the pastoral tone is stronger in some than in others, but all of them include some social or political argument.

Virgil's Latin in these marvelous poems (and in the *Georgics* and the *Aeneid*) – its rich vocabulary, its supple metre, its compelling syntax – is extraordinarily beautiful and effective. Here is the Latin of the five lines translated above:

> *Tityre, tu patulae recubans sub tegmine fagi*
> *siluestrem tenui Musam meditaris auena;*

---

[7] In the form of alternating speeches; the technical term is 'amoebean'.

> *nos patriae finis et dulcia linquimus arua.*
> *nos patriam fugimus; tu, Tityre, lentus in umbra*
> *formosam resonare doces Amaryllida siluas.*
>   (*Eclogue* 1.1–5)

The excellences of Virgil's Latin cannot, alas, be reproduced in translation. Fortunately the available English translations include some very good ones, which do retain some echo of Virgil's poetry, and which give us his words as faithfully as can be done in another time and place. (See the section on Translations below.)

The Georgics

Two-and-a-half times as long as the *Eclogues* – 2188 lines to 829 – the four books of the *Georgics* are ostensibly a didactic account of various aspects of Roman farming practice (*Georgica* comes from a Greek word meaning 'husbandry'). Book 1 deals with field crops; Book 2 with trees and vines; Book 3 with domestic animals; and Book 4 with bees. The work does in fact contain useful teaching on these subjects – though much is omitted – but it is not only, or even primarily, a farmer's handbook. Virgil's intention, rather, was to show how the greatness of Italy was based on a rural life of hard work undertaken in harmony with nature, a life not without difficulties but one which would deserve the rewards of divine providence. In this poem – dedicated to his patron Maecenas, but with an eye on Octavian – Virgil's country life is adapted, not from the idealised pastoral of Theocritus, but from the more down-to-earth *Works and Days* of Hesiod with its moral-didactic insistence on the importance and value of work, and its acceptance of divine rule (see pp. 41–2 above).

The farmer can never relax his efforts:

> for everything by nature's law
> Tends to the worse, slips ever backward, backward.[8]
> As with a man who scarce propels his boat
> Against the stream: if once his arms relax,
> The current sweeps it headlong down the rapids.
>
> The farmer's labour is a treadmill:
> All round the year he treads in his own tracks.

---

[8] *Naturam expelles furca, tamen usque recurret* ('You drive Nature out with a fork, but she always comes back', Horace, *Epistles* I. 10. 24).

Nevertheless:

> How lucky, if they know their happiness,
> Are farmers, more than lucky, they for whom,
> Far from the clash of arms, the earth herself,
> Most fair in dealing, freely lavishes
> An easy livelihood.
>> (*Georgics* 1.199–203, 2.401–2, 458–60, trs. by L.P.
>> Wilkinson, 1982, Penguin Classics, pp. 63, 90, 91–2)

Bee-keeping served Virgil's underlying purpose especially well in the fourth book of the *Georgics*, since bees' communities are easy to consider anthropomorphically as models of moral and social behaviour. He tells Maecenas:

> I will show you a spectacle
> To marvel at, a world in miniature,
> Gallant commanders and the institutions
> Of a whole nation, its character, pursuits,
> Communities and warfare.
>> (*Georgics* 4.3–5, trs. by L.P. Wilkinson. 1982, Penguin
>> Classics p. 124)

In fact, although the practice of bee-keeping was well understood in ancient times, using smoke to approach the hives and so on, the biology of bees was not: Virgil believed that the queen bee was a king (the 'gallant commander' of this extract, who led his troops out to war), and that the bees' young were spontaneously generated in leaves and fragrant herbs from which the workers collected them in their mouths. Virgil was able to make good use of the military metaphor: Octavian, who had recently forced Antony to commit suicide after defeating him at Actium, would have approved of the advice given to the bee-keeper following a battle between two swarms:

> But when you have recalled from the field of battle
> Both captains, single out the inferior
> And put him to death, for fear his wasteful presence
> Obstruct the work, and leave the palace free
> For the better one to rule.
>> (*Georgics* 4.88–90, trs. by L.P. Wilkinson, 1982, Penguin
>> Classics p. 127)

The last book concludes with the story of Aristaeus's loss of his bees by disease and their subsequent replacement, as an encouraging parallel to the story of Orpheus's unsuccessful attempt to recover Eurydice from the underworld. In the final eight-line epilogue, the humbly born Virgil sums up his work, his contribution so far to the greatness of Caesar and Rome:

> This song of husbandry of crops and beasts
> And fruit-trees I was singing while great Caesar
> Was thundering beside the deep Euphrates
> In war, victoriously for grateful peoples
> Appointing laws and setting his course for Heaven.
> I, Virgil, at that time lay in the lap
> Of sweet Parthenopé,[9] enjoying there
> The studies of inglorious ease, who once
> Dallied in pastoral verse and with youth's boldness
> Sang of you, Tityrus, lazing under a beech-tree.
>> (*Georgics* 4.559–66, trs. by L.P. Wilkinson, 1982, Penguin Classics p. 143)

The *Aeneid*

The very first words of Virgil's Roman epic both define the noble subject of the poem and make respectful reference to its great predecessors:

> *Arma virumque cano, Troiae qui primus ab oris*
> *Italiam fato profugus Lauiniaque uenit*
> *litora.*

> Arms I sing and the man who first from the coasts of Troy, exiled
> by fate, came to Italy and Lavinian shores.
>> (*Aeneid* 1.1–3, trs. by H. Rushton Fairclough, 1916, Loeb p. 241)

The man, of course, is Aeneas, the Trojan hero who was the ancestor of the founders of Rome; while 'arms' and 'the man' bring to mind the two Homeric epics to which Virgil is indebted for his form and inspiration, the *Iliad* with its armed warfare, and the *Odyssey* with its 'allround man'.

The myth of Aeneas had settled into the form in which Virgil knew it by the third century BC. The story, which he used as the framework of his epic, was that Aeneas, the son of Anchises (a prince of the junior branch of the Trojan royal house) and the goddess Aphrodite, made an adventurous voyage to the west after the fall of Troy. Finally reaching Italy, he founded Lavinium, a settlement on the coast 25k south of Rome.[10] Romulus, the founder of Rome, was

---

[9] Naples.
[10] Archaeological evidence shows that Lavinium (now Prática di Mare) was an early Latin settlement that had direct links with the Greek world.

his direct descendant, as were the early kings of Rome; and he thus formed the link that the Romans sought between themselves and the Greek world of the heroic age. Since the Julian *gens*, to which both Julius Caesar and Octavian belonged, claimed descent from Aeneas[11] (and therefore from Aphrodite/Venus as well), this myth was the perfect vehicle for Virgil's greatest work, celebrating the greatness of Rome in general and of Octavian in particular.

The *Aeneid* is in twelve books of hexameters totalling 9,896 lines (compared with the 15,000 of the *Iliad* and the 12,000 lines of the *Odyssey*) so that it is just over one-third of the length of both the Homeric epics put together. The overall plan of Virgil's epic was plainly Homeric, with its main elements reversed: now the odyssey of the man comes first and the armed fighting follows it; but the Homeric parallels are many and obvious.

In Book 1 Aeneas and his comrades have just sailed from Sicily for Italy, but their ships are wrecked in a storm stirred up by Juno, the enemy of Troy. Neptune sees them safe ashore on the north African coast, where they are welcomed in Carthage by the Phoenician queen Dido; and Venus arranges for Dido to fall in love with Aeneas.

In Book 2 Aeneas relates the story – told only briefly by Homer – of the final fall of Troy to the deceitful Greeks with their wooden horse, of the last-ditch stand of the Trojan heroes, and of Aeneas's escape with his father Anchises and his infant son Iulus, but without his wife Creusa, who has died in the mêlée and whose ghost tells him of his destiny.

Book 3 continues the tale of Aeneas's adventures, which are strongly reminiscent of those of Odysseus. The Trojans are told by oracles to sail to the land of their fathers. At first they believe this to be Crete, but then learn that it is Italy, and further troubles befall them on the way: they are attacked by the foul Harpies, they have an unexpected meeting in Illyria with Priam's son Helenus and Andromache (formerly Hector's wife), they rescue a member of Odysseus's crew who has been accidentally marooned with the Cyclopes, and old Anchises dies. But in the end they reach Libya and the unfortunate Dido.

Book 4 rises to an emotional climax. Dido knows she should not betray the memory of her dead husband, but her sister encourages

---

[11] The etymology was supposed to be: from Ilium (Troy) comes Iulus (the son of Aeneas, also known as Ascanius), from which is derived Iulius, the name of the Julian *gens*.

her in her passionate love for Aeneas, while Juno and Venus arrange for it to be consummated in a cave during a thunderstorm. For a while the two lovers are happy together, but then Jupiter sends Mercury to remind Aeneas of his duty, and he prepares to leave for Italy. Dido is devastated: she raves, she pleads, she is furious; Aeneas is sorry, he is shifty, he is adamant. He sails away, and Dido, cursing him, commits suicide.

Book 5 sees the Trojans' departure from Carthage, Dido's funeral pyre blazing in the background. A storm carries them back to Sicily, where they hold Games: an exciting boat race, a foot race (with some cheating), an archery contest, boxing, and a display of horsemanship by the young Trojans led by Aeneas's son Ascanius. The Trojan women, tired of travelling, try to burn the ships of the expedition, but a miraculous storm prevents their destruction, and Aeneas sets off again for Italy with a reduced company; on the way Palinurus the helmsman falls asleep and is drowned.

In Book 6 Aeneas reaches Cumae (a Greek settlement on the Italian coast a little way north of Naples), where a prophetess tells him of the difficulties he will experience in Latium, and enables him to seek information and advice by entering the underworld. Aeneas crosses the Styx with Charon, avoids Tartarus (Hell) and enters Elysium where the souls of the virtuous live in Paradise. Here he meets the spirit of his father Anchises, who shows him the souls of the Roman heroes to come – the descendants of Aeneas, including Romulus, Julius Caesar, and Augustus – who are waiting to be reborn. At the end of Book 6, the centre-point of the work, Anchises exhorts one of them (it must be the soul of the future Augustus):

> 'Others, I do not doubt it, will beat bronze into figures that breathe more softly. Others will draw living likenesses out of marble. Others will plead cases better or describe with their rod the courses of the stars across the sky and predict their risings. Your task, Roman, and do not forget it, will be to govern the peoples of the world in your empire. These will be your arts – and to impose a settled pattern upon peace, to pardon the defeated and war down the proud.' (6.847–53, trs. by David West, 1990, Penguin Classics p. 159)

Now Aeneas's odyssey is ended and the fighting is about to start.

Book 7 begins the second half of the poem with the arrival of Aeneas and his company at the mouth of the Tiber. We learn that King Latinus of Latium has a beautiful only daughter, Lavinia, who is being wooed by Turnus, the king of the Rutulians. Latinus is told by the prophetic shade of his father that she must be married, not to

Turnus, but to a stranger, whom he understands to be Aeneas. Juno, still opposed to the Trojans, stirs up opposition to this plan, first in the heart of Latinus's queen, and then among the tribes of Latium led by Turnus. The scene is set for another war fought for possession of a princess, this time Lavinia instead of Helen.

In Book 8, advised by the river-god of the Tiber, Aeneas makes an alliance with the Arcadian king Evander, who rules from a settlement on the Palatine Hill in what is to be the city of Rome; and he is encouraged by a good omen (a sow with her litter) which he had been told to expect. Venus asks Vulcan to make Aeneas a set of armour; it includes a shield embossed with representations of the future glories of Rome down to Augustus's victory over Antony at Actium (this recalls the armour and shield made by Hephaestus for Achilles, *Iliad* 18).

In Book 9 the war begins in earnest, the advantage going now to the forces of Turnus, now to the Trojans. Turnus tries to destroy the Trojans' ships, but Neptune turns them into sea-nymphs. Ascanius kills in battle for the first time. Turnus is cut off but escapes by jumping into the river Tiber.

Book 10 continues the story of the fighting. The Olympian gods discuss the conflict, some led by Jupiter supporting Aeneas, others led by Juno opposing him. Aeneas enlists another ally, Tarchon king of the Etruscans, and they return to the attack supported by Pallas son of Evander; Pallas is killed. Aeneas wins the day, killing Turnus's ally Mezentius and his son Lausus.

In Book 11 a truce is arranged, and it is proposed that Turnus shall meet Aeneas in single combat, but the Latins hear that the Trojans and Etruscans are advancing to attack them. The Volscian cavalry, led by Turnus's ally Camilla, is thrown into the battle, but is defeated by Tarchon.

Book 12 brings the war to an end with the victory of the Trojans. Preparations are made for the duel between Turnus and Aeneas, but again it is postponed by a battle between the two armies. Aeneas, wounded by an arrow, is healed by Venus. The Latins' stronghold is stormed and captured; the Latin queen who has opposed Aeneas commits suicide; and the duel between Aeneas and the maddened Turnus finally takes place. The disagreements between Jupiter and Juno are resolved; and the poem ends (rather abruptly) with the death of Turnus at the hands of Aeneas. The reader knows that the descendants of Aeneas and Lavinia will found Rome and lead it to the heights of empire.

For us, Books 1–6 of the *Aeneid*, describing the odyssey of Aeneas from Troy to Latium and his affair with Dido, are likely to be more engrossing than the second half of the poem with its many battles and intrigues (rather in the way that the romantic *Odyssey* may appeal to us more than the martial *Iliad*); but Virgil, like Homer, is a master storyteller, the narrative never flags, and his didactic and celebratory purposes are splendidly achieved. Although it is a Homeric epic, the *Aeneid* is permeated with the glories of Roman history, Roman religious understanding, and the ethical values of the Roman people. It is, finally, a celebration of the Roman language, Latin poetry in the perfection of its riches of vocabulary, imagery, and usage.

Virgil's reputation and influence

Virgil was recognised even in his own lifetime as a great writer, and when the *Aeneid* was published posthumously his work was accepted in the Roman world as being canonical. He was, indeed, venerated: his tomb was treated as a shrine, and his books were used for soothsaying.[12] His works were widely used as school texts in both ancient and modern times; and the early Christians were eager to claim him as a fellow-Christian born before his time. For Dante he was the greatest of all poets, the one chosen to guide the narrator of the *Divine Comedy* through the *Inferno* and up to the gates of Purgatory. Virgil has been recognised ever since as one of the great nodes of western literature, like Dante and Shakespeare, his work drawing in the literature of the past, then spreading out again to influence the literature that was to come.

Translations

Theocritus

The complete *Idylls* and selected *Epigrams* of Theocritus are admirably translated and annotated by Robert Wells (1988) in Penguin Classics.

Virgil

The whole of Virgil is published in Oxford World's Classics in the translations of Cecil Day Lewis: the *Eclogues* (1963) and the

---

[12] In the *sortes virgilianae*, lines chosen at random from his books were believed to foretell the future.

Georgics (1940), in one volume with notes by R.O.A.M. Lyne (1983); and the *Aeneid* (1952) in another volume with notes by Jasper Griffin (1986). These are spirited translations in loose un-rhymed hexameters, but I personally find them too loose, and prefer some of the Penguin Classics versions.

The *Eclogues* and the *Georgics* are available in splendid Penguin Classics translations by Guy Lee (1980) and L.P. Wilkinson (1982) respectively; Lee keeps very close to the Latin in unrhymed hexam-eters, while Wilkinson translates the *Georgics*, again with admir-able fidelity, into attractive five-stress blank verse. Both volumes have excellent notes and apparatus, Lee's *Eclogues* including the Latin text in parallel.

Penguin Classics offers three translations of the *Aeneid*. There is, first, the magnificent, freely translated version in heroic couplets by John Dryden (1697), which is itself a major work of art; and it is, perhaps, a more successful approach to a great classical poem than is Pope's version of the *Iliad*, in that the Neoclassicism of the seventeenth and eighteenth centuries looked back to the literature of Augustan Rome, not to that of Archaic Greece; it is well edited by Frederick M. Keener. There are then two prose translations, by W.F. Jackson Knight (1956), and by David West (1990); West's version is the plainer and more accurate of the two, and is recommended for first-time readers of the poem. All the Penguin versions have some editorial matter, but the only one to have adequate notes is the Day Lewis translation in Oxford World's Classics.

To help readers choose between three of these translations, here is a moving passage from Book 4 of the *Aeneid* (4.314–24) in which Dido pleads with Aeneas not to leave her, in the original Latin and in the versions by Dryden, Day Lewis, and West:

> *mene fugis? per ego has lacrimas dextramque tuam te*
> *(quando aliud mihi iam miserae nihil ipsa reliqui),*
> *per conubia nostra, per inceptos hymenaeos,*
> *si bene quid de te merui, fuit aut tibi quicquam*
> *dulce meum, miserere domus labentis et istam,*
> *oro, si quis adhuc precibus locus, exue mentem.*
> *te propter Libycae gentes Nomadumque tyranni*
> *odere, infensi Tyrii; te propter eundem*
> *exstinctus pudor et, qua sola sidera adibam,*
> *fama prior. cui me moribundam deseris, hospes,*
> *hoc solum nomen quoniam de coniuge restat?*
> (*Aeneid* 4.314–24)

See, whom you fly; am I the Foe you shun;
Now by those holy Vows, so late begun,
By this right Hand, (since I have nothing more
To challenge, but the Faith you gave before;)
I beg you by these Tears too truly shed,
By the new Pleasures of our Nuptial Bed;
If ever *Dido*, when you most were kind,
Were pleasing in your Eyes, or touch'd your Mind;
By these my Pray'rs, if Pray'rs may yet have Place,
Pity the Fortunes of a falling Race.
For you I have provok'd a Tyrant's Hate,
Incens'd the *Lybian*, and the *Tyrian* State;
For you alone I suffer in my Fame;
Bereft of Honour, and expos'd to Shame:
Whom have I now to trust, (ungrateful Guest,)
That only Name remains of all the rest!

> (*Virgil's Aeneid*, trs. by John Dryden, 1697, Penguin Classics
> pp. 100–1)

Am I your reason for going? By these tears, by the hand you gave
    me –
They are all I have left, today, in my misery – I implore you,
And by our union of hearts, by our marriage hardly begun,
If I have ever helped you at all, if anything
About me pleased you, be sad for our broken home, forgo
Your purpose, I beg you, unless it's too late for prayers of mine!
Because of you the Libyan tribes and the Nomad chieftains
Hate me, the Tyrians are hostile: because of you I have lost
My old reputation for faithfulness – the only thing that could have
    made me
Immortal. Oh, I am dying! To what, my guest, are you leaving me?
'Guest' – that is all I may call you now, who have called you husband.

> (*Virgil: The Aeneid*, trs. by C. Day Lewis, 1952, Peters, Fraser &
> Dunlop pp. 102–3)

Is it me you are running away from? I beg you, by these tears, by the pledge
you gave me with your own right hand – I have nothing else left me now in
my misery – I beg you by our union, by the marriage we have begun – if I
have deserved any kindness from you, if you have ever loved anything about
me, pity my house that is falling around me, and I implore you if it is not too
late for prayers, give up this plan of yours. I am hated because of you by the
peoples of Libya and the Numidian kings. My own Tyrians are against me.
Because of you I have lost all conscience and self- respect and have thrown
away the good name I once had, my only hope of reaching the stars. My
guest is leaving me to my fate and I shall die. 'Guest' is the only name I can
now give the man who used to be my husband.

> (*Virgil: The Aeneid*, trs. by David West, 1990, Penguin Classics pp. 90–1)

16 Horace: epigram, lyric, and satire

Catullus

Before we get to Horace, the main subject of this chapter, we should look at the work of Gaius Valerius Catullus (c.84–c.54 BC), a predecessor who developed a new form of Latin lyric poetry based on Hellenistic Greek models. The 116 (or 117) poems of Catullus are known to us by the merest chance of a single manuscript of them having survived into the fourteenth century, when two further copies were made of it. All three of these manuscripts have since disappeared, but we do have copies that were made of the two fourteenth-century copies. Not surprisingly the text was by this stage marred by perhaps a thousand copying errors, accumulated over many centuries, but textual scholars have largely repaired them and we appear to have the collection in more or less the form and order in which Catullus left it.

Of Catullus himself we know little but what he tells us in the poems. Like Virgil, he came from Cisalpine Gaul, the son of a wealthy magistrate, and spent most of his life in Rome as a man-about-town. He claimed in his verse to be having a passionate love affair with a married woman who is addressed as 'Lesbia' in twenty-five of the poems; he lost a brother to whom he was devoted; he had several very close friends; he was acquainted with Julius Caesar; and he spent a year on the staff of the governor of Bithynia in Asia Minor. He was probably only about thirty when he died.

The poems are arranged with some deliberation in three major groups. Poems 1–60 are fairly short, some of them pithy and epigrammatic, many of them in the 'elegiac' metre that was used for – amongst other things – love lyrics; then come four long poems, 61–4, which include a 'mini-epic' (poem 64); and then another large group of mostly short poems, 65–116 (65–8 being longer than the rest), many of them cast in the form of epigrams. Poem 51 to Lesbia imitates the poem by Sappho which is given on p. 58 above; poem 66 is a translation of a poem by Callimachus about the Berenice whose lock of hair became a constellation in heaven. Some of the shorter poems in the first and last groups were defamatory of well-known people, and a considerable number of them were obscene. In all of them Catullus wrote in a witty, scintillating Latin, a language that was both racy and erudite, and he used a number of Greek metres, some of them difficult, which were then new to Latin verse.

The poems that have lasted best are those addressed to 'Lesbia', which progress from the expression of passionate love, through increasing anger at Lesbia's infidelity, to contempt and dismissal. The whole cycle of emotions is covered in poems 2, 3, 5, 7, 8, and 11, and the other Lesbia poems in the first and third groups can be fitted into it. Here is poem 8, describing the pivotal moment at which the poet reluctantly recognises that Lesbia is slipping away from him:

> Wretched Catullus, you should stop fooling
> And what you know you've lost admit losing.
> The sun shone brilliantly for you, time was,
> When you kept following where a girl led you,
> Loved by us as we shall love no one.
> There when those many amusing things happened
> Which you wanted nor did the girl not want
> The sun shone brilliantly for you, truly.
> Now she's stopped wanting, you must stop, weakling.
> Don't chase what runs away nor live wretched
> But with a mind made up be firm, stand fast.
> Goodbye, girl. Catullus now stands fast,
> Won't ask or look for you who're not willing.
> But you'll be sorry when you're not asked for.
> Alas, what life awaits you now, devil?
> Who'll find you pretty now? What type touch you?
> Whom will you love and whose be called henceforth?
> Whom will you kiss? and you will bite whose lips?
> But you, Catullus, mind made up, stand fast.
>   (*Catullus: The Complete Poems*, trs. by Guy Lee, 1990,
>   Oxford World's Classics p. 9)

But did Lesbia even exist? – for poets have always been apt to personify their erotic obsessions. Apuleius said later that she was really called Clodia; and the likeliest candidate of this name is Clodia Metelli, the wife of a former provincial governor, who was attacked by Cicero in 56 BC as an unashamed nymphomaniac in *Pro Caelio*, his hard-hitting and successful speech for the defence of a young man who was accused of stealing from and trying to poison her. But this Clodia had two sisters of the same name who are also possibilities, so that, even if there was a real Lesbia, we cannot be sure that it was she.

Horace

Quintus Horatius Flaccus (65–8 BC), the second of the three giants of Augustan poetry, was five years younger than his friend Virgil, and he was also acquainted with Ovid, who was a generation younger than himself. It is not easy to make sense of what we are told, by Horace himself in his verse and later in a brief *Life* by Suetonius, about his background and career. He was, it appears, the son of a freedman of Venusia in southern Italy – that is a man who had been freed from slavery during his lifetime – but a freedman who had become rich enough from his percentages as an auctioneer's middle-man to take his boy to be educated by the best teachers in Rome and then to send him to study philosophy in Athens. And there in Greece, despite his seemingly humble background and complete lack of military experience, the youth was appointed by Marcus Brutus to be a military tribune in his republican army, a rank second only to the commander of a Roman legion, a commissioned officer who might have to take command in the absence of the legate. One suggestion is that Horace's father had been a prominent man who was enslaved following the Social War in which Venusia rose against Rome in 90–88 BC, and that when he was pardoned and freed he was still sufficiently well off and well connected to give his son a leg up.

Going back to Horace's military appointment at the age of twenty-one, he served with Brutus and Cassius until they were defeated by Octavian and Antony at Philippi in 42 BC where, he says, he ran away. He then returned to Italy, where his family's property had been confiscated, obtained a pardon, and bought – what with? – a 'quaestorship', a government post in the treasury. Now poor, he tells us, he took to writing poetry to support himself.

There really is something very odd about Horace's account of how he got on in the face of what should have been insuperable difficulties. We should remember, however, first that autobiography – and particularly autobiographical poetry – is an unreliable form of history; and secondly that Horace was an ironical parodist, especially where he himself was concerned. We do not have to take his account of his own life at face value.

The story now becomes more straightforward. Horace's poetry brought him into contact with Virgil, who in 38 BC introduced him to his patron Maecenas. Horace's first book of *Satires* was published in 35 BC, and soon after that Maecenas bought him a modest country estate in the Sabine hills near Tivoli, some 25km east of Rome. Here Horace – a short and tubby man – lived very happily for the rest of his life: nurturing his friendships, tending his estate, writing superlative poetry, enjoying food and drink and girls, and staying out of politics. Augustus took to him, and saw him as a sort of poet laureate; he even offered him a job as a private secretary, but Horace politely turned it down. The *Epodes* and *Satires* II came out in 30 BC, *Odes* I–III in 23, *Epistles* I in 19, *Carmen Saeculare* in 17, and finally *Odes* IV and *Epistles* II in 14–13. He died in 8 BC at the age of fifty-seven, a few months after Maecenas, and they were buried in adjacent graves in Maecenas's estate in Rome.

Horace's poetry was various in its metres and subjects; and much of it was so compressed and allusive that it is more than usually difficult to communicate in English. Technically (like most of the Roman poets from Catullus onwards) he adapted Greek metres to Latin verse: hexameters for the *Satires* and *Epistles*, and a variety of elegiac and lyric metres from Sappho, Anacreon, Alcaeus, and Pindar for the *Epodes* and *Odes*. Here is an 'autobiographical' passage from the first book of *Satires*:

> I revert now to myself – only a freedman's son,
> run down by everyone as only a freedman's son,
> now because I'm a friend of yours, Maecenas, before
> because as a military tribune I commanded a Roman legion.
> The two factors are different; a person might have reason
> to grudge me that rank, but he shouldn't grudge me your friendship too,
> especially as you are so careful to choose suitable people,
> and to hold aloof from twisters on the make. I could never say
> I was lucky in the sense that I *just happened* to win your friendship.
> It wasn't chance that brought you into my life. In the first place
> the admirable Virgil and then Varius told you what I was.
> When I first met you in person I just gulped out a few words,
> for diffidence tied my tongue and stopped me from speaking plainly.
> I didn't pretend that I had a distinguished father or possessed
> estates outside Tarentum which I rode around on a horse.
> I told you what I was. As usual you answered briefly. I left.
> Nine months later you asked me back and invited me to join

your group of friends. For me the great thing is that I won
the regard of a discriminating man like you, not by having
a highly distinguished father but by decency of heart and character.
> (*Satires* I.6.45–64, trs. by Niall Rudd, 1973, Penguin Classics p. 68)

Although it is superficially similar, this is not a serious autobiographical poem on the lines of Wordsworth's *The Prelude*. What is apparent even in this earliest of Horace's publications is the sly irony of his self-description, the sense we get that he is unobtrusively making fun of himself and his patron, knowing that Maecenas will get the joke. This ironical tone of self-satire, sometimes slipping into self-parody, is a feature of much of Horace's verse.

Irony of a more obvious sort is found in *Epode* 2. This longish poem in direct speech celebrates the joys of the country life of a small farmer like himself, starting:

> 'Fortunate the man who, free from cares,
>   like men of old still works
> his father's fields with his own oxen,
>   encumbered by no debt.
> No soldier he, aroused by bugle's blare,
>   nor does he fear the angry sea.
> The Forum he avoids, and lofty doors
>   of powerful citizens.
>
> And so, to daughters of the vine when they are come
>   of age, he weds tall poplars;
> in sheltered valley sees his wandering herds
>   of lowing cattle;
> or with his sickle prunes the useless growth
>   and grafts more fruitful shoots;
> or stores pressed honey in clean jars,
> or shears his helpless sheep.

And on in the same strain for sixty-six lines about trees and vines and hunting and family life and good food and wine. Is this an affectionate parody of Virgil's *Georgics*, one wonders – until the last four lines, where the direct speech breaks off and the poem ends:

> When Alfius the money lender said all this,
>   resolved at last, at last, to be a countryman,
> he called in all his money on the Ides –
> and on the Kalends now he tries to place it out again.[1]
> > (*Epodes* 2, 1–16, 67–70, trs. by David West, 1997, Oxford World's
> > Classics pp. 4, 6)

---

[1] The Ides were the thirteenth or fifteenth day of the month, and the Kalends the first day of the following month, a fortnight after the Ides.

And the whole thing turns out to have been the fantasy of a grasping money-lender, who, when it comes to the point, cannot bring himself to invest his loot in a dream-farm, but goes straight back to money-lending.

In the *Odes*, one of the key collections of poems in world literature, Horace comes nearer to revealing the things that are closest to him. *Ode* I.29 is ostensibly a not-so-gentle rebuke to a former friend:

> Iccius, are you eyeing
> Arabian treasures, preparing a dire foray
> against Sabaean kings never before
> conquered and forging fetters
>
> for the gruesome Mede? What exotic
> virgin, her fiancé killed, shall attend you?
> What palace boy with unctuous curls,
> taught to aim Eastern arrows
>
> with his father's bow, shall be your
> cupbearer?[2] Who will deny that descending
> streams may well flow back to the heights
> and Tiber reverse his course
>
> when you, who promised so well, intend to swap
> the illustrious books of Panaetius,[3]
> collected far and wide, plus
> the Socratics, for a Spanish armour?
>> (*Odes* I.29, trs. by W.G. Shepherd, 1983, Penguin Classics
>> pp. 94–5)

Here Horace is comparing, unfavourably, his friend's life of action, ambition, and ostentation with his own ideal of leisure and study. He may also be addressing, with a smile, the stout little poet who lives a self-indulgent life on his Sabine farm and takes his pleasure with slave-girls.

But Horace can as easily drop the irony and self-parody. One famous *Ode* advises 'Thaliarchus' – as with the 'Iccius' of the last poem, Horace uses Greek pseudonyms in place of people's real names – to enjoy wine and dancing and the love of a girl now, while age is still unimaginable to him; the whole poem being set in a winter scene symbolic of the ageing of his sentimental friend the poet. It is given here both in Latin and English, to illustrate the extraordinary,

---

[2] 'Cupbearer' would have been understood to mean a boy lover.
[3] The Stoic philosopher, see p. 145 above.

controlled compression of Horace's verse, even when compared
with the translation of a poet who achieves an unusual degree of
compression in English:

Uides ut alta stet niue candidum
Soracte, nec iam sustineant onus
    siluae laborantes, geluque
        flumina constiterint acuto.

dissolue frigus ligna super foco
large reponens atque benignius
    deprome quadrimum Sabina,
        o Thaliarche, merum diota:

permitte diuis cetera, qui simul
strauere uentos aequore feruido
    deproeliantis, nec cupressi
        nec ueteres agitantur orni.

quid sit futurum cras fuge quaerere et
quem Fors dierum cumque dabit lucro
    appone, nec dulcis amores
        sperne puer neque tu choreas,

donec uirenti canities abest
morosa. nunc et campus et areae
    lenesque sub noctem susurri
        composita repetantur hora,

nunc et latentis proditor intimo
gratus puellae risus ab angulo
    pignusque dereptum lacertis
        aut digito male pertinaci.

Look how the snow lies deeply on glittering
Soracte. White woods groan and protestingly
    Let fall their branch-loads. Bitter frost has
        Paralysed rivers: the ice is solid.

Unfreeze the cold! Pile plenty of logs in the
Fireplace! And you, dear friend Thaliarchus, come,
    Bring out the Sabine wine-jar four years
        Old and be generous. Let the good gods

Take care of all else. Later, as soon as they've
Calmed down this contestation of winds upon
    Churned seas, the old ash-trees can rest in
        Peace and the cypresses stand unshaken.

Try not to guess what lies in the future, but
As Fortune deals days enter them into your
    Life's book as windfalls, credit items,
        Gratefully. Now that you're young, and peevish

Grey hairs are still far distant, attend to the
Dance-floor, the heart's sweet business; for now is the
    Right time for midnight assignations,
        Whispers and murmurs in Rome's piazzas

And fields, and soft, low laughter that gives away
The girl who plays love's games in a hiding-place –
    Off comes a ring coaxed down an arm or
        Pulled from a faintly resisting finger.
            (*Odes* I.9, trs. by James Michie, 1964, HarperCollins
            p. 35)

The last book of *Odes*, Horace's final publication, contains a miraculous poem of man's beginning and ending, combining their joy and melancholy: *Diffugere niues*, translated here by another notable poet (and classical scholar), A.E. Housman:

The snows are fled away, leaves on the shaws
    And grasses in the mead renew their birth,
The river to the river-bed withdraws,
    And altered is the fashion of the earth.

The Nymphs and Graces three put off their fear
    And unapparelled in the woodland play.
The swift hour and the brief prime of the year
    Say to the soul, *Thou was not born for aye.*

Thaw follows frost; hard on the heel of spring
    Treads summer sure to die, for hard on hers
Comes autumn, with his apples scattering;
    Then back to wintertide, when nothing stirs.

But oh, whate'er the sky-led seasons mar,
    Moon upon moon rebuilds it with her beams:
Come *we* where Tullus and where Ancus are,
    And good Aeneas, we are dust and dreams.

Torquatus, if the gods in heaven shall add
    The morrow to the day, what tongue has told?
Feast then thy heart, for what thy heart has had
    The fingers of no heir will ever hold.

When thou descendest once the shades among,
    The stern assize and equal judgment o'er,
Not thy long lineage nor thy golden tongue,
    No, nor thy righteousness, shall friend thee more.

Night holds Hippolytus the pure of stain,
  Diana steads him nothing, he must stay;
And Theseus leaves Pirithoüs in the chain
  The love of comrades cannot take away.
    (*Odes* IV.7, trs. by A.E. Housman, *Poems*, Clarendon Press 1997,
    pp. 118–19)

Reading these poems, what are we to make of Horace? For one thing, they are works of art, not fragments of autobiography. Of course Horace, like all artists, puts parts of himself into his work, but with him especially it is unwise to take the glimpses he gives as a fair picture of the poet. Certainly there was a fat little man called Horace who charmed his friends and enjoyed the good things of life – Maecenas said so, and so did Augustus – but in him there was another Horace: clever, wry, amusing, but also subversive, melancholy, and too clear-sighted for his own comfort. Like Shakespeare, of whose personality we know so little, he has something for everyone, and he is the best of company.

Juvenal

Virtually nothing is known about Decimus Junius Juvenalis and his life but that he came orignally from Aquinum, 105km south-east of Rome; that he lived and worked in Rome early in the second century AD; and that he wrote sixteen *Satires* in Latin hexameters, probably published in five separate 'books'.

Juvenal claimed Lucilius (a satirist of the second century BC, whose work is almost entirely lost) and Horace as his guides, but he does not follow the wry autobiographical bent of Horace's *Satires*, and his bitter invective has little in common with Horace's mellow humour. Juvenal writes biting, rhetorical satire as we now understand the term, his aim being to expose the vices and the everyday perils of the age, the grotesque self-indulgence of the rich and the pathos of the poor. He is explained best in his own words. Here is a passage, for instance, about rich men and their 'parasites':

Weary old clients trudge away from the porches, resigning
what they had yearned for, though nothing stays with a man so long
as the hope of a dinner. Cabbage and kindling have to be purchased.
Meanwhile the magnate will lounge alone among empty couches,
chewing his way through the finest produce of sea and woodland.
(Yes, off all those antique tables, so wide and so stylish,
they gobble up their ancestors' wealth at a single sitting.)
Soon there'll be no parasites left. But who could abide

that blend of luxury and meanness? What size of gullet could order
a whole boar for itself, an animal born for parties?
But a reckoning is nigh. When you strip and, within that bloated body,
carry an undigested peacock into the bath-house,
death steps in, too quick for a will; old age is cancelled.
At once the joyful news goes dancing around the dinners.
The funeral cortège departs to the cheers of indignant friends.
> (*Satires* 1.132–46, trs. by Niall Rudd, 1991, Penguin Classics p. 7)

Another fine example is *Satire* 3, on the evils of the big city, which
was much admired by later writers and was the inspiration of
Samuel Johnson's 'London' (1738). It is nearly all told in the first
person by 'Umbricius', a Roman who can't stand life in the city any
longer, and is leaving for the old Greek settlement of Cumae. Here
he is on expensive prostitutes:

A free-born Roman's son concedes the inner position
to a rich man's slave. The latter pays as much as a tribune
of a legion earns in a year to Calvina or Catiena
to shudder on top of her once or twice; but you, however,
when you fancy Chíone's looks, will have to stop and think twice
before helping the dolled-up harlot down from her chair.

And here on how a man is judged, with a savage epigrammatic
conclusion:

they are interested first in his money (the *last* question concerns
his integrity): how many slaves does he keep, how many acres
of land does he own, how large and how many the plates on his table?
Whatever amount of cash a person has in his strong-box
that's the extent of his credit. If a poor man swears by the altars
of Sámothrace and of Rome, people assume that he's flouting
the gods and their thunderbolts, with the consent of the gods themselves.
That same man, moreover, provides a cause and occasion
for universal amusement if his cloak is ripped and muddy,
if his toga is a little stained, and one of his shoes gapes open
where the leather is split apart, or if several scars are apparent
where coarse new thread proclaims that a wound has been sewn together.
Of all that luckless poverty involves, nothing is harsher
than the fact that it makes people funny.
> (*Satires* 3.131–6, 140–53, trs. by Niall Rudd, 1991, Penguin Classics p. 19)

Translations

Catullus

The complete poems of Catullus are available both in Penguin
Classics translated by the poet Peter Wigham (1966), and in Oxford

World's Classics in a parallel-text translation by Guy Lee (1990). Wigham's poems are striking, but they often depart some way from Catullus's Latin, and the better choice is Lee's accurate but still exciting translation into loose unrhymed verse of various metres, which has the additional advantage of including the Latin text and outstandingly good introduction and notes.

Horace

The whole of Horace's work is available in several good translations, samples of which are given in the poems and extracts quoted above. The *Satires* and *Epistles* (together with the *Satires* of Persius) are well translated and introduced by Niall Rudd (1973) in Penguin Classics. The *Epodes* and *Odes* are translated and annotated by W.G. Shepherd with an introduction by Betty Radice (1983) in Penguin Classics; and by David West with his introduction and notes (1997) in Oxford World's Classics. Both these versions include the *Carmen Saeculare* and Suetonius's *Life* of Horace. I slightly prefer Shepherd's translation and West's notes, but both are very good. There is another excellent Penguin Classics translation of the *Odes* (now out of print) by James Michie (1964), which gives the Latin text on facing pages.

Juvenal

The *Satires* are admirably translated by Niall Rudd (1991) in Oxford World's Classics, with a valuable translator's preface, and introduction and notes by William Barr. The Penguin Classics translation is by Peter Green (revised edition 1998).

17 Ovid: love poetry and the novel

Ovid

Publius Ovidius Naso (43 BC to 17 AD) was born at Sulmo in the hill-country of the Abruzzi, 120km east of Rome, the second son of a prosperous knight. We know – or think we know – a lot about his life, chiefly because of an autobiographical poem that he wrote late in his life;[1] but, as with Horace, we should beware of putting too much faith in the historical accuracy of autobiographical poetry. As Ovid himself said on another occasion:

> The poet's fruitful freedom knows no bounds,
> and takes no oath to tell it as it happened.
> *(Amores* III.12.41–2, trs. by E.J. Kenney, in Ovid,
> *Metamorphoses,* trs. by A.D. Melville, 1986, Oxford
> World's Classics p. xix)

The story is that Ovid and his brother were destined by their father for a senatorial career, which was frustrated in both cases, by the death of the brother and by Ovid's preference for poetry. Ovid was married off at about sixteen to an even younger wife who was probably unfaithful to him; they were divorced after two years, and then his brother died. He went abroad on a tour of Greece, the eastern provinces, and Sicily when he was about twenty, and then embarked unenthusiastically on the training and minor government jobs that were the necessary preliminary to a career in public life. During this period he wrote his first group of poems, the *Amores* or 'Loves', inspired by 'Corinna', a married mistress. Ovid remarried, happily this time but again briefly; his second wife died soon after the birth of a daughter, perhaps in about 14 BC, when he was twenty-nine or thirty.

---

[1] *Tristia* IV. 10.

From this time onwards, Ovid gave up any intention of pursuing a public career, and settled down to writing poetry, presumably supported by an allowance from his father and with the patronage of Messala Corvinus, a supple and powerful lawyer-politician. Ovid was a member of a group of brilliant young writers, intellectuals, and socialites, which included the notable elegiac poet Propertius, a few years older than Ovid. He married for a third time, perhaps in about 5 BC, again successfully; and his father died, aged ninety, around the turn of the century. This period saw the production of his *Heroides*, verse letters of legendary heroines; the second group of amatory poems, *Ars amatoria*, the explicit 'Art of Love'; *Metamorphoses*, a 12,000-line collection in epic style of stories from myth and legend; and *Fasti*, a poetical calendar of the Roman year.

Then disaster struck. In 8 AD, when he was fifty-one, Ovid was exiled by Augustus to the distant and unattractive settlement of Tomis (now Constantsa, south of the Danube delta on the west coast of the Black Sea), the equivalent for him of the far end of Siberia. The cause of his banishment, Ovid said, was a poem and a mistake. The poem was the *Ars amatoria*, which had been published about eight years earlier and had conflicted with Augustus's campaign for moral reform and his stern disapproval of adultery. We do not know what the mistake was; the most likely possibility is that Ovid was implicated, perhaps as an unwilling witness, in some scandal or plot involving members of Augustus's family – something that he should have reported but kept to himself.

And there, in Tomis, Ovid stayed for the rest of his life, his loyal third wife remaining in Rome to work for his pardon. He went on writing elegant, sad poems – the elegiac *Tristia* ('Sorrows'), and *Epistulae ex Ponto* ('Letters from the Black Sea') – and he went on hoping that they would cause him to be remembered and forgiven and allowed to return home; but they never did. He died in exile in 17 AD, when he was sixty.

The *Amores*, which was originally in five books but was later pruned down to three, is written in Ovid's favourite elegiac metre, couplets of alternating six- and five-foot lines. It begins:

> I'd meant in solemn metre to rehearse
> A tale of arms and war and violence,
> Matching the weighty matter with my verse,
> All lines alike in length, no difference;
> > But Cupid laughed (they say)
> > And filched one foot away. [...]

> Poor me! That boy's sure arrows never stray.
> I'm burning. In my vacant breast love reigns.
> So in six beats my verse must rise today,
> And settle back in five. Farewell you strains
>   Of steely war! Farewell to you,
>   And to your epic metre too!
> > (*Amores*, I.1.1–4, 25–30, trs. by A.D. Melville, 1990, Oxford
> > World's Classics pp. 3, 4)

In a later, equally self-conscious, poem the poet fears that his verses
have caused his 'Corinna' to be so admired that she has become
common property:

> What day was it, birds of ill omen, that you croaked your portents
>   Above this eternally love-struck head of mine?
> What unlucky star has crossed me, what gods are planning
>   My downfall? That girl whom the town
> Spoke of – till lately – as *mine*, my solitary obsession,
>   I fear I must now share
> With all comers. Could my poems have made her a public figure?
>   That's it: *she* was prostituted by *my* art,
> And serve me right for trumpeting her beauty abroad! If my darling's
>   On the market, it's all my fault –
> I've pimped her charms, I've marked up the route for lovers,
>   It was I who let them in at her front door.
> What good have my poems done me? They've brought nothing but
> trouble,
>   Made men envy my success.
> > (*Amores* III.12.1–14, trs. by Peter Green, 1982, Penguin Classics
> > p. 160)

The *Ars amatoria* is not a collection of passionate love lyrics like
Amores, but three long, mock-didactic poems of 700–800 elegiac
lines each – two for men and one for women – which describe
techniques for carrying out seductions and successful adulteries.
Addressed to the hedonistic smart set of Rome, the book is light-
hearted and amusing, but it caused much offence to Augustus and
his moralistic supporters.

Metamorphoses, from about the same period as *Ars amatoria*,
is a collection of stories from myth and legend retold in fifteen
books of hexameters, a form but not a subject that recalls earlier
epic poetry. Ovid says at the beginning what the poem is going to be
about:

> Now I am ready to tell how bodies are changed
> Into different bodies.

I summon the supernatural beings
Who first contrived
The transmogrifications
In the stuff of life.
You did it for your own amusement.
Descend again, be pleased to reanimate
This revival of those marvels.
Reveal, now, exactly
How they were performed
From the beginning
Up to this moment.

> (*Metamorphoses* I.1–4, paraphrased by Ted Hughes in
> *Tales from Ovid*, 1997, Faber p. 3)

But it turns out that metamorphosis, miraculous change of form, is a less important feature of the book than the entertainment provided by the wonderful tales the poet tells – a great chronological sequence from the creation down to his own times – and the skill and care with which the poem is composed. *Metamorphoses* is an unprecedented collection of traditional stories told with a charm and brilliance that has affected western writing ever since. This is where Shakespeare got several of his notions, including the story of Pyramus and Thisbe which he caricatured in *A Midsummer Night's Dream* (c.1594–5). Here is the passage which relates how a lioness bloodied Thisbe's shawl, given in Ovid's economical Latin (56 words), and in translations in prose (97 words) and verse (73 words):[2]

> uenit ecce recenti
> caede leaena boum spumantis oblita rictus
> depositura sitim uicini fontis in unda;
> quam procul ad lunae radios Babylonia Thisbe
> uidit et obscurum timido pede fugit in antrum,
> dumque fugit, tergo uelamina lapsa reliquit.
> ut lea saeua sitim multa conpescuit unda,
> dum redit in siluas, inuentos forte sine ipsa
> ore cruentato tenues laniauit amictus.
> (*Metamorphoses* IV.96–104)

But suddenly a lioness, fresh from the kill, her slavering jaws dripping with the blood of her victims, came to slake her thirst at the neighbouring spring. While the animal was still some distance off, Thisbe saw her in the moonlight. Frightened, she fled into the darkness of a cave, and as she ran her veil slipped from her shoulders, and was left behind.

---

[2] See also the paraphrase by Ted Hughes in his *Tales from Ovid*, Faber 1997, p. 250. which brilliantly amplifies Ovid's scene; and *A Midsmmer Night's Dream*, V. 1. 217–64.

When the savage lioness had drunk her fill, and was returning to the woods, she found the garment, though not the girl, and tore its fine fabric to shreds, ripping it with bloodstained jaws.

(trs. by Mary M. Innes, 1955, Penguin Classics pp. 96–7)

> But lo! a lioness,
> Her jaws all bloody from a recent kill,
> Came to the spring nearby to slake her thirst.
> In the bright moonlight Thisbe watched her come
> And fled in terror to a shadowy cave,
> And running dropped her shawl. The savage beast
> Drank deep and quenched her thirst, then, turning back
> Into the woods, chanced on the delicate wrap
> (But not the girl!) and with her bloody jaws
> Tore it.

(trs. by A.D. Melville, 1986, Oxford World's Classics p. 77)

The *Metamorphoses* was the work on which Ovid wished to be judged, and he concluded it with an envoi reminiscent of Horace's *Odes* III.30, 'I have built a monument more lasting than bronze':[3]

> Now stands my task accomplished, such a work
> As not the wrath of Jove, nor fire nor sword
> Nor the devouring ages can destroy.
> Let, when it will, that day, that has no claim
> But to my mortal body, end the span
> Of my uncertain years. Yet I'll be borne,
> The finer part of me, above the stars,
> Immortal, and my name shall never die.
> Wherever through the lands beneath her sway
> The might of Rome extends, my words shall be
> Upon the lips of men. If truth at all
> Is stablished by poetic prophecy,
> My fame shall live to all eternity.

(*Metamorphoses* XV.871–9, trs. by A.D. Melville, 1986, Oxford World's Classics p. 379)

The poems of exile were Ovid's attempt – part resentful, part melancholy – to get the attention of the authorities in Rome, and to remind them of his great talent and the monstrous harshness of his punishment. One of the most interesting of them is *Tristia* IV.10, in which Ovid both indulges in autobiography –

---

[3] *Exegi monumentum aere perennius.* This has been a recurring theme in the poetry of all ages.

Who was this I you read, this trifler in tender passions?
  You want to know, posterity? Then attend –

and ends by making his peace with his Muse and his readers:

So the fact that I live still, to grapple with such grim hardships,
  unwearied, yet, of the light and all it brings,
I owe, my Muse, to you: it's you who afford me solace,
  who come as rest, as medicine to my cares;
you my guide and comrade, who spirit me from the Danube
  to an honoured seat on Helicon; who have
offered me that rare benefit, fame while still living,
  a title rarely granted till after death.
Nor has Envy, belittler of all that's present, sunk her
  malignant fangs into any work of mine:
for although our age has produced some classic poets,
  Fame has not grudged my gifts renown.
There are many I'd rank above me: yet I am no less quoted
  than they are, and most read throughout the world.
So if there's any truth in poetic predictions, even
  should I die tomorrow, I'll not be wholly earth's.
Which I was it triumphed? True poet or fashion's pander?
  Either way, generous reader, it is you I must thank.
      (*Tristia* IV.10.1–2, 115–32, trs. by Peter Green, 1994, David
      Higham Associates pp. 79, 82–3)

Translations

Ovid

The *Amores* and *Ars amatoria* are available in fine translations by
Peter Green (*Ovid: The Erotic Poems*, 1982) in Penguin Classics, and
by A.D. Melville (*Ovid: The Love Poems*, 1990) in Oxford World's
Classics; extracts from both, which are equipped with good
introductions and notes, are given above. *Metamorphoses* is translated into pleasant five-stress blank verse by A.D. Melville (1986) in
Oxford World's Classics; and into rather flat prose by Mary M. Innes
(1955) in Penguin Classics. Ted Hughes's free-verse paraphrases of
some of the stories from *Metamorphoses* (*Tales from Ovid*, Faber
1997) are splendid, though they can stray some way from the Latin.
Heroides is translated into loose blank verse by Harold Isbell (1990)
in Penguin Classics. *Tristia* and *Epistulae ex Ponto* are again very
well translated with good apparatus by Peter Green (*Ovid: The
Poems of Exile*, 1994) in Penguin Classics, and by A.D. Melville
(*Ovid: Sorrows of an Exile*, 1992) in Oxford World's Classics.

The novel

Any reasonably broad definition of the novel – such as 'nearly always an extended fictional prose narrative, although some novels [...] have been written in verse'[4] – can be stretched to include a good deal of classical literature, starting, for instance, with the *Odyssey*. Long fictional narratives were written in prose in classical times – mostly in Hellenistic Greek – but only a few examples have come down to us in more than fragmentary form. Of these, we shall look at one of the five surviving Greek novels, and at both the two Latin novels that have survived.

Longus

The early Greek novel appears to have been developed in the Hellenistic age, but the novels that we know about mostly belong to the late second and early third century AD. Characterisation was primitive, but they had strong, simple plots on the lines of: boy meets girl / they overcome various difficulties, including separation / they are reunited / there is a happy ending. The best of the surviving examples is *Daphnis and Chloe*, but nothing is known about its author except that he was called Longus, a Roman name that may mean that he was a Greek living in Italy.

Daphnis and Chloe, we learn, were separately exposed by their parents in early infancy in the country near Mytilene in Lesbos where, protected by Pan and the Nymphs, they were suckled by a nanny-goat and a ewe respectively. The babies were discovered by neighbouring families of agricultural slaves, and brought up as their children. Daphnis, now a goat-herd aged fifteen, and Chloe, a shepherdess of thirteen, are constant companions on the grazings, and are beginning to fall in love with each other. Despite seeing the mating of their animals, they are sexually naive, and can do no more than hug and kiss. Various adventures befall them: another young man wants to marry Chloe; they get into trouble with a party of visiting rowdies; their district is invaded by a hostile fleet from another part of Lesbos which carries off Chloe and her sheep (but Pan intervenes and she escapes); and Daphnis learns all about sex from an old man's young wife who fancies him. Finally the owner of the estate – and of Daphnis and Chloe and of

---

[4] Chris Baldick, *The Concise Oxford Dictionary of Literary Terms*, Oxford University Press 1990, p. 151.

their foster-parents, for they are all slaves – arrives with his family, and agrees to give the handsome Daphnis to his son's homosexual servant, who wants him as a lover. But at the last moment the foster-parents save the day by producing the tokens which they had found with Daphnis and Chloe when they saved them from exposure. It emerges that Daphnis is the younger son of his 'owner' and that Chloe is the only daughter of a rich neighbour. Daphnis and Chloe can be married at last – Chloe's virginity having survived all these dangers – and we are told that they will have children of their own and grow old together, happy in the countryside that they love.

This charming, sentimental romance, far removed from the realities of peasant life, has a pastoral setting deriving primarily from the *Idylls* of Theocritus (see pp. 154–5 above), in which another Daphnis is celebrated. It has a central theme that transcends its fairy-tale plot and the naivety of its characterisation: the inevitable triumph of Love (Eros), aided by Pan and the Nymphs, over the difficulties that are put in its way by Fate.

Until recently regarded as mildly pornographic, *Daphnis and Chloe* has had a lasting influence on western literature. It has been known in expurgated translations since the mid-sixteenth century (and in a complete French version since 1810); and, together with ideas from Rousseau, it inspired Saint-Pierre's hugely successful *Paul et Virginie* (1788). It was particularly admired by Goethe, who wrote: 'One would do well to read it every year, to be instructed by it again and again, and to receive anew the impression of its great beauty.'[5]

Petronius

The *Satyricon* is part of a long Roman novel that probably dates from the 60s AD. Its author, Petronius, has been plausibly identified with T. Petronius Arbiter, a former consul and a voluptuary who was the companion in luxury of the Emperor Nero, and who was obliged, as a result of a false charge of treason, to commit suicide in 65.[6] It would be hard to imagine an early novel that differed more radically in tone from the pastoral felicities of *Daphnis and Chloe*

[5] Quoted by Paul Turner in his Penguin Classics *Longus*, p. 16.
[6] Scholars are not all agreed on this point, but the apparent relevance of the description of Petronius Arbiter given by Tacitus (*Annals* 16. 17–20) makes the identification difficult to avoid.

than does the *Satyricon*, and yet there is a connection between them; for it is likely that Petronius was satirising, amongst other things, the sentimental Hellenistic romances from which *Daphnis and Chloe* was to derive.

What we have is parts of Books 14, 15, and 16 of the *Satyricon*, of which 15 is more or less complete; plus a few minor fragments from earlier parts of the novel. (There is much disagreement about how long it was originally, some critics suggesting a length of up to 400,000 words, but this is probably an exaggeration.) The 'heroes' are the homosexual pair Encolpius (the narrator) and Giton, whose lustful exploits are 'satyric', after the fashion of satyrs; while the tale of their adventures gives the opportunity for satire, a 'satirical' commentary on the persons and manners of contemporary Roman society.

The novel as we have it is episodic, with the interpolation of a variety of tales and poems that parody more serious works. There are sexual encounters with changing partners, legacy-hunting, a visit to 'Circe' in one of many references to Homer, and – the centre-piece of the fragments – the lengthy and astonishing tale of a dinner given by the immensely rich, vulgar freedman Trimalchio, which is itself a parody of Plato's *Symposium*. The ignorant snobberies and posturing of both narrator and host at this absurd dinner, the outrageous displays of wealth, the gross nature and quantity of the food and drink, the humiliation of the slaves: the whole thing is a remorseless attack on the shabby values and open vulgarity of Nero's Rome.

Vilification and contempt, however amusing, can be tedious if they are unrelieved by anything positive, and not everyone will regret that we do not have the whole of the *Satyricon*. But the plain-spoken vitality of the book has attracted readers since early Christian times. It was especially admired in the late seventeenth century (the first English translation appeared in 1694); but it then went out of favour for most of the eighteenth and nineteenth centuries, partly no doubt because of its descriptions of perverse sexual activities, but more perhaps because it depicted aspects of first-century Rome that admirers of Roman virtues and Roman art did not want to see. Its influence on a number of European and American modernists – Pound, Eliot, Fitzgerald, Miller – was marked in the early twentieth century, when its reputation as an obscene text ceased to matter (though its paedophilia and voyeurism could still give offence). Since then it has been frequently translated.

Apuleius

Coming to *The Golden Ass*, after smiling at the innocent simplicity of *Daphnis and Chloe* and scenting the corruption of the *Satyricon*, is to discover a lively and entertaining novel that belongs to a more familiar tradition of fiction; and indeed *The Golden Ass* has probably had a greater influence on the development of the western novel than any other work of classical literature. It is a fantasy incorporating fable and folk tale, and it is considerably more outspoken about sex and bodily functions than was commonly acceptable in Europe in the period after the Renaissance and before the twentieth century. Nevertheless its approach to structure, characterisation, and narration foreshadowed the kind of fiction that has come to be the dominant form of literature over the past three centuries.

Apuleius was born in the mid-120s AD in what is now Algeria, the son of one the chief magistrates of the Roman colony of Madaurus. He was a polymath, with interests encompassing philosophy, the law, agriculture, medicine, astronomy, music, arithmetic, and magic as well as literature, and he wrote and lectured about them with charm and vitality. Having married a rich widow in his early thirties, he was accused by her disappointed relatives of having bewitched her, but in the subsequent trial (in which he defended himself) he was acquitted. He seems to have spent the rest of his life in Carthage, writing and teaching; to have written *The Golden Ass*[7] in the 160s; and to have died not before c.170.

Apuleius took the basic plot of *The Golden Ass*, in which a first-person narrator called Lucius is transformed into an ass, from an early Greek novel of which an abridged version survives, and expanded it with new material, probably doubling its length but retaining its original Greek setting. We meet the hero Lucius on a journey to Thessaly, where his adventures begin and he shows an unhealthy interest in the practice of magic. Before long he persuades a slave girl, with whom he is having an affair, to steal a magic ointment from her mistress, who is a witch; but, instead of turning him temporarily into an owl as he had hoped, the ointment turns him into an ass, and for most of the rest of the tale Lucius relates his largely disagreeable experiences as a beast of burden before he finally returns to human form. As an ass, he tells us, he is

---

[7] Also known (like Ovid's poem) as *Metamorphoses*.

used and abused by a succession of cruel, greedy, and careless owners; and he takes the opportunity to interpolate a large number of stories within the main story, ranging from trivial anecdotes that are at best entertaining, through a splendid spoof trial, to the great fable of Cupid and Psyche told in the third person, which occupies a sixth of the whole novel and is placed at its centre. Lucius is finally rescued by the mother-goddess, who allows him to become a man again, and to be purged of his former dabblings in magic as he is initiated into the great mysteries of the religion of Isis: a parallel to the apotheosis of Psyche following her living death.

The Golden Ass has the basic three-part structure of fiction, situation/action/resolution, both in the main story and in the subsidiary tales; and in the fable of Cupid and Psyche there are glimpses of elements of later fairy tales, including the Ugly Sisters of Cinderella and the magic castle of Beauty and the Beast. There is a first-person narrator (Lucius) and a third-person narrator (for Cupid and Psyche), who use both direct and reported speech. The best-developed character is of course that of Lucius, the forerunner of the numerous first-person narrators of the novels of the past three hundred years; but we can also see that Psyche foreshadows many of the misused heroines of later literature.

As with the poetry of Catullus, we are lucky to have *The Golden Ass* at all, for at one point its survival depended on a single manuscript copied in Italy in the eleventh century. But having got it, later writers and readers have made good use of it. Between 1518 and 1566 it was translated into Italian, French, Spanish, German, and English; and most of the major European writers of the sixteenth century used or referred to it. It was Shakespeare's favourite novel – his most obvious borrowings being in *A Midsummer Night's Dream*, in which Bottom the Weaver is turned into an ass and Titania is made to fall in love with him in his animal form[8] – and its echoes can still be heard in the mainstream fiction of later periods, for instance in the English first-person novels of the eighteenth century. The influence of the fable of Cupid and Psyche was also pervasive in western literature and visual art from the sixteenth to the nineteenth century, from Spenser to William Morris, from Raphael to Rodin.

---

[8] In *The Golden Ass* (10.19–22) a lascivious woman becomes enamoured of the ass Lucius, and has sex with him.

Translations

The novel

It is strange to think that when Paul Turner's agreeable translation of *Daphnis and Chloe* first appeared as a Penguin Classic in 1956 it was expurgated; and that it was not until 1968 (well after the end of the *Chatterley* ban and the Beatles' first LP) that Penguin ventured on the unexpurgated version which is still in print, with revised introduction and notes; *Daphnis and Chloe* is not yet included in Oxford World's Classics.

The Oxford World's Classics translation of the *Satyricon* by P.G. Walsh (1997) is outstanding, and has a full and up-to-date apparatus; there is also a good Penguin Classics translation by J.P. Sullivan (1965, revised 1986).

There are excellent, well-annotated translations of *The Golden Ass* both in Oxford World's Classics, by P.G. Walsh (1994), and in Penguin Classics, by E.J. Kenney (1998).

18 Tacitus and Roman history

Roman historians

The major Roman historians may be divided into three groups according to their different approaches to writing history. They are named here with the periods during which they were active; and they will be discussed in this order, the main emphasis being on the work of Tacitus:

> *A Military Autobiographer*
> > Julius Caesar, mid-first century BC
>
> *Three Historians of the Roman State*
> > Sallust, mid-first century BC
> > Livy, early first century AD
> > Tacitus, early second century AD
>
> *Two Historical Biographers*
> > Plutarch (writing in Greek, not Latin), early second century AD
> > Suetonius, early second century AD

The chronological table lists the major events of the two centuries from 100 BC to 100 AD with which much of their work was concerned.

Caesar and the Gallic War

We have already looked at Xenophon's gripping memoir of the expedition to Persia of the Ten Thousand in 401 BC (see pp. 95–8 above); now we have another soldier's personal account of his campaigns, but one which is on an altogether grander scale. In the course of his climb to power, Gaius Julius Caesar (100–44 BC) spent most of the summer campaigning-seasons of the fifties BC conquering Gaul for Rome, returning to northern Italy, where he was governor, for the winters. The huge area he sought to control – and so to

190

BC

100	Julius Caesar b.
90–88	Social War
86	Sallust b.
84	Catullus b.
82–80	Reforms of Sulla
73–71	Slave revolt under Spartacus
70	Virgil b.; consulate of Crassus and Pompey
65	Horace b.
63	Octavian (Augustus) b. (d. 14 AD); Cicero Consul; Catiline conspiracy
60	'First Triumvirate' of Crassus, Pompey, and Caesar
59	Livy b.; Caesar Consul
58–57	Cicero exiled
58–51	Caesar's campaigns in Gaul and Britain; Caesar, *Gallic War*
54	Catullus d.
53	Crassus defeated at Carrhae in Mesopotamia; Crassus d.
49	Civil War; Caesar crosses the Rubicon
48	Caesar defeats Pompey at Pharsalus; Pompey d.
47–44	Caesar dictator
45–35	Sallust, *Histories*
44	Caesar assassinated
43	Ovid b.; Second Triumvirate of Antony, Lepidus, and Octavian; Cicero murdered
42	Brutus and Cassius defeated at Philippi
37	Virgil, *Eclogues*
35	Sallust d.
31	Antony defeated at Actium; Horace, *Satires* I
30	Antony d.; Horace, *Epodes* and *Satires* II
29	Virgil, *Georgics*
29 to 17 AD	Livy, *Histories*
27	Augustus (Octavian) emperor
23	Horace, *Odes* I–III
20	Ovid, *Amores* (five books)
19	Virgil d.; Virgil, *Aeneid*; Horace, *Epistles* I
14	Horace, *Odes* IV and *Epistles* II
c.10–1	Ovid, *Ars amatoria* and *Metamorphoses*

| 8 | Horace d. |
| 4 | Seneca b. |

AD

8	Ovid exiled
8–17	Ovid, *Tristia* and *Epistulae ex Ponto*
9	Varus's legions lost in Germany
14	Tiberius emperor
17	Livy and Ovid d.
37	Caligula emperor
41	Claudius emperor
43	Britain invaded
c.46	Plutarch b. (d. c.120)
54	Nero emperor
56/7	Tacitus b. (d. 117+)
60	British revolt
64	Fire of Rome
65	Seneca d.; Pisonian conspiracy
66–70	Jewish revolt
68–9	Four emperors: Galba, Otho, Vitellius, Vespasian
70	Suetonius b. (d. 120+)
78–85	Agricola governor of Britain
79	Titus emperor; destruction of Pompeii and Herculaneum
80	Colosseum dedicated
81	Domitian emperor
96	Nerva emperor
98	Tacitus, *Agricola* and *Germania*
98–117	Trajan emperor

enhance his own power and prestige at home – was the whole of modern France except for Provence (which was already under Roman rule), the whole of Belgium, and the parts of Holland and Germany lying to the south and west of the Rhine. They were inhabited for the most part by tribes of warlike Celtic peoples, who often fought each other, but who sometimes managed to unite in opposition to Rome.

Astonishingly, Caesar successfully performed this enormous task with only three (later five or six) Roman legions of heavy infantry, plus their auxiliary cavalry and light infantry (see pp. 135–6 above). There is no doubt that he was a general of genius – fast-thinking, resilient, innovative – not only in his battle tactics, but perhaps even more importantly as a leader of men who could get the best out of his small, well-trained army. In addition to this, he was a writer of great accomplishment, who compiled an annual *Commentary* (notes, or memoirs, written in the third person) recording the season's campaign in simple, lucid Latin, probably for dispatch to Rome. He wrote seven *Commentaries* on the Gallic War (58–52 BC), to which an additional *Commentary* was added by Aulus Hirtius for his final Gallic campaign of 51 BC; and he wrote a further, uncompleted set of *Commentaries* on his conduct of the Civil War against Pompey in 49–48 BC.

It is a pity that generations of beginners have been put off Caesar's *Gallic War* by being made to use it as an elementary Latin text, for it is an enthralling – and indeed unparalleled – work of military history. Despite Caesar's understandable tendency to play up his many successes and play down his few failures, and to distance himself from massacres carried out by his troops which he may have condoned at the time, there is no better (or better-written) account of any war and its individual engagements written by the commander-in-chief himself.

Of course neither Caesar nor the Roman army was infallible: not all the unit commanders were as good as they should have been, and discipline occasionally broke down. It also appears that the two expeditions to Britain in 55 and 54 BC, which in the event served no purpose beyond adding to Caesar's prestige at home, were excessively risky: he did not realise that combined operations in the stormy Channel would be more hazardous than those in the Mediterranean, and the landings very nearly ended in disaster. But the *Gallic War* does illustrate Caesar's superb generalship on land: his flexible tactics, his methods of command and presentation of himself as commander, and his application of the latest Roman technology in bridging and other engineering works. And the book brings us nearer to understanding Caesar's unique qualities: the clarity of his mind, his daring and ruthlessness in pursuit of success tempered by leniency and forgiveness when it was achieved, and his unrivalled political skills put at the service of a relentless ambition to reach the top.

Sallust

The commander of one of Caesar's legions in the Civil War in 49 BC was Gaius Sallustius Crispus (86–35 BC), a former tribune of the people who had been expelled from the Senate in 50, allegedly for immorality (though the power of his political enemies may have had most to do with his expulsion). In 46, following an African campaign, he was appointed the first governor of Nubia, which he plundered; and he would have been convicted of malpractice there but for Caesar's intervention on his behalf. He then retired from public life as a very rich man, and spent his last decade writing history at his luxurious houses in Rome and Tivoli.

Sallust completed monographs on the Catiline 'war' – really a 'putsch' – of 63 BC and on the Jugurthine War of 107–104 BC, which have survived; and he began a general history of Rome since 78 BC which is nearly all lost. His monographs took the writing of Roman history a stage beyond the somewhat mechanical annals that had traditionally recorded the events of previous centuries. He had a clear view of the causes and motives involved in political events, the knack of sharply characterising the leading players, and an eye for the most interesting stories. On the other hand he does not seem to have consulted documentary sources, and he was often careless about the accuracy of what he wrote.

Sallust's story of the Catiline conspiracy (the *Bellum Catilinae*, c.42–41 BC) is freshly and interestingly told with the aim of showing up the degeneracy which Sallust believed was destroying the society and government of the Republic (while of course ignoring his own degeneracy); and it deals with extraordinary events that took place in Sallust's own lifetime, when he was in his early twenties. However, if it is compared with the speeches and letters that Cicero wrote about the conspiracy at the time, discrepancies of fact are discovered where Cicero's contemporary evidence must be preferred to Sallust's later history.[1] This combination of a definite point of view, an ability to tell a good story well, and a lack of rigour in sifting the historical evidence continued to be characteristic of the Roman historians of the next two centuries.

---

[1] On Cicero's part in defeating the Catiline conspiracy see pp. 147–8 above.

Livy

Although Titus Livius (59 BC–17 AD) is yet another ancient notable about whose life we know relatively little, it is clear that he was one of the earliest professional historians, a scholar whose whole life was devoted to the writing of history. He was born in Padua, probably to an affluent family of Republican sympathies, and stayed for some time in Rome as an adult; there he was befriended by Augustus and he encouraged the future Emperor Claudius in his historical studies. His great work was *Ab urbe condita libri*, 142 'books from the foundation of the city' of Rome down to 9 BC, which he began in 29 BC and published in instalments, completing it shortly before his death in 17 AD. Thirty-five of his 142 books have survived (Books 1–10 and 21–45), together with brief summaries of nearly all the rest. This was one of the most extensive literary works of antiquity: the translator of the Oxford World's Classics *Livy: Books 1–5* estimates that, if we had the whole of Livy's *History*, it would occupy some twenty-five substantial volumes of that series.

Livy explains the aims of the work in the Preface to Book 1: his purpose is to record the notable events in Rome's history in order to demonstrate how it became the world's leading nation, and how its greatness has recently been threatened by the decline in morals of the first century BC (a point of view with which Sallust would have agreed). 'The special and salutary benefit of the study of history,' Livy continues, 'is to behold evidence of every sort of behaviour set forth as on a splendid memorial; from it you may select for yourself and for your country what to emulate, from it what to avoid, whether basely begun or basely concluded.'[2] Livy intends to improve on the earlier historians from whom he adapts most of his material by teaching a moral lesson in a narrative that is dramatic and well told; he is not much concerned with finding out whether they got their facts right. Nor had Livy been a soldier, and his accounts of war and battles are inevitably less expertly handled than those of Caesar and Sallust.

In any case, the early parts of his work (which are all that we have in full) dealt largely with legendary material, and there it was the myth that counted, not the facts; as he said, 'In matters so ancient, I

---

[2] *Livy: The Rise of Rome: Books 1–5*, trs. by T.J. Luce (1998), Oxford World's Classics p. 4.

am satisfied to accept as true what has the appearance of truth' (5.21).[3] The first five books (which take the reader from the fall of Troy down to the sack of Rome by the Gauls in 390 BC) include the famous, and stirringly told, tales of the rape of Lucretia by King Tarquinius, Brutus's execution of his sons, Horatius holding the bridge, Cincinnatus summoned from the fields, and Mucius Scaevola thrusting his right hand into the fire to impress Lars Porsenna. In the ancient world Livy's *Ab urbe condita* was accepted as the definitive history of the Roman Republic, and his immediate successors did not attempt to improve on it. Today we are likely to admire him more as a literary artist than as a historian; and to enjoy the stories (familiar to British readers from, for instance, Shakespeare's *Rape of Lucrece*, 1594, and Macaulay's *Lays of Ancient Rome*, 1842) as splendid fictions.

Tacitus

Cornelius Tacitus (c.56 to after 117 AD), whose *praenomen* is not certainly known, came from a patrician family, possibly settled in Provence. He was in Rome by 75, where he followed a senatorial career, keeping his head down in the difficult times under the Emperor Domitian, and rising to be Consul in 97 and Proconsul of Asia for 112–13 under the more genial rule of Nerva and Trajan. He was married to the daughter of a senior senator, also from Provence, whose biography, the *Agricola*, he was to publish in 98. This first historical monograph was followed in the same year by an ethnographical monograph on the German tribes (the *Germania*).

These notable short books were followed by the *Histories*, a general account of the period 69–96 AD (from the year of the four emperors to the end of Domitian's reign); it was written c. 106–7, in twelve or fourteen books of which we have the first four and part of the fifth. This was followed by the *Annals*, another general history – despite its title – of the years 14–68 AD, written c.116 in about sixteen books of which parts of Books 5–6, the whole of 7–10, and most of 16 are lost. Thus the *Histories* and the *Annals* between them covered most of the first century AD, 14–96,[4] from the beginning of Tiberius's reign to the end of Domitian's.

[3] Compare Thucydides on 'speeches', p. 84 above.
[4] This is as if a historian born in 1956 were to write, early in the twenty-first century, a history of the period from the beginning of the First World War to the end of the Soviet Union.

Tacitus did consult some public records, and he wrote where he could from his own experience; but he relied to a considerable extent – like most other ancient historians – on the work of earlier historians, annalists, and travellers. Indeed he seems to have compiled his detailed accounts of Britain and Germany without having visited either country himself. They are nevertheless valuable records of conditions there in the first century, which richly supplement the background material in Caesar's *Gallic War*. The *Agricola* of 98 AD is a eulogistic biography of Tacitus's father-in-law, C. Julius Agricola (40–93 AD), whose senatorial career had included a consulship in 77 or 78, but who had served chiefly in Britain. Here Agricola had been a military tribune in c.61, commander of the Twentieth Legion in 70–3/4, and governor from 78 to 84. Tacitus pauses after his introduction to describe the British Isles (Chapters 10–12) and to summarise the history of the early conquest (Chapters 13–17), after which he follows Agricola's victorious career in the province (Chapters 18–38), and ends with a brief account of his subject's later life and death. This does very well as biography – Agricola emerges as having been an admirable soldier and statesman – but equally interesting are Tacitus's accounts of Britain and its inhabitants, and of the background to Agricola's military campaigns against the north Britons, culminating in the conclusive defeat of the Caledonians at Mons Graupius[5] in 84.

The *Germania*, also 98, is an account of Germany and the German tribes, a detailed (and hitherto unparalleled) geographical and ethnographical survey of a foreign country that had successfully withstood the power of Rome, and threatened it still. Although Tacitus's main interest here is in describing this extraordinary place for the benefit of Rome's security, the book has the subsidiary purpose of contrasting the institutions, character, beliefs, and customs of the uncorrupted Germans – which remind Tacitus of the moral strengths of early Rome – with the corrupt decadence that has overtaken the Rome of his own time.

The first of Tacitus's two major works, the *Histories* of 69–96 AD (written c.106–7), is maddeningly incomplete in its surviving form, covering only the year 69 and nine months of 70. This period is nevertheless of great interest, to us as well as to Tacitus, for 69 was the year of the four emperors, and 70 saw the rising of the Batavian (= Dutch) tribes under Civilis. This substantial work of history is

---

[5] Which may have been Bennachie, 42km north-west of Aberdeen.

also the first full manifestation of Tacitus's strengths and weaknesses as a historian. His strengths were his well-controlled narrative and sheer readability; his searching analysis of causes and motives; his economical, acerbic style of writing, adorned with epigrammatic reflections; and his ironical pessimism about the state of Rome. On the other hand he readily invented 'speeches' of the sort that were used by all the ancient historians (see p. 84 above); and he relied on dubious sources of information, which led to the repetition of some of the factual errors of his predecessors.

Tacitus is at his best when his narrative stretches out, as it does in *Histories* 1.12–49, the brilliantly constructed and absorbing account of the last fortnight of Galba's tenure of the throne, and of the usurpation plotted by Otho and carried out by his bloodthirsty soldiers. It cannot be quoted at length here (it runs to twenty-three pages in the Oxford World's Classics translation), but its beginning shows Tacitus plunging into his story, and its ending is a fine example of his pungent, paradoxical style:

> A few days after 1 January [69] a dispatch arrived from Belgica, in which the procurator Pompeius Propinquus announced that the legions of Upper Germany had broken their oath of allegiance and were clamouring for a new emperor, but that by way of tempering their treason they referred the final choice to the Senate and People of Rome. Galba had already been deliberating and seeking advice from associates as to the adoption of a successor,[6] and this occurence hastened his plans.

It ends with Tacitus's damning faint praise of the emperor, who was assassinated on 15 January:

> Such was the end of Servius Galba, who for seventy-three years had enjoyed prosperity under five different emperors, happier in their reign than his own. He came of an old and noble family and possessed great wealth. His own character was mediocre, rather free from vices than rich in virtues. Though not indifferent to fame, he did not flaunt it. Not greedy of other people's money, he was careful of his own, and a miser with public funds. Towards friends and freedmen, if they happened to be honest, he was irreproachably tolerant; when they were not, he was culpably blind. But his distinguished origin and the perils of the time disguised his apathy, which passed as prudence. In the flower of his youth he served with distinction in Germany. As pro-consul he governed Africa wisely, and in later years showed the same fairness in Nearer Spain. When he was a commoner he seemed too big for his

---

[6] Galba felt the need to 'adopt' a successor because he was old and ill and the Julio-Claudian imperial house was now extinct. He chose L. Calpurnius Piso but, when the throne was usurped by Otho, Piso as well as Galba was killed.

station: the universal view was that he had the qualifications to be a ruler – if
only he had not ruled.

> (*Histories*, 1.12, 49, trs. by W.H. Fyfe, 1912, revised by D.S.
> Levene, 1997, Oxford World's Classics pp. 9, 31)

We have considerably more of the *Annals* of Tacitus (ten and a half
books) than we do of his *Histories* (four and a half books), but again
the lacunae are unfortunate, depriving us of the accounts of two
years of Tiberius's reign (30–1 AD); the whole four years of the reign
of Caligula and the first six years of Claudius (37–41, 41–7); and the
last years of Nero (66–8). But the narrative that remains is just as
brilliant and exciting as that of the *Histories* – and Tacitus was
writing about an extremely exciting time – and just as hard to illustrate in a short space. Some of the *Annals* (along with Suetonius's
Lives of the Caesars) inspired Robert Graves in writing his two
Claudius novels, such as this extract concerning the unmasking and
death of Claudius's wife Messalina in 48. Messalina's sexual
excesses – she was probably then aged about 30 to Claudius's 58 –
had culminated in a form of marriage with a handsome young senator called Gaius Silius while Claudius was away in Ostia. Claudius
was told about it by his freedmen, and exhorted to take action
against the lovers:

> Meanwhile, Messalina was indulging in unprecedented extravagances. It
> was full autumn; and she was performing in her grounds a mimic grape-
> harvest. Presses were working, vats overflowing, surrounded by women
> capering in skins like sacrificing or frenzied Maenads. She herself, hair
> streaming, brandished a Bacchic wand. Beside her stood Silius in ivy-wreath
> and buskins, rolling his head, while the disreputable chorus yelled round
> him. Vettius Valens, the story goes, gaily climbed a great tree. Asked what
> he saw, his answer was: 'A fearful storm over Ostia!' There may have been
> a storm. Or it could have been a casual phrase. But later it seemed
> prophetic.
>
> Rumours and messengers now came pouring in. They revealed that
> Claudius knew all, and was on his way, determined for revenge. So the
> couple separated, Messalina to the Gardens of Lucullus, Silius – to disguise
> his alarm – to business in the Forum. The others too melted away in every
> direction. But they were pounced on and arrested by staff-officers of the
> [Praetorian] Guard, in the streets or in hiding-places. Messalina was too
> shaken by the catastrophe to make any plans. But she instantly decided on
> the course that had often saved her – to meet her husband and let him see
> her.
>
> (*Annals* 11.31–2, trs. by Michael Grant, 1956, revised 1989,
> Carcanet Press pp. 247–8; cf. Robert Graves, *Claudius the God*,
> 1934, Chs 28–9)

But this time Messalina's wiles did not succeed in getting round Claudius, and she and Silius were both killed.

Despite his shortcomings, Tacitus remains the best as well as the most readable of the Roman historians: the one who gives us the clearest idea of what his times felt like to an intelligent, sardonic, melancholy member of the ruling class who experienced them.

Plutarch

We met Plutarch (c.46 to after 120 AD) – the Greek philosopher and historian – at the beginning of Chapter 1 (pp. 14–15 above); and, although he wrote in Greek, he is included here among the Roman historians because he was a Roman citizen who was writing as much, if not more, for the instruction of the educated Romans of the empire as he was for his fellow-Greeks. To recapitulate: he came from a distinguished and prosperous family settled in the small city of Chaeronea, 30km east of Delphi; he admired the power of Rome as much as its complement, the culture of Greece; and he wrote about both with elegance and charm. His writings were so much appreciated, both in antiquity and afterwards, that a large number of them have survived: some 78 miscellaneous works and 50 *Lives*[7] of Greek and Roman worthies, out of an original total of at least 227 items. Most of the miscellaneous works concerned moral philosophy, rhetoric, and antiquarian matters; but perhaps his greatest achievement was as a historian with his *Parallel Lives* of Greek and Roman worthies, from the legendary founders of Athens and Rome, Theseus and Romulus, down to more recent heroes such as Alexander and Julius Caesar.

Plutarch claims at the beginning of his *Life* of Alexander the Great that he is not writing history at all:

> I am not writing history but biography, and the most outstanding exploits do not always have the property of revealing the goodness or badness of the agent; often in fact, a casual action, the odd phrase, or a jest reveals character better than battles involving the loss of thousands upon thousands of lives, huge troop movements, and whole cities besieged. And so, just as a painter reproduces his subject's likeness by concentrating on the face and the expression of the eyes, by means of which character is revealed, and pays hardly any attention to the rest of the body, I must be allowed to devote more

---

[7] Twenty-three pairs of parallel lives, and four separate lives.

time to those aspects which indicate a person's mind and to use these to
portray the life of each of my subjects, while leaving their major exploits and
battles to others.

(*Greek Lives*, Alexander 1, trs. by Robin Waterfield, 1998, Oxford
World's Classics p. 312)

But history, as we now understand it, is more than the record of
outstanding exploits and great battles. The biography of famous
men and women is certainly a form of history; and Plutarch chose to
write his history in this way because it was particularly apt for
serving the underlying purpose (common to most ancient historians) of conveying moral instruction about how men should think
and behave. (It was indeed this purpose, at its plainest in Plutarch,
that was partly responsible for the ancient historians' relative lack
of interest in accuracy and original research, their preference for
what should have been said and done over what probably was.)
Plutarch's biographies are instructive in this way, but they are also
elegantly written and thoroughly readable. They are, moreover, in
many cases the only accounts that have survived of the people and
events that they portray; and, where it is possible to check them
against parallel accounts, they are found to be sufficiently accurate
by the standards of ancient history.

Although the current paperback translations present Plutarch's
Greek and Roman subjects in separate volumes, he undoubtedly
intended that each Greek and Roman pair should be read together
and considered in relation to each other, writing a 'comparison' as
the conclusion to many of the pairs of *Lives*. There are obvious
pairs, such as the orators Demosthenes and Cicero, and less obvious
ones such as the Athenian statesman and thinker Solon and the man
of action Publius Valerius Publicola (or Poplicola, reputedly Consul
in 509 BC, who may have helped his colleague Lucius Junius Brutus
to expel the Tarquins and to establish the Republic). But, whether
the subjects were famous or not, the fact remains that the stories of
each pair were supposed to be mutually enlightening, and it is
unfortunate that they are separated in the Penguin Classics and
Oxford World's Classics volumes.

Suetonius

Gaius Suetonius Tranquillus (c.70–c.130 AD) was a middle-class
scholar and advocate who wrote in Greek as well as Latin on a wide
range of subjects, most of his work being lost. He held imperial

secretaryships under Trajan and Hadrian in the early second century, but was dismissed for unknown reasons by Hadrian in about 121, and died a few years later. As a historian he specialised in biography, and we have a fragmentary *Lives* of Roman men of letters and, most importantly, a nearly complete *Lives of the Caesars*: biographies of the twelve emperors from Julius Caesar to Domitian. The fullest lives are those of Julius Caesar and Augustus, and Suetonius appears to have had access to the imperial archives while he was writing them; he may have written the other ten biographies after his dismissal from the palace.

In writing his biographies Suetonius used a thematic as well as a chronological structure, beginning with his characters' backgrounds and ending with their deaths, but arranging what happened in between by subjects such as public finances, buildings, and shows. His approach is gossipy and anecdotal, and he took even less care than usual to check his facts or to qualify material that was plainly fictional. Nevertheless the *Lives of the Caesars* is a lively, readable work, full of fascinating details about these extraordinary rulers.

Here, to end with, are two brief extracts, about the pride of the greatest of the Roman emperors, and the vanity of one of the worst of them:

[Augustus] came to the conclusion that the Elder and the Younger Julia[8] had both been indulging in every sort of vice; and banished them. When Gaius then died in Lycia, and Lucius eighteen months later at Massilia,[9] Augustus publicly adopted his remaining grandchild, Agrippa Postumus and, at the same time, his step-son Tiberius; a special bill to legalize this act was passed in the Forum. Yet he soon disinherited Postumus, whose behaviour had lately been vulgar and brutal, and packed him off to Surrentum.

When members of his family died Augustus bore his loss with far more resignation than when they disgraced themselves. The deaths of Gaius and Lucius did not break his spirit; but after discovering his daughter Julia's adulteries, he refused to see visitors for some time. He wrote a letter about her case to the Senate, staying at home while a quaestor read it to them. He even considered her execution; at any rate, hearing that one Phoebe, a freedwoman in Julia's confidence, had hanged herself, he cried: 'I should have preferred to be Phoebe's father!' Julia was forbidden to drink wine or enjoy any other luxury during her exile; and denied all male company, whether free or servile, except by Augustus's special permission and after he had been given full particulars of the applicant's age, height, complexion,

[8] His daughter and granddaughter respectively.
[9] His grandsons, brothers of the younger Julia, whom Augustus had adopted as his heirs.

and of any distinguishing marks on his body – such as moles or scars. He kept Julia for five years on a prison island before moving her to the mainland, where she received somewhat milder treatment.

> *(The Twelve Caesars*, Augustus 65, trs. by Robert Graves 1957, revised by Michael Grant 1979, Penguin Classics pp. 89–90)

[Nero's] dominant characteristics were his thirst for popularity and his jealousy of men who caught the public eye by any means whatsoever. Because he had won so many stage victories, most people expected him to take part in athletic contests at the next Olympiad. For he practised wrestling all the time, and everywhere in Greece had watched the gymnastic competitions like the judges, squatting on the ground in the stadium, and if any pair of competitors worked away from the centre of the ring, would push them back himself. Because of his singing he had been compared to Phoebus Apollo and because of his chariot-riding to the Sun-God; now, apparently, he planned to become a Hercules, for according to one story he had a lion so carefully trained that he could safely face it naked before the entire amphitheatre; and then either kill it with his club or else strangle it.

Just before the end Nero took a public oath that if he managed to keep his throne he would celebrate the victory with a festival, performing successively on water-organ, flute, and bagpipes; and when the last day came would dance the role of Turnus in Virgil's *Aeneid*. He was supposed to have killed the actor Paris because he considered him a serious professional rival.

> *(The Twelve Caesars*, Nero 53–4, trs. by Robert Graves, 1957, revised by Michael Grant 1979, Penguin Classics p. 245)

Translations

Caesar

The translation of *Caesar: The Gallic War* by Carolyn Hammond (1996) in Oxford World's Classics is first rate, with excellent introduction and apparatus; the Penguin Classics version, *Caesar: The Conquest of Gaul*, is by S.A. Handford, revised by Jane Gardner (1982).

Sallust

The Penguin Classics *Sallust: The Jugurthine War/The Conspiracy of Catiline* is pleasantly translated by S.A. Handford (1963), but lacks adequate notes. Sallust is not yet included in Oxford World's Classics.

Livy

There are three collections of work by Livy in Penguin Classics, but the one recommended is the Oxford World's Classics version of

Books 1–5 in *Livy: The Rise of Rome* translated by T.J. Luce (1998), which has a good introduction and apparatus.

Tacitus

The *Agricola* and *Germania* are available in an old but well-revised translation by H. Mattingly (1948, revised 1970) in Penguin Classics; it has Mattingly's original introduction and notes. The *Histories* is available in both series: in Penguin Classics translated by Kenneth Wellesley (1964), and in Oxford World's Classics translated by W.H. Fyfe as long ago as 1912, revised and updated with excellent editorial matter by D.S. Levene (1997). The Penguin Classics *Annals* is translated by Michael Grant (1956, revised 1989), and has good apparatus. The *Agricola, Germania* and *Annals* of Tacitus are not yet in Oxford World's Classics.

Plutarch

The Oxford World's Classics *Plutarch: Greek Lives* is a selection of nine lives well translated by Robin Waterfield (1998) with introduction and notes by Philip A. Stadter; it is to be followed by a collection of Roman lives in the same series. The Penguin Classics *Plutarch: Makers of Rome*, which also contains nine lives translated by Ian Scott-Kilvert (1965), lacks notes. There is little overlap between these collection of Greek and Roman *Lives,* and to read them in pairs as Plutarch intended it is necessary to go back to the Loeb parallel-text edition.

Suetonius

The Penguin Classics version of *Suetonius: The Twelve Caesars* (which is not yet included in Oxford World's Classics) is in Robert Graves's readable translation of 1957, revised with a good apparatus by Michael Grant (1979).

Afterword

The Greek and Latin classics remained at the heart of European secondary and higher education from the later Renaissance until the mid-twentieth century. Any education above the elementary level began with learning Latin; and more advanced studies successively embraced the exciting discoveries of the Renaissance; the Augustan enthusiasm of the Neoclassical period; cool Victorian Hellenism; and the shift back from Greek to Latin in the early twentieth century. Until then classical studies were valued more highly than any other for the cultural and mental training of the civilised adult.

It was not until Greek was dropped as a requirement for entrance to Oxford and Cambridge universities shortly after the First World War, followed by the dropping of compulsory Latin shortly after the Second, that the classics gradually gave up their place as the foundation of British secondary and higher education to modern humanities and the sciences. The moral and cultural lessons to be learned from classical studies came to be perceived by many – by teachers as well as by pupils – to be irrelevant in the modern world, and the learning of dead languages to be a distraction from more useful subjects of study.

But, whether or not we come upon classical literature in our formal education, it is still there: in the literature that has descended from it in the west from the Middle Ages onwards, in the general set of our minds, and in the very ways that we think and speak. The Greek and Latin authors remain in print in cheap, readable, and well-edited translations; they can be bought – and they are bought – in general bookshops everywhere. I hope that this book has helped to show why reading them is still eminently worth while.

The survival of ancient texts

The survival of ancient texts has been, for the most part, a chancy business. The texts of the small number of authors who were regarded as being canonical in ancient times have survived virtually complete, and in reasonably good order. But for the rest time has winnowed out much – in some cases all or nearly all – of what they wrote. The texts of the works that did survive were marred by inaccuracies and gaps as a result of the many times that they were copied and recopied.

There were various reasons for the disappearance of so many texts. In the first place, papyrus rolls were fragile and wore out, when they might or might not be recopied, perhaps as codices. But eventually codices wore out too, or were reused as palimpsests,[1] and again there was a chance that early texts might not be recopied. Texts dropped out of the school curriculum (or were never in it), authors went out of fashion, or were considered irreligious or obscene. Dramatic texts, even of the greatest playwrights, which were originally intended for performance rather than for reading, disappeared in huge numbers.

The result of all this was that a very large number of classical texts, even if they survived into late antiquity (say until the sixth to the eighth century AD), were lost by the time of the revival of interest in the classics during the early Italian Renaissance of the thirteenth and fourteenth centuries; and we constantly come across references in works that do survive to other works that do not, even those of major writers. Of the ten primary authors treated in this book, we appear to have most of Homer, Herodotus, Virgil, Horace, and

[1] A palimpsest is a document of parchment or vellum from which the original writing has been erased by washing and scraping so that it could be written on again. Sometimes, but not always, the original writing can be read by multi-spectral imaging.

Ovid; but substantial portions of Pindar, Sophocles, Plato, Cicero, and Tacitus are lost. Of the rest, much of the work of Sappho, Anacreon, Aeschylus, Euripides, Aristophanes, the pre-Socratics, Xenophon, Aristotle, Demosthenes, Plautus, Seneca, Petronius, Apuleius, Livy, Plutarch, and Suetonius had also disappeared by the early medieval period. Even where a work has survived, it has sometimes been by the merest chance. In the early Middle Ages many works which we now value, but which were then largely neglected, appear to have been represented by a single manuscript: Cicero's *Letters*, Apuleius's *Golden Ass*, the whole of Catullus, and the surviving fragments of Livy, Tacitus, and many others. Any of these single manuscripts might easily have been irrevocably lost before they were copied.

The transmission of texts

The accurate transmission of classical texts was hindered up to the end of the manuscript period in the later fifteenth century in three main ways. First, there was the difficulty of interpreting manuscripts of earlier periods because they might be written in scripts that were unfamiliar to later copyists; a particular problem was that in Classical times Greek and Latin texts were written continuously without word divisions, and without line divisions in poetry, which led to misunderstandings. Secondly, the process of transcribing any text inevitably introduces errors: words misread, words wrongly spelled, words added, words or lines missed out; sometimes a whole section or page might be omitted by accident; and such copying errors accumulated each time a text was recopied. Thirdly, when the manuscript of a text was wearing out, or was judged to be in an unacceptably old-fashioned form, it might not be thought worth while to make another copy of the whole of of it. Scholars, librarians, and directors of scriptoria did their best from Hellenistic times onwards to avoid or overcome these problems, but they could not always succeed.

Textual scholarship

It was recognised by the sixteenth century that early manuscripts were more likely to represent the original text than later copies, and a system was evolved for constructing a 'family tree' of manuscripts that would trace the descent of a text, hypothesising where necessary 'ancestor' texts that no longer existed. This system, refined in later centuries, has proved very successful in identifying the best texts, or

parts of texts, for editors to work on – for even the best texts still
have errors which require emendation. The result of the devoted and
often inspired work of textual scholars since the late Middle Ages is
the great corpus of classical texts that is available to us today; texts
which are about as good as human ingenuity can make them, and of
which the chief remaining imperfections are the losses or hopeless
corruptions sustained early in the chain of transmission.[2]

History and archaeology

Classical history has continued to be studied and written in medieval and modern times, picking up where the ancient historians left
off, and necessarily being based to a large extent on their work. The
improvements in historical method made by these later historians
have chiefly been in their critical reassessment of the reliability of
the ancient sources, and in their insistence on getting the facts right
as far as they can. And of course modern historians then reinterpret
the early evidence in the light of their own thinking.

Not many hitherto unknown written documents of the ancient
world are likely to turn up now; but new physical evidence of the
past is being discovered all the time by archaeologists, and is adding
in important ways to our understanding of ancient cultures and
events. Archaeological research, if we include in it the collection of
ancient sculptures and ceramics, and the study of inscriptions (epi-
graphy) and old coins (numismatics), has been going on since the
Renaissance; and ancient sites have been excavated since the eighteenth century. The early excavations, of Pompeii for instance, began
as treasure hunts, but digs have become increasingly professional,
and late-twentieth-century archaeology makes use of carbon-dating,
pollen-analysis, and DNA testing as well as the traditional methods
of laboriously uncovering and recording, layer by layer, the physical
evidences of the past. This period has also seen the development of
under-water archaeology, primarily the investigation of wrecks in
the Mediterranean by divers using breathing apparatus, which has
revealed complete time-capsules surviving from the ancient world,
to be surveyed *in situ* before the evidence is disturbed.

As a result of modern historical research, as well as of changing
social attitudes, we are now inclined to see the ancient world with

---

[2] For the classics in schools and universities, see the Afterword on p. 205.

less uncritical admiration than was common before the twentieth century. For rich and privileged men in ancient Greece and Rome there were indeed many material, spiritual, and artistic benefits to be enjoyed in beautiful surroundings. However, it is clearer now that these advantages were accompanied by political insecurity, by a culture of deliberate cruelty, and by the constant wars that impinged on the lives of people of all classes. For everyone else it was by no means a golden age: the freedom of women was limited; the lower classes were kept down; ordinary town-dwellers lived in squalor; slaves were abused; and the masses of the rural poor were trapped in their poverty and suffered recurrent famine.

Reference bibliography

This bibliography does not have an author section, for three reasons. First, the best books about particular classical authors are aimed at students specialising in classical studies, and commonly expect the reader to have some basic knowledge of Latin, and often of Greek as well. Secondly, the well-edited paperback texts mentioned above in the notes on translations of each author – especially the Penguin Classics and Oxford World's Classics translated (or at least introduced and annotated) in the late 1980s and the 1990s – will be found to serve general readers, as well as students studying the classics, very well; and they are equipped with good reading lists. And thirdly, there are a number of excellent general reference books and introductions to particular aspects of classical studies, as follows.

General reference

The most comprehensive and up-to-date encyclopedia of classical studies is the third edition of *The Oxford Classical Dictionary*, ed. by Simon Hornblower and Antony Spawforth, Oxford University Press 1996, which is arranged alphabetically. It is addressed to classical specialists, though anyone can make good use of it; but it is very expensive (£70 at the time of writing), so that most people will have to consult it in a library.

More accessible (in every sense) is the second edition of *The Oxford Companion to Classical Literature*, ed. by M.C. Howatson, and issued as a revised paperback by Oxford University Press in 1997. General readers will find that this well-organised alphabetical reference book is easy to use and that it will answer nearly all their questions.

For a general introduction to the history and culture (including the literature) of the ancient world, Charles Freeman's *Egypt,*

Greece, and Rome: Civilisations of the Ancient Mediterranean,
Oxford University Press 1996, is outstanding: a thorough, agreeable
historical narrative, with good illustrations, maps, and chronology.

Routledge publishes two well-indexed paperback atlases of the
ancient world: Michael Grant's *The Routledge Atlas of Classical
History*, fifth edition 1994, with 92 pages of simplified maps that
are very easy to read, with limited explanatory matter; and *Atlas of
Classical History*, ed. by Richard J.A. Talbert, 1985, with 177 pages
of more detailed maps and extensive explanatory text. Each of these
inexpensive black-and-white atlases has its virtues, and there is
much to be said for using both.

Subject guides

Greece

The following three books, all available in paperback, are collec-
tions of articles by different hands: *The Oxford History of
Greece and the Hellenistic World*, ed. by John Boardman, Jasper
Griffin, and Oswyn Murray, Oxford University Press 1986;
Ancient Greek Literature, ed. by Kenneth Dover, second edition,
Oxford University Press 1997 (half the articles being by the
editor); and the more specialised *The Cambridge Companion to
Greek Tragedy*, ed. by P.E. Easterling, Cambridge University
Press 1997.

Rome

The Roman World, ed. by John Boardman, Jasper Griffin, and
Oswyn Murray, Oxford University Press 1986–8, is again a collection of articles by different hands; as is the more specialised
The Cambridge Companion to Virgil, ed. by Charles Martindale,
Cambridge University Press 1997. Adrian Keith Goldsworthy's
The Roman Army at War 100 BC–AD 200, Oxford University Press
1998, is also a specialist monograph, but will appeal to anyone
interested in military history. These three books are all available in
paperback.

Peter Salway's *The Oxford Illustrated History of Roman Britain*,
Oxford University Press 1993, is superb, a scholarly work that is a
pleasure to read and is copiously illustrated. It may be used in
conjunction with the Ordnance Survey's historical map and guide,
Roman Britain, fourth edition, 1991.

Art

The Oxford History of Classical Art, ed. by John Boardman, Oxford University Press 1993, is a magnificently illustrated collection of articles, arranged chronologically, by different hands; available now in paperback, it covers artistic developments (including architecture) from pre-Classical Greece to the later Roman Empire.

Simplified phonetic spellings are given in parentheses after the Greek and Latin names and other words in the Index, the suggested pronunciations being those generally used today by English readers of Classical literature. There are many inconsistencies caused by – amongst other things – mixtures of old and new pronunciation of Latin (see pp. 5–7 above). The phonetic equivalents of these spellings in the Received Pronunciation of British English are:

a as in *cat*	*oh* as in *slow*
ah as in *bath*	*oi* as in *coin*
ai as in *air*	*oo* as in *boot*
aw as in *raw*	*oor* as in *moor*
ay as in *may*	*ow* as in *cow*
e as in *bet*	*u* as in *bus*
ea as in *beer*	*ur* as in *curse*
ee as in *meet*	*ch* as in *loch*
ew as in *hew*	*s* as in *kiss*
g as in *get*	*sh* as in *sheep*
i as in *hit*	*th* as in *thick*
eye as in *kite*	*yaw* as in *your*
o as in *got*	

The neutral vowel, or schwa, is represented by the symbol 'ə', as in the English words *sofa*, 'SOHfə', *about*, 'əBOWT', and *passion*, 'PASHən'.